This book studies the development of ideas on freedom, coercion, and power in the history of economic thought. It focuses on the exchange of goods and services and on terms of exchange (interest rates, prices, and wages) and examines the nature of choice – that is, the state of the will of economic actors making exchange decisions. In a social context, anyone's range of choice is restricted by the choices made by others. The first to raise the question of the will in this economic context were the medieval scholastics, drawing on noneconomic analytic models inherited from antiquity and mainly from Aristotle. From these origins, views on economic choice, coercion, and power are recorded, as they gradually change over the centuries, until they manifest themselves in contemporary disputes between different branches of institutional economics.

The legacy of scholasticism in economic thought

Historical Perspectives on Modern Economics

General Editor: Craufurd D. Goodwin, Duke University

This series contains original works that challenge and enlighten historians of economics. For the profession as a whole, it promotes better understanding of the origin and content of modern economics.

Other books in the series:

The legacy of scholasticism in economic thought

Antecedents of choice and power

Odd Langholm
Norwegian School of Economics

CAMBRIDGE
UNIVERSITY PRESS

PUBLISHED BY THE PRESS SYNDICATE OF THE UNIVERSITY OF CAMBRIDGE
The Pitt Building, Trumpington Street, Cambridge CB2 1RP, United Kingdom

CAMBRIDGE UNIVERSITY PRESS
The Edinburgh Building, Cambridge CB2 2RU, United Kingdom
40 West 20th Street, New York, NY 10011–4211, USA
10 Stamford Road, Oakleigh, Melbourne 3166, Australia

First published 1998

Printed in the United States of America

Typeset in Baskerville

Library of Congress Cataloging-in-Publication Data
Langholm, Odd Inge (date)
The legacy of scholasticism in economic thought : antecedents of
choice and power / Odd Langholm.
p.   cm. – (Historical perspectives on modern economics)
Includes bibliographical references and index.
ISBN 0-521-62159-3
1. Economics – History – to 1800.   2. Economic history – Medieval,
500 – 1500.   3. Scholasticism.   I. Title   II. Series.
HB79.L363   1998
330.1 – dc21   97–26895
                                                          CIP

*A catalog record for this book is available from
the British Library.*

ISBN 0 521 62159 3 hardback

Contents

Preface

Historians of economic doctrine now recognize that modern theory is the product of continuous growth over a much longer period of time than was previously assumed. There is also, among historians in general, a renewed interest in the Middle Ages. The combination of these factors invites the question of what was the main and lasting contribution to economics of the medieval scholastics, that is, of the masters who taught and wrote in the first centuries of the European universities. The present volume contains the author's considered reply to that question. I first touched upon the subject some fifteen years ago in a brief article whose title, "Economic freedom in scholastic thought," may still serve as a clue. "Economic freedom" has been used as a label on a number of quite different things. For the medieval scholastics, it derived its principal meaning from an issue that has lain at the core of Christian philosophy since its origin, that of the freedom of the human will. In scholastic economic thought, freedom in that sense was brought to bear on two of the elements of all market economies, namely, the phenomenon of need in the face of scarcity and the arrangement of need satisfaction by means of exchange. The question of freedom then became the question of the state of the will of a person who consents to certain terms of exchange because of need. Conversely, it became the question of compulsion by need or, in a personalized sense, of compulsion (or coercion) by one party to the exchange taking advantage of the other party's need. Since the time of the scholastics, this issue has remained as an irritant in the body of economic doctrine, encapsulated for long periods of time by dominant schools, but occasionally breaking to the surface and issuing in ideological and ethical controversy.

There are several possible points of entry into the material presented here in order to record and explain these developments. A set of alternative reader's guides may be useful. First, of course, I should prefer the book to be read in the order in which it is presented. It then takes on the character of a sort of literary history of comments on the opening chapter of Book III of the *Nicomachean Ethics* of Aristotle, which deals with compulsion and the voluntary (much as value theory can be

read as a history of comments on *Ethics*, V,5, on justice in exchange).
All the channels described in Part I – philosophical, theological, and
legal – through which the scholastics received the building blocks for
their theory of the will in economic relationships, originated in ancient
Greece, and the most direct line back leads to *Ethics*, III,1. Economists,
for whom this volume is primarily intended, will probably find Chapters
1–3 more difficult than the rest. I nevertheless urge anyone who wants
to trace the prehistory of current disputes about economic freedom
and coercion to accept the challenge of Part I at some point, preferably
but not necessarily at the outset.

Second, to persons primarily interested in scholastic economic
thought as such, I suggest that Part I be bypassed or postponed. There
is virtually no economics in Part I. As told in Part II, it was the medieval
scholastics who restated the Aristotelian and related ancient traditions
in terms of need and applied them to economic exchange in this altered form. This main, second part of the book was written with the
idea in mind that it should be able to stand alone as a record of this
one central theme in medieval and early modern thought. If Chapters
4–7 should whet the reader's curiosity about what went before and what
came after, so much the better.

Third, and perhaps surprisingly in the economic context, I offer this
book as a contribution to Hobbes studies, suggesting an entry in Chapter 8, which opens Part III. Thomas Hobbes is the only author who has
a chapter all to himself in the book. Taking Hobbes on compulsion,
the will, and justice as a point of departure, the rest of Part III can be
read as a sketch of what his contribution led to in the field of economics, whereas Parts I and II explain the scholastic–Aristotelian *economic*
doctrines against which he reacted so violently. Finally, let the partici-
pant, or observer, of current disputes between different branches of
institutional economics read the concluding Chapter 10 first. It will
indicate to him the modern issues whose long history is told in this
book and may cause him to go back to one or another of the earlier
entry points suggested previously.

It is hardly possible in a book that spans more than two millennia
and ranges over a number of the human and social sciences to avoid
making blunders. There are undoubtedly in this volume passages that
will offend specialists in this or that area. I can only hope that it will
be received in the spirit in which it was written. I am convinced that
economics is a science in need of greater self-understanding and that
one way to achieve this is by extending its scope, historically and thematically. With no intention of shifting responsibility, I extend my
thanks to all those persons – historians, philosophers, philologists, and

jurists, as well as economists – whose advice I have sought and generously been given. I thank the Norwegian School of Economics for granting me time and funds for research. Special thanks are due, once more, to Elisabeth Stiegler, who took my manuscript through its different stages with exemplary skill and good cheer. Last, but most of all, I thank my wife, Grethe, for companionship and encouragement on our joint expeditions into medieval Europe.

Introduction

This book is a study of the development of one particular subject in the history of Western economic thought. It is directly concerned only with that part of economic activity that has to do with the exchange of goods and services, including loans. If it touches upon production and distribution, it is merely indirectly and by implication. More specifically, the study deals with the will of economic actors making exchange decisions, that is, with the nature of economic choice. Because of scarcity, any economic actor's range of choice is restricted, in a social context, deliberately or not, by the choices made by other economic actors. We shall therefore be primarily occupied with what used to be called compulsion but is now more often referred to as economic coercion. The story starts in the Middle Ages with the scholastics, or "schoolmen." I use these terms loosely to include both the university masters of theology and law and those who applied their ideas from the pulpit or in the confessional. On the subject in question, the scholastics taught the official doctrine of the Catholic Church, while drawing extensively on the heritage of classical antiquity. From this medieval origin, views on economic choice and compulsion/coercion will be recorded, as they gradually change over the centuries, until they manifest themselves in contemporary ideological and scholarly disputes.

There is one early-twentieth-century author who offers his readers a most revealing perspective on this subject. This is Max Weber. Because I am writing in English, I shall quote Weber's *Wirtschaft und Gesellschaft* in the English edition, *Economy and Society*. No alteration will be made to this admirable translation except for the reintroduction of a certain notation that is to be found in the original but has all but disappeared in the English version (this fact is food for thought in itself). Among different forms of socioeconomic relations discussed by Weber, particular attention is paid to power ("Macht") in a general sense and to domination ("Herrschaft") in a more specific sense. The former is "the probability that one actor within a social relationship will be in a position to carry out his own will despite resistance, regardless of the basis on which this probability rests." This concept is "sociologically amorphous," however, because all kinds of qualities in a person and

1

combination of circumstances can enable him to impose his will in a given situation. Hence the need for the more precise concept of domination, which is "the probability that a command with a given specific content will be obeyed by a given group of persons."[1] It would seem that this is not a particularly fortunate way of describing what takes place in the economic sphere, where words like "command" and "obedience" have a somewhat foreign ring to them. Perhaps for this reason, the distinction between the two concepts tends to become blurred when the author turns to economic relationships. These represent a main area of sociological research, because a frequent, and frequently intended, result of domination, as well as one of its most important instruments, is the possession of, or control ("Verfügung") over, economic goods. This represents economic power ("ökonomische Macht"). A comprehensive taxonomy is out of the question, but it is useful to posit two limiting cases. These are

domination by virtue of a constellation of interests (in particular: by virtue of a position of monopoly), and domination by virtue of authority, i.e., power to command and duty to obey. The purest type of the former is monopolistic domination in the market; of the latter, patriarchal, magisterial, or princely power. In its purest form, the first is based upon influence derived exclusively from the possession of goods or marketable skills guaranteed in some way and acting upon the conduct of those dominated, who remain, however, formally "free" and are motivated simply by the pursuit of their own interests. The latter kind of domination rests upon alleged absolute duty to obey, regardless of personal motives or interests.

Even sellers in positions of incomplete monopoly can thus influence prices without imposing any obligation on buyers to submit to their domination. Similarly, in capital markets, banks have the power to dictate, or to influence strongly, interest rates and other loan conditions.

The potential debtors, if they really need the credit, must in their own interest submit to these conditions and must even guarantee this submission by supplying collateral security. The credit banks do not, however, pretend that they exercise "authority," i.e., that they claim "submission" on the part of the dominated without regard to the latter's own interests; they simply pursue their own interests and realize them best when the dominated persons, acting with formal "freedom," rationally pursue their own interests as they are forced upon them by objective circumstances.

From markets in goods and money, Weber in the sequel extends his range of examples to the hiring of labor, referring to employment

---

[1] For this and the following quotations from Weber, cp., successively, *Wirtschaft und Gesellschaft*, 28–9; 603–5; 71; 179; and *Economy and Society*, 53; 942–5; 127–8; 305.

based on a "contract concluded in the labour market by formally 'equal' parties through the 'voluntary' acceptance of terms offered by the employer." Elsewhere he speaks in much the same terms of "formally 'free' labour," namely, labor according to a contract that is formally free on both sides but that may be subject to substantial regulation. In all these areas, power relations may in principle be reversed. In the case of labor, the author does not fail to point out that there may be a certain monopolistic element present in the possession of an acquired professional skill. This is also a form of economic power.

The different classes of economic acts and agreements described in these quotations are those that are to be examined in the main, second part of this book: moneylending, exchange of commodities, the hire of labor. If Max Weber provides an apt introduction to our theme, it is because of his insistence on putting words like "free" ("frei") and "voluntary" ("freiwillig") in quotation marks when describing such acts and agreements, as though hedging against their unconditional use. The reason for this reluctance on the part of such a scrupulous author will naturally arouse the reader's curiosity and may invite reflections and explorations along ideological, analytic, and historical lines. It is the latter line that is to be pursued in this book. Something must be said about the problem of entangling this line from the other two.

By indicating no more than that persons subjected to the economic power of others act "freely" and "voluntarily" in a certain formal sense, Weber evidently attempts, as far as possible, to avoid committing himself to any specific economic ideology. There is an old and firmly established tradition in European thought for the idea that neither party to a mutually free and voluntary agreement can be said to suffer injustice. According to one ideological view, no one has cause to complain if economic powers are left unrestrained, for those upon whom such powers are brought to bear act as freely and voluntarily as those who apply those powers. "Free" is simply free, and "voluntary" is simply voluntary. According to a different view, those who are in the economic power of others indeed have cause to complain, because they are being exploited: "Free" is really unfree and "voluntary" is really involuntary. The picture of capitalism as a society that functions for the greatest benefit of all because all are left free to pursue their own best interests, and the picture of the same system as a society of virtual slavery, where one class is forced by need to accept economic conditions on the level of subsistence, mark the extreme points on a scale. No social scientist, even if his conscious purpose is descriptive and explanatory, can hope successfully to hide his position on this scale under the cloak of his grammar. Some argue that it is best for any author not to try to do so but to state his position openly. For the historian, this dilemma will presumably be the more acute the closer to the present he brings his story. If it affects this book, it is mainly in Part III. All I wish to say is that my conscious purpose there is to show how both conflicting modern ideologies to some extent tie in with the much older literary traditions examined in Parts I and II.

To the extent that Max Weber succeeded in eliminating ideological implications, his *Wirtschaft und Gesellschaft* became a pioneering scientific study of one aspect of modern sociology (along with that of other aspects inspired in other works). It can reasonably be argued that one of the most important contributions to economics in the twentieth century was not rendered by economists but by social and political scientists studying the nature of power and dependence, freedom, and voluntary cooperation. For this line of research, Weber provided a typology, which invited the construction of systematic theories. A sideline to this, most relevant from the point of view of the present study and subtly invited by the notation in question, is the study of the nature of coercion (as the current literature mostly styles it), or compulsion (in the terminology of earlier traditions). In abstract terms, coercion is not defined exactly the same way by all authors. The following would seem to be more or less standard. If A does a* rather than a, with the consequence that B does b* rather than b, A can, under certain conditions, be said to coerce B. These conditions may include the proviso that a* and b* are in some sense extraordinary acts compared with a and b, and it is usually assumed that A intends to influence B's behavior as described. This general definition clearly includes cases where A represents authority, exercising "patriarchal, magisterial, or princely power" (as Weber has it). It seems more often to be assumed, however, that A and B are private individuals, the question of the lawfulness or not of the acts envisaged appearing merely as a factor limiting the practical applicability of the theory.

A case of pure economic coercion or, in Weber's terminology, of the exercise of private economic power, then, is that of a monopolist coercing a hungry or sick person, in fear of starvation or death, to agree "freely" and "voluntarily" to pay an abnormally high price for food or medicine. In modern society, exploitation of need in this crude sense is obviously only one among myriad means by which, or circumstances under which, one party to an economic relationship, involving capital, commodities, or labor, can obtain an unusual profit (lawful or not) by coercing the opposite party according to the abstract definition of coercion cited previously. Many such cases are described in the literature. A stronger analytical model is being developed, which might, technically, be applied to historical source material as well. I shall have some occasion to refer to modern methodology, but in the main, true to a different research principle, I shall present the ideas on compulsion, the will, and freedom recorded in my primary sources in the much simpler analytical schemes in which they were originally set down. If lines can be drawn from Weber's peculiar notation, applied three quarters of a century ago, to contemporary ideological disputes and to future social science, there is a third line, which takes us back through the centuries to medieval scholastic philosophy. Taking leave of him here for the time being, it is useful to recall that Max Weber, before gaining fame as a sociologist, and indeed before applying himself to the study of religion and gaining notoriety for his thesis about the economic concomitants of Protestantism, was a medievalist.

It was a medieval master associated with the fledgling University of Paris who first raised the question of justice and validity of contracts in cases involving economic compulsion or coercion in the sense indicated above, that is, in the sense that one party to a contract does not agree to it or to its terms entirely freely and voluntarily but because of economic need. The earliest extant record of a discussion in these terms dates from the second decade of the thirteenth century, but there is some internal evidence to indicate that the tradition is somewhat older. It is clear, anyhow, that it consists in an adaptation to purely economic categories of an analytical model that originated in ancient Greece. It was transmitted to the Latin West through three distinct though occasionally confluent literary channels, namely, by way of translations of the relevant part of Aristotle's *Ethics* or of paraphrases on it, by way of Roman law, and by way of patristic moral theology. In Part I, a chapter is devoted to tracing each of these ancient traditions until their reinterpretation in economic terms.

In its original form, the model would not normally involve economic terms at all. The advantage obtained by the compeller would not be of an economic character, and the threat would be entirely physical. Moreover, in the ancient and early medieval periods, the questions raised by philosophers and theologians in connection with compulsion in this sense would not relate to justice but rather to the moral responsibility or culpability of the person succumbing to the threat. The model was applied to the question of justice and validity of contracts in classical Roman law, but authors in the legal tradition, including the early medieval Romanists, would insist on limiting the cases considered to those involving physical compulsion, the terms of contract being obtained by threats of death or physical violence. Aristotle described acts performed under compulsion as being "mixed" as regards their voluntary or involuntary nature: In the ensuing traditions, alternative terminologies appeared: The threatened person's action or consent would not be "absolutely" or "simply" voluntary but merely "conditionally" voluntary or voluntary "in a certain respect."

The kinship between these expressions and those of Weber is very obvious, but there is a difference as regards their dialectic signification. Whereas the twentieth-century social scientist will seek to preserve his "Wertfreiheit" by constructions like these, the medieval and early modern authors whose works are to be examined in the sequel would construct a detailed casuistry, considering different kinds and degrees of compulsion, different consequences of withstanding or succumbing to the compulsion, and would discuss how this affected the moral responsibility or culpability of the compelled, or the justice of the contract obtained by the compeller. When this model was fully adapted to economic categories, the casuistry was extended to a variety of economic contracts, to different kinds and degrees of need, and to various moral and legal questions relating to the profits obtained by compulsion. This is the scholastic tradition on need, the will and justice, which will be recorded and analyzed in Part II, the main part of this book. In the course of the approximately five centuries that it covers, opinions would change, new attitudes would appear, and different schools would be established, which, as will be indicated in Part III, tie in with conflicting modern ideologies.

When the ancient model of compulsion and the voluntary was applied to economic compulsion in the early thirteenth century, the first cases considered did not relate to the sale and purchase of necessaries like food or medicine but rather to the lending and borrowing of money. This might nearly amount to the same thing, in that it seems originally to have been assumed that the money in question was to be used for the purchase of necessaries. Unless the potential debtor agrees to pay usury, the potential creditor will refuse to lend. The consequences of this refusal may in the end be physical enough. When I call this economic compulsion distinct from the kind of physical compulsion long since considered by the Romanists, it is because the physical consequences do not appear in the form of violence threatening at the hands of the creditor or his henchmen but in the form of the want and possible starvation and death threatening the debtor if the loan is refused. Economic compulsion is compulsion by a person's own need, utilized by another person to his advantage. Before long, cases involving usury were extended to loans for different purposes, including that of profitable investment, calling for critical assessment of compulsion and justice in relation to an ever-extending concept of economic need. Before the century was over, application of this analytical model had been made to the sale and purchase of necessary commodities as well, and it was later to be extended to luxuries. More than two centuries were to pass before cases of labor and wage contracts were similarly subjected to analysis in terms of compulsion by need in relation to consent and justice.

Some readers will no doubt recognize a certain scheme of historical periodization in this chronological sketch. The problem of usury is very old, arising even in mainly agrarian societies. Usury was discussed, and largely condemned, in Mediterranean cultures as far back as the written evidence extends. Problems relating to the just price of commodities and the validity of monetary exchange contracts will come to the fore with the growth of commercial capitalism. The question of the just price of labor, in the broad sense of a just remuneration of labor laid down in work offered for sale, will arise simultaneously and can be discussed by analogy with or, indeed, as an aspect of, the question of the just price of commodities. In the narrower sense of the just wage, this question will attract attention with the gradual replacement of slavery by hired labor in domestic service and with the appearance of industrial capitalism. In Part II, one chapter will be devoted to money and usury, two chapters to commodities and price, and one chapter to labor and wages. By the turn of the fifteenth and sixteenth centuries, a general paradigm, long since established, was at last being applied to the analysis of all these three main classes of economic contracts as regards need, the will, and justice. Within a few decades, however, the first signs of a decomposition of this paradigm had appeared, heralding both the long-drawn-out decline of scholastic economics and the rearguard struggle to preserve its essential principles.

The primary source material supporting the analysis in Part I (prescholastic sources) is relatively limited and easily accessible (see Bibliography). Most of the authors cited are prominent historical figures; moreover, a selection of secondary critical literature is referred to in notes. Part II is more problematical from a biographical and bibliographical point of view. The material analyzed (scholastic sources, including most of the manuscript sources) is much larger and may seem complex and obscure. Scholasticism is understood in this book in a broad sense. It is taken to include not only the works of theologians and philosophers but also those of some Romanists and canonists as well as many works occupying border areas between these various disciplines. All are relevant insofar as they contribute to the establishment, development, and criticism of the central doctrines analyzed in Part II. To the specialist in any of these areas of study, the authors representing his particular area will be thoroughly familiar figures as well. As we are to range over a number of such special areas, however, there is a danger of swamping the general reader (as well as the narrow specialist) with names and titles that tell him very little. The obvious way out of this dilemma is by simplification and selection, but this has all too often been done in medieval economics studies, usually at the cost of precision and variety in historical reconstruction, and this is something I very much want to avoid. As an alternative, I have supplied the bibliography of scholastic sources with the barest vital data about the authors (as far as they are known). On the basis of the following brief overview, and on further particulars supplied in the text as we proceed, I then trust that the titles of works listed will indicate where each author belongs within the broad compass of scholasticism. Some secondary critical studies will also be referred to here for additional information regarding different schools and periods, but very few of these touch, even peripherally, on the main theme of the present book.

As indicated previously, examination of the question of economic need and the will in connection with justice was initiated in Parisian academic circles. The authors in question were theologians with a notable leaning toward canon law. This is an expression of a general dependence of the subsequently dominant theological tradition of scholastic economics on a previous tradition in law. From the twelfth century, doctrines regarding moneylending and trade in commodities were developed in connection with the study of Roman and, mainly, canon law. These schools of law were based in Northern Italy with centers at Bologna but drew students and teachers from other regions as well. Some of the foremost proponents of economic doctrine in the canon law context were of Spanish origin. The just-price teaching of the early Romanists and canonists was studied by Baldwin, 1959. This scholarly work is still unsurpassed in its particular field. In other fields, the best works available are even older. McLaughlin, 1939–40, reports on the usury teaching of the early canonists. Canonistic culpability doctrine was examined by Kuttner, 1935, who refers briefly to the question of compulsion and the will. Most of the twelfth-, thirteenth-, and fourteenth-century lawyers quoted in the present book appear in one or more of these studies. For valuable bio-bibliographical information mention may also be made of a recent general introduction to medieval canon law by Brundage, 1995, and of the impressive repertory by Kuttner, 1937.

In the first couple of centuries after the foundation of the University of Paris, scholasticism was associated with this institution and primarily with its faculties of philosophy and theology. These schools, in their heyday, represent the first great flourishing of scholastic thought. Paris attracted scholars from all parts of Europe. Besides some Frenchmen, the towering figures of medieval scholasticism include natives of Italy, Germany, Belgium, and Britain. Most of them were men who had studied and taught for a period in the schools of Paris and had received much of their inspiration there. As regards norms of economic behavior, which was a peripheral though relevant subject from the point of view both of moral philosophy and of moral theology, the contributions made by some British masters may be more significant than is generally recognized. Anyhow, scholastic economic doctrine found much of its lasting form in this academic milieu. This is true of the characteristic medieval paradigm regarding need, the will, and justice, which was to shape arguments and determine cases long after Paris had lost its prominent position. On the economic doctrines of the Paris theologians of the thirteenth and early fourteenth centuries, I refer to my recent comprehensive study, Langholm, 1992. Economic compulsion is mentioned there but is not a dominant theme. The book contains fuller information about authors quoted in the present one, and their works in theology and adjacent fields, as well as a more extensive bibliography of secondary sources. The economic doctrines developed in the philosophical traditions inspired from Paris (that is, mainly the commentary traditions on Aristotle's *Ethics* and *Politics*) are the subjects of two earlier works, Langholm, 1979, 1983. Both extend beyond the main Paris period and contain additional information about authors and their works. The first of them can be consulted thematically on the scholastic doctrine of justice in exchange, but the question of economic compulsion and the will is not raised.

The ravages of war, famine, and pestilence that struck Europe in the fourteenth century affected its intellectual life as well. In the aftermath of the Black Death, and for many decades to come, academic teachers discussing usury, trade, and related subjects were mostly content with copying the medieval masters. When scholastic economics resumed some of its vigor in the early fifteenth century, its center of gravity had moved eastward, to the more recently founded German universities. On the eve of the Renaissance, it crossed the Alps and came to rest in Northern Italy, where it remained until after the Reformation. The Council of Trent marks the end of Italian hegemony in this area. The last great flourishing of scholasticism is then often associated with Salamanca and other Iberian universities in Spain's golden age, when economic subjects naturally found their place in the academic curriculum. The German contribution will be noted in works covering a more extended period. One trustworthy critical study of this kind is that of Noonan, 1957, a work that deals with more than usury, which is the only subject announced in the title. Some of the works on the late Spanish scholastics to be mentioned also look back to their German predecessors, as well as to some of the Italians. In the case of the latter, these selective flashbacks cannot do justice to the contribution of Italian Renaissance scholasticism to the development of economic thought.

Some of the main thirteenth-century contributors to the formation of scholastic economic doctrine in the Paris theological tradition were born and taught for much of their lives in the Mediterranean region, and their ideas lived on there. While the influence of Paris declined and transalpine theology gradually lost touch with its source of inspiration in canon law, legal studies continued to flourish in Italy throughout the fourteenth and fifteenth centuries. In the early Renaissance, a growing commercial and industrial economy, the techniques and institutions that served it, and, not least, the mentality that was both its motive power and its product, all called for a reexamination of moral guidelines. This need was felt primarily by the friars, the successors of the great friar theologians of the Paris schools, but these were friars with a legal background as well. They caused the two academic traditions to merge once more, creating a characteristic set of economic doctrines in the border area between theology and canon law.

In view of the wealth of documentation and analysis of life and letters in Renaissance Italy, these doctrines represent a curiously neglected aspect of it. Such historical studies as have appeared tend to focus narrowly on one of the early itinerant preachers and on the mid-fifteenth-century author of a theological *summa*, both important figures. On the economics of these two Tuscan saints, there is a valuable study with much useful information and further references by De Roover, 1967. The main literary vehicles of the tradition, however, were the books of instruction *(summas)* and briefer manuals for confessors or penitents. They were not originally a Mediterranean genre, but they developed in Italy from the thirteenth century and flourished throughout this Italian phase of scholasticism. The question of justice in connection with need and the will was a frequent issue, and it was in Italy that attitudes to this question started to change. For general bio-bibliographical information, the best reference is Michaud-Quantin, 1962. Doctrinal studies of other subjects in these works have appeared. A monograph on their economics should be a promising research project.

The contribution to economic thought made by late Spanish scholasticism is the subject of a number of studies. Those of Dempsey, 1948; W. Weber, 1959, 1962; and Grice-Hutchinson, 1952, 1978, tend to focus on monetary doctrine, but their scope is, in fact, broader. Exchange and value doctrine is examined by Gómez Camacho, 1978, 1981, and labor and wages doctrine by Rocha, 1933. Chafuen, 1986, covers all these areas. Traditional scholastic genres are still represented in the source material at this final stage, including the *summa* for confessors (which had extended with time to multivolume size), but the typical literary vehicle was the treatise "on justice and right," a combination of moral theology and law in a new format. Some of the authors treat extensively of economic subjects. In these academic circles and literary contexts, the medieval paradigm regarding need and the will was explicitly reconsidered and rejected. The tradition is sometimes referred to loosely as the School of Salamanca to indicate its origin and nucleus, but a number of its major contributors were, in fact, based elsewhere in the Iberian Peninsula, and with Spain's domination it spread to the north, particularly to the Netherlands. It influenced the Protestant natural law tradition and thereby, eventually, modern professional economics.

PART I

Compulsion and the will:
three ancient traditions

A questo punto voglio che tu pense
che la forza al voler si mischia, e fanno
sì che scusar non si posson l'offense.
Voglia assoluta non consente al danno;
ma consentevi in tanto, in quanto teme,
se si ritrae, cadere in più affanno.

Dante, *Paradiso,* IV, 106–11

CHAPTER 1

The Aristotelian tradition

1.1 Aristotle on compulsion and the voluntary

Aristotle's occupation with questions relating to the voluntary can be explained on the basis of the literary context of his ethical works, as well as on the basis of the broader cultural and historical circumstances.[1] As a disciple of Plato, Aristotle was one of the first to try to make sense of what came to be known as the moral paradox of Socrates, namely, that no person acts against his own better judgment.[2] He was perhaps the first to declare that this proposition "plainly contradicts the observed facts."[3] That remark occurs in the seventh book of the *Nicomachean Ethics*, in the course of Aristotle's discussion of ἀκρασία, usually rendered by English translators as "incontinence" (following the Latin tradition), but occasionally as "weakness of will."[4] These chapters in Book VII contain Aristotle's most penetrating analysis of the nature of the voluntary and the involuntary, but already in Book III there is a preliminary discussion of certain aspects of this question. It is presented by way of a general introduction to the analysis of the virtues and the vices. A person can be praised or blamed only for actions that he performs voluntarily. This is not merely a question of judgment and strength of will, but also of circumstances.

It is disputable whether Aristotle in some contexts should be inter-

---

[1] On the literary and historical background of Aristotle's analysis of the voluntary in *Ethics*, III, cp. Burnet, 1900, 108; Joachim, 1951, 95–6; Dirlmeier, 1964, 322; and Gauthier and Jolif, 1970, II,1, 168–9.

[2] Most explicitly in *Georgias*, 460B–C, 509D–E, and *Protagoras*, 345C, supported by passages in other early dialogues of Plato and permeating his moral teaching in *Republic*. Cp. also Xenophon, *Memorabilia*, III,9,5.

[3] EN, VII,1: 1145b27–8.

[4] Ross, whose translation is mostly followed here, is among the great majority who adopt Grosseteste's *incontinentia*, but cp. Burnet, 1900, 280, who has found some recent followers as well. On the concepts of absolute and conditional will in connection with the analysis of ἀκρασία in *Ethics*, VII, with quotations from some medieval theologians and Aristotle commentators, cp. Saarinen, 1994.

preted as being a psychological determinist. He is perhaps best under-stood in the present context as though he was not, but the issue is not decisive for our purpose. Regardless of how the formation of the will is to be understood, suffice it to say that Aristotle considered a person to be the master of his own acts and therefore morally (and legally) responsible for them provided that he acted on the right information and in the absence of external hindrances.[5] The question raised in *Ethics*, III,[6] is whether and to what extent responsibility is withdrawn in the case of acts done through ignorance or under compulsion. As in Plato, much more space is devoted to ignorance than to compulsion.[7] As regards the latter, one form of it is unproblematical (Ross's trans-lation): "That is compulsory of which the moving principle is outside, being a principle in which nothing is contributed by the person who is acting or is feeling the passion, e.g., if he were to be carried some-where by a wind or by men who had him in their power."[8]

The *Eudemian Ethics* provides another graphic example: A person takes hold of another person's hand and, against his will, strikes a third person with it.[9] Imputability does not extend to such acts, which the agent, being overpowered by an external force, is physically incapable of preventing. In *Protagoras*, however, Socrates recognizes that men are

[5] For a closely argued study of responsibility in Aristotle, with regard to external as well as internal factors and with useful further references, cp. Irwin, 1980. See also note 12 below.

[6] When the *Ethics* of Aristotle is referred to without an adjunct, I shall mean the *Nicomachean Ethics*, on which the medieval commentary tradition was largely based, rather than the *Eudemian Ethics*, to which I shall refer occasionally by its full title.

[7] In each of the ancient literary traditions that form the subjects of this and the two following chapters, ignorance and compulsion appear (under various designations) as analytical pairs. In medieval economics, the question of fraud, which mostly pertains to ignorance through faulty or insufficient information, drew a volume of critical literature that greatly exceeds the literature on economic compulsion. Despite the fact, however, that Aristotle in *Ethics*, III, on the pages following our quotations, proceeds to discuss ignorance at length, he does not appear to have inspired medieval economic thought on this subject at all. An indirect influence is evident, mainly via Roman law. But *Ethics*, III, was not read in the medieval schools with a view to economic fraud the way some scholastic masters found that it could be read with a view to the abuse of economic power. Nothing more needs therefore to be said about Aristotle on ignorance.

[8] EN, III,1: 1110a1–4.

[9] EE, II,8: 1224b11–14.

sometimes said to be governed by other forces, "now by passion, now
by pleasure, now by pain, at times by love, and often by fear *(φόβος)*."[10]
Most of these forces are internal, but fear (when rational) is externally
provoked. It is "an expectation of evil."[11] This line of thought is pursued by Aristotle. It makes the question of the voluntary and the involuntary more complicated. For purposes of reference, I insert some
words and phrases of Robert Grosseteste's medieval Latin translation
in the English version by Ross. The key term, in the *Ethics* as in *Protagoras*, is φόβος.[12]

But with regard to the things that are done from fear of greater evils *(propter
timorem maiorum malorum)* . . . (e.g., if a tyrant were to order one to do something
base, having one's parents and children in his power, and if one did the action
they were to be saved, but otherwise would be put to death), it may be debated
whether such actions are involuntary or voluntary. Something of the sort happens also with regard to the throwing of goods overboard in a storm; for in the
abstract no one throws goods away voluntarily *(simpliciter quidem enim nullus eicit
voluntarius)*, but on condition of its securing the safety of himself and his crew
any sensible man does so. Such actions, then, are mixed *(mixtae)*, but are more
like voluntary actions *(assimilantur autem magis, voluntariis)*; for they are worthy
of choice *(voluntariae)* at the time when they are done, and the end of an action
is relative to the occasion. Both the terms, then, "voluntary" *(voluntarium)* and
"involuntary" *(involuntarium)*, must be used with reference to the moment of
action. Now the man acts voluntarily *(volens)*; for the principle that moves the
instrumental parts of the body in such actions is in him, and the things of
which the moving principle is in a man himself are in his power to do or not
to do. Such actions, therefore, are voluntary, but in the abstract perhaps involuntary *(Voluntaria utique talia; simpliciter autem forsitan, involuntaria)*; for no one
would choose any such act in itself *(Nullus enim utique eligeret secundum se ipsum,
talium facere)*.[13]

The voluntary nature of such acts is confirmed by the fact that men
are sometimes praised for them. On the other hand, if the pressure is
too great, those who cannot withstand it are sometimes pardoned,

---

[10] *Protagoras*, 352B: Lamb's translation, LCL 165, 227.
[11] Ibid. 358D: 247; cp. *Laches*, 198B: Lamb's translation, LCL 165, 73: "fear
(δέος) is expectation of coming evil."
[12] The following presentation and discussion of Aristotle's theory of
compulsion and the voluntary are strictly limited to what is relevant as a
background for its medieval Latin reception. For some recent critical
analyses of the theory in its classical Greek context, cp. Sorabji, 1980, 259–
63, and Kenny, 1979, 27–48 (with a comparison between the version of the
Nicomachean Ethics and that of the *Eudemian*, which is generally considered
to be the more satisfactory one).
[13] EN, III,1: 1110a4–19.

though there are perhaps some acts to which a man cannot be forced (Grosseteste: *non est cogi*); it would be better to face a painful death. What kind of acts, then, are rightly to be called "compulsory" (βίαια; Grosseteste: *violenta*)? Following these reflections, this question is answered in a brief summing-up:

Without qualification *(simpliciter)* actions are so when the cause is in the external circumstances and the agent contributes nothing. But the things that in themselves are involuntary *(secundum se ipsa quidem involuntaria)*, but now and in return for these gains are worthy of choice *(nunc autem et pro hiis voluntaria)*, and whose moving principle is in the agent, are in themselves involuntary, but now and in return for these gains voluntary *(voluntaria)*. They are more like voluntary acts; for actions are in the class of particulars, and the particular acts here are voluntary *(Operationes enim, in singularibus. Haec autem, voluntaria).*[14]

In the course of this analysis, Aristotle makes a distinction (though neither term appears as a noun in the excerpts quoted) between βία and ἀνάγκη. Both words can be rendered in English as "force," but whereas the former is the kind of force that overpowers a person completely and renders him passive, the latter is the force implied in a threat. Aristotle's "mixed acts" thus occur in cases of ἀνάγκη. This distinction is to be found in the *Magna Moralia* as well. It is less clear-cut in the *Eudemian Ethics*. Of a person who finds himself in external circumstances in which he does something he would not otherwise have done, Aristotle says there that he acts through βία in a sense, but not absolutely.[15] This immediately suggests an association between the Greek dichotomy and the medieval jurists' *vis absoluta* versus *vis compulsiva*, which will be encountered in subsequent chapters, and there can be no doubt about an actual historical influence. As regards the word "compulsion," it will be used here more or less interchangeably with "force," according to common usage, referring to either class of cases. As long as it is clear that the reference is to ἀνάγκη or *vis compulsiva*, Aristotle's intention is hardly violated by saying that someone is compelled or forced by fear or by a threat.

Having established these matters of terminology, a nice symmetry of Aristotle's analysis in the *Nicomachean Ethics* should be observed. It will illustrate some of its essence, as well as a certain limitation of its scope. Four cases are being considered. A person is subjected either to βία or to ἀνάγκη, by an external force that is either personal or impersonal. Note first that the personal or impersonal character of this external force is irrelevant in cases of βία (in the absolute sense). Whether being

[14] Ibid., 1110b1–7.
[15] EE, II,8: 1225a12.

carried away helplessly by the elements or by other persons who have
him in their power, the person in question is unable to influence the
course of events and thus is without responsibility for what ensues –
unless he voluntarily or through gross negligence placed himself in
those circumstances. Except for this, which we need not go into here,
cases of βία are irrelevant to ethics as far as the person compelled is
concerned. Then note, however, that Aristotle addresses the question
at issue as though the personal or impersonal character of the external
force is irrelevant in cases of ἀνάγκη as well. Whether the person is
faced with the threatening sea or with a tyrant threatening the life of
his family, Aristotle's analysis is strictly unilateral; it is focused entirely
on the responsibility of the person forced to act in a certain way. When
the external compeller is personal, a potentially important aspect of
the problem is missed.

In most human encounters, moral judgment requires a bilateral approach, considering the motives and circumstances of both parties involved. Aristotle devoted a different book of the *Ethics* exclusively to
this subject and thereby greatly influenced European thought on justice. Intent on another analytical purpose, he deliberately ignores this
complicating factor in *Ethics*, III, choosing for his example a human
compeller who is distant and unyielding. Just as the storm cannot be
stilled, there is no question of making the tyrant withdraw his threat.
The external compelling force, whether personal or impersonal, is simply a datum to the analysis of the position of the person compelled.
There is no question but that this approach imported a curious sense
of alienation to the tradition that developed from this text. When Aristotle's influence spread from the narrow textual commentaries to
other literary genres, he was frequently quoted piecemeal. His authority
was granted to arguments stretched far beyond their original context.
Thus, when justice was being considered in cases of compulsion in
immediate personal encounters, Aristotle's conclusion regarding the
voluntary could be made to decide the issue unilaterally, as though
there were no other person involved than the one compelled. As a
matter of fact, in scholastic economic literature, the case of the captain
who jettisons cargo became the standard example, while I am at a loss
to point to a single mention of the unfortunate fellow threatened by
the tyrant.

Aristotle's original context does not call for a bilateral view. His sole
concern in *Ethics*, III, is the nature of a person's will when he acts as
he would not otherwise have done, because he is being threatened,
regardless of how or by whom. The captain would obviously have preferred to sail his ship safely into harbor with its cargo. When the storm

breaks, this option is closed. He must choose between two inferior alternatives,[16] namely, either to throw some of the cargo overboard in order to snug the ship down or to risk shipwreck. So the captain decides to jettison cargo. Does he will this? Is this "mixed act," performed "from fear of greater evils," a voluntary act? Aristotle hedges about his reply to this question in the *Nicomachean Ethics*, saying, in effect, yes and no; in the circumstances, yes, though adding that such acts are, in the final analysis, "more like voluntary acts." This vagueness may indicate a certain doctrinal uncertainty. The *Eudemian Ethics* suggests that at least some acts, performed in circumstances where alternative courses are in principle open to the agent, are nevertheless involuntary, namely, if the threat is particularly severe.[17] The *Magna Moralia* has the distinction between βία and ἀνάγκη but does not state clearly whether acts of the latter class are voluntary or not.[18] On the other hand, if the question is to be answered only in terms of Aristotle's ἑκούσιος, which Grosseteste rendered as *voluntarius* and modern English translators render consistently as "voluntary," it would seem to be difficult to be more precise. Joachim, perhaps the finest modern commentator on the *Nicomachean Ethics*, preferred to speak of the actions of a person under compulsion as "willing" or "unwilling,"[19] and it seems now to be generally recognized that the question is mainly semantic. Aristotle lacked words to distinguish "willing" from "voluntary" and "unwilling" from "involuntary"; the Greek ἑκούσιος and ἀκούσιος can mean either the

[16] It would be logically more correct, as well as a better literal translation of Aristotle, to describe the situation not as that of choosing between two alternative *acts* but as that of weighing the pros and cons of a certain act ("to do something base," "to throw goods overboard"), the alternative being to *do nothing* and suffer the consequences. Cp. Joachim, 1951, 98. In economics, the "decision alternatives" are frequently of this nature; for instance, either to buy at the price asked by the seller (to do something) or not to buy on these conditions (to do nothing).

[17] EE, II,8: 1225a25–33.

[18] MM, I,14–15: 1188a38–b24. The author of this work, however, gives the latter class a very wide definition. It applies, "for instance, whenever a man receives some damage by way of alternative to some other greater, when compelled by circumstances. For instance, 'I found it necessary to hurry my steps to the country; otherwise I should have found my stock destroyed.' " The step from a conception like this to economic compulsion in the scholastic sense is very short indeed, but on this point I can find no evidence of an influence of the *Magna Moralia* on the medieval Latin commentary tradition on the *Nicomachean Ethics*.

[19] Joachim, 1951, 97–8.

one or the other.[20] It could perhaps be said that the ship's captain
jettisons cargo voluntarily but unwillingly (in the sense of reluctantly).
The Latin Aristotelians inherited this problem, for *voluntarius* carries
the same double meaning. In addition, the translation introduced dif-
ficulties of its own.

1.2   The early tradition to Grosseteste

The complete text of the *Nicomachean Ethics* was rendered into Latin
from Greek by Robert Grosseteste, bishop of Lincoln, and his assistants,
and the work was finished in 1246 or 1247. This version was sometimes
referred to as the *Translatio lincolniensis*, to distinguish it from several
fragments of earlier Latin translations. One of these, covering Books II
and III and known as the *Ethica vetus*, had been in circulation at least
since before the turn of the century. It was known to Grosseteste, who
used it critically.[21] These Latin translations are, on the whole, narrowly
literal, at times cryptic and hard to make sense of. Fortunately, they
were accompanied by a varied and interesting commentary tradition
that did something to clarify Aristotle's meaning and sometimes suggested original interpretations.

Almost a century before Grosseteste, and perhaps antedating the *Ethica vetus*, Burgundio of Pisa translated, from the Greek, a learned treatise that came to be known in Latin as *De natura hominis*. Attributed by
scholastic authors (including Thomas Aquinas, who used it copiously)
to Gregory of Nyssa, it is, in fact, the work of Nemesius, a fifth-century
Syrian Neoplatonist and bishop of Emesa. He drew on the Stoa and on
scriptural traditions, as well as on Aristotle. A series of chapters contains
paraphrases of the analysis of the voluntary in the *Nicomachean Ethics*.[22]
Some years before this, Burgundio translated, as *De fide orthodoxa*, a
work by the eighth-century theologian St. John Damascene. It was used
by Aquinas and others and contains a brief paraphrase of Aristotle on

---

[20] Cp. Hardie, 1968, 152–3; Kenny, 1979, 27.
[21] All the medieval Latin versions of the *Nicomachean Ethics* were critically
edited in *Aristoteles Latinus* (AL), XXVI, 1–3. The *Ethica vetus* is in Fasc. 2,
and Grosseteste's translation in its pure form (the *lincolniensis* as quoted
here) is in Fasc. 3. See also note 26.
[22] This work, in the original Greek, with a different Latin translation, is in
PG 40, 503–818. *De natura hominis*, in the version of Burgundio of Pisa, was
critically edited in *Corpus Latinum commentariorum in Aristotelem Graecorum*
(CLCAG), Suppl. 1, 1975.

compulsion and the voluntary.[23] Averroës's work on the *Ethics* also reached the Latin West early on. His "middle commentary" was translated from the Arabic by Herman the German in 1240. It was known in its Latin version as the *Liber Nicomachiae*.[24]

When Grosseteste's assistants brought home Greek manuscripts for the Lincoln translation, they added some Greek commentaries, recently compiled at Constantinople from material of varying ages and origins. They included a set of anonymous scholia on Book III, perhaps dating from the third century. Translated and copied alternately with the text, these commentaries exerted considerable influence in the scholastic milieu, both directly and indirectly, in that they served as aids for the translation of Aristotle's original.[25] To this impressive collection of text and commentaries, Grosseteste further contributed a large number of his own notes. Interlinear and marginal, grammatical and doctrinal, some brief, some quite lengthy, they include a large subset of notes that explain his own translation or suggest alternative translations. Selections of these notes (often confusingly intermingled with later notes in similar hands) are preserved in a few precious manuscripts of Grosseteste's corpus on the *Ethics*.[26]

The significance of these translations is partly terminological and partly substantive. They introduced a set of Latin terms by which to describe conditional and absolute will and to explain why and in what sense that which is done under compulsion can be said to be done voluntarily. It should also be noted that the direct Latin translations of

---

[23] In the Greek original, this paraphrase is in Book II, Chapter 24, and is to be found in PG 94, 954–5. Burgundio's Latin version is in Chapter 38; critical edition, 1955, 146–7.

[24] This work is lost in the Arabic original, and there is as yet no critical edition of Herman's translation. I quote it from a Vatican manuscript, Urbin. lat. 221.

[25] The anonymous scholia on *Ethics*, III, are in *Commentaria in Aristotelem Graeca* (CAG), Vol. 20, 141–75. The Latin translation by Robert Grosseteste was critically edited in CLCAG, Vol. VI,1, 236–306.

[26] There is as yet no critical edition of the several strata of notes in the early Latin manuscripts of the *Ethics*. Numerous notes, believed to be those of Grosseteste, with occurrences in different manuscripts, are recorded by Gauthier in his edition of the pure text of the *lincolniensis* in AL, XXVI, 1–3, Fasc. 3. Only a few years after the publication of the pure text in 1246/7 revised text appeared (cp. ibid., Fasc. 4), which served as a basis for many of the scholastic commentaries. Occasionally, Grosseteste's notes influenced the revision and thereby these commentaries. Cp. Langholm, 1979.

the *Ethics* persisted in a confusing error on a crucial point in Aristotle's argument. To get his true meaning, medieval users of the Lincoln translation would have had to have recourse to the supporting note and commentary material.

In the second (the longer) of the sequences quoted verbatim in the preceding section, Aristotle teaches that, were it not for the circumstances, no one would throw goods overboard; but for the circumstances, such actions must be said to be involuntary. This phrase corresponds to one used by Burgundio of Pisa: No one would choose to do things like that *sine circumstantia*.[27] In *De natura hominis*, this is a literal translation of ἄνευ περιστάσεως.[28] The original in the *Ethics*, however, is ἁπλῶς[29] ("simply," "plainly," "absolutely," or, as Ross has it in both instances, "in the abstract"). In the third excerpt quoted, Ross renders ἁπλῶς as "without qualification,"[30] a phrase also preferred by Joachim.[31] The medieval Latin versions *(vetus and lincolniensis)* consistently render this word as *simpliciter*. At the second occurrence of *simpliciter* in the longer verbatim quotation (toward the end), a number of manuscripts of the *Translatio lincolniensis* have a marginal or interlinear gloss reading, *id est secundum se ipsa considerata*,[32] and in the sequence it is stated in the text that no one would choose "in itself" *(καθ' αὐτό; vetus: per se; lincolniensis: secundum se ipsum)* to do the thing that the circumstances force him to do.[33] This terminology is confirmed in the last verbatim quotation.[34]

These acts are nevertheless "more like voluntary acts," and the penultimate line quoted in the preceding paragraph provides the clue to Aristotle's reason for saying this. While not chosen *secundum se*, acts performed through fear are the result of a choice. This does not come through as clearly in the Lincoln translation as in the Greek original, for on this point Grosseteste failed to correct what can only be called an error in the *Ethica vetus*. The long middle passage in the last verbatim quotation from the *Ethics* is reduced to a meaningless tautology

---

[27] Chapter 29: CLCAG, Suppl. 1, 121.
[28] PG 40, 721 (in Chapter 30).
[29] 1110a9; a18.
[30] 1110b1.
[31] Joachim, 1951, 97.
[32] At 1110a18 in Stockholm KB V.a.3, f.38rb; Cambridge Peterhouse 116, f.54rb; Eton College 122, f.41va (three of the manuscripts of the Lincoln corpus richest in original notes), and in others.
[33] 1110a19.
[34] 1110b3.

in the Latin versions because two key words are both rendered *volun-taria*. In the first instance the original is αἱρετά ("desirable," or "choice-worthy").[35] The correct sense of Aristotle's argument is that, granted that we would not otherwise have done this particular thing, and provided that the moving principle in doing it is in ourselves, we choose to do it under the given circumstances in view of what we gain by it in comparison to the feasible alternative,[36] and therefore such actions must, after all, be said to be voluntary.

The translators of the commentaries and paraphrases on the *Ethics*, mentioned previously, had chosen some other Latin words by which to convey Aristotle's meaning better. Someone who does a certain thing "from fear of greater evils," says Nemesius of Emesa, "does it by option or by choice, and at the time when they are performed [such actions] are worthy of choice (αἱρεταί)."[37] Burgundio translates, *facit . . . secundum optionem vel secundum electionem, et tunc sunt hae tales eligibiles cum geruntur.*[38] A similar expression is to be found in the *Liber Nicomachiae*. In Herman the German's translation of Averroës, the word *spontaneus* is used for the voluntary. At the time when an action compelled by a threat is performed, the agent *spontaneus est et eligens.*[39] The word used by both these translators appears also in the translation of the ancient anonymous scholiast on Book III that was included in the Lincoln corpus. That which we do because of the circumstances *eligimus et desideramus et ut desiderata volumus.*[40] In connection with the translation of the *Ethics* itself, Grosseteste ties in with this terminology only in the note material. The word αἱρεταί also occurs in the longer excerpt from the *Ethics* quoted verbatim in the preceding section. It is rendered *voluntariae.*[41] But at this word several manuscripts carry a note suggesting an alternative reading: *seu eligibiles*; and in some manuscripts there are different versions of a longer note as well, stating that because throwing goods overboard in a storm to save one's life is *in electione*, it is, in a sense, a voluntary act.[42] The first generations of scholastics using Gros-

---

[35] 1110b4.

[36] The original expression is ἀντὶ τῶνδε ἑκούσια, suggesting rather "voluntary, following a weighing of the advantages and disadvantages of the action against one another." Cp. note 16 and Joachim, 1951, 98.

[37] PG 40, 721.

[38] CLCAG, Suppl. 1, 120.

[39] Vat. Urbin. lat. 221, f.197ra.

[40] CLCAG VI,1, 238; cp. CAG 20, 141.

[41] 1110a12.

[42] One version of this extensive note is to be found in Eton College 122,

seteste's translation seem to have had access to the full Lincoln corpus. Unfortunately, as demand for copies of the translation multiplied, the accompanying notes and commentaries tended to be omitted, and so one of Aristotle's main points regarding compulsion and the voluntary was left in obscurity.[43]

The captain elects or chooses to jettison cargo.[44] The fact that he did not elect to be in the situation in which this seems the best course of action does not render his choice involuntary in the situation. John Damascene says of such acts that they are in the middle (μέσα; Burgundio: *media*)[45] between the voluntary and the involuntary.[46] According to Aristotle, they are "mixed" as regards the will. The word used is the same in the original Greek (μικταὶ), in the medieval Latin translations *(mixtae)*, and in English. To the scholastic authors citing Aristotle, it became a common description of compelled choice. The dialectical convenience of such a construction is evident. It is adaptable to directly opposing argumentative purposes, lending support both to claims to moral extenuation or, if the compeller is personal, to injustice, and to claims to moral responsibility or justice. In the commentary tradition of the thirteenth and fourteenth centuries, the latter view was favored by the commentators' emphasis on the voluntary nature of "mixed" acts.

f.41va: "Et haec videtur melior littera. Ex hoc enim quod in electione est proicientis sua de navi in tempestate ut ipse salvetur, sequitur quod eius actio sit aliquo modo voluntaria." A variant is in Stockholm KB V.a.3, f.38ra, and in Paris Arsenal 698, f.30vb. The question of the origin of the notes and glosses in these manuscripts is complicated. Grosseteste's authorship to the note cited here is still hypothetical.

[43] When the *lincolniensis* was revised (see note 26), some of the alternative readings suggested in glosses found their way into the text. This did not happen in either of the instances where αἱρετός is rendered *voluntarius*.

[44] Dirlmeier, 1964, 323, notes the Greek practice of putting the decision to jettison cargo to the vote among those on board. This would demonstrate its deliberate character to Aristotle's listeners and may explain his choice of this particular example. The medieval authors, to whom this became a favorite standard case of behavior caused by "fear of greater evils," would seem to have been unfamiliar with this factual background and to have thought of it as an individual decision on the part of the captain.

[45] PG 94, 956; cp. ed. Buytaert, 147.

[46] The idea of such a middle position may derive from Plato. In *Laws*, IX, at 861E, certain acts are described as being "partly voluntary and partly involuntary" and at 867A as "lying midway between the voluntary and the involuntary" (Lamb's translation, LCL 192, 227, and 245). Cp. Walzer, 1929, 110.

1.3   Scholastic commentaries

The first commentator on the Latin translations of the *Nicomachean Ethics* was Albert the Great. In *De bono,* an early work, citing the *Ethica vetus* as well as *De natura hominis,* he examines the question of the voluntary and the involuntary in circumstances involving compulsion. Albert questions the use of the word *simpliciter.* In principle, he agrees that only that can be said truly to be involuntary whose efficient cause is external, "being a principle in which nothing is contributed by the person who is acting." Before confirming Aristotle's conclusion, he considers a number of objections, including one based on the example of the captain who "throws valuables from his ship in a storm in order not to endanger the ship." Such actions are said by Aristotle to be *simpliciter* involuntary, and yet the moving principle is in the agent. Albert replies with Aristotle that they are mixed acts and more like voluntary ones. As to the key word,

> *"simpliciter"* can be used in two different ways. Namely, with regard to what is done, without adding the circumstances of the event and the time. And thus it is true that what is done is *simpliciter* involuntary, *"simpliciter"* having regard only to the action considered *in se.* But if *"simpliciter"* is meant to refer to the cause of the action, then it is *simpliciter* voluntary, because it is *simpliciter* in respect of an intrinsic principle in which the agent participates.[47]

This would prove to be a pivotal statement. Albert the Great did not repeat it in the first of his two full-length commentaries on the *Nicomachean Ethics.* In *Super Ethica,* a close textual exposition with questions, composed shortly after the publication of the Lincoln translation, Albert is merely concerned with explaining Aristotle. He defines *simpliciter* as *universaliter.* The captain's action is voluntary at the moment *(secundum nunc),* but it is *simpliciter* involuntary, that is, involuntary when considered in the abstract, removed from time and circumstances.[48] This terminology is retained in *Ethica,* a later and freer commentary, but this work contains a passage that recalls Albert's original, unconventional usage as well. In *Ethica,* *"simpliciter* voluntary" is predicated, not merely on the cause *(causa)* of the compelled action, as in *De bono,* but on its end or purpose *(finis).* The jettison of cargo in a storm is an action *simpliciter* involuntary, that is, involuntary without the circumstances *(sine circumstantia),* for no one would choose to do a thing like that but

---

[47] *De bono,* I,4,3: 51–3.
[48] *Super Ethica,* III,1: 140.

for the circumstances; however, the purpose of the action, namely, to save the ship, is *simpliciter* voluntary.[49]

Thomas Aquinas took the decisive next step, predicating "*simpliciter* voluntary," directly and exclusively, of the compelled act as such. The crucial passage is to be found in his *Summa theologiae*. Like his teacher, Albert the Great, Aquinas referred to the case of the captain who jettisons cargo in other works besides his commentary on the *Ethics* itself. His terminology and interpretations are not consistent throughout these works but are clearly influenced by their different contexts. Though we shall have more to say about the theological tradition on compulsion and the voluntary in a later chapter, it seems best to anticipate Aquinas's contribution because it influenced later textual commentators on the *Ethics* as well.

In *De malo*, Aquinas considers the classic question whether sin primarily consists in voluntary acts and records the objection that that which is done through necessity is not voluntary and therefore not sinful. He replies that absolute force absolves from blame, but that there is another kind of necessity that is mixed with the voluntary, citing Aristotle's example. One who sins under such circumstances is not blameless, for his act is more voluntary than involuntary, as stated in *Ethics*, III.[50] In a later question in the same work, the author is clearly influenced by Albert the Great. "Voluntary" can refer both to the act and to the purpose of the act. A sick man who wants to be cured also wants to drink his bitter medicine, and a merchant [sic: *mercator*] who throws goods overboard in order to save his ship does so voluntarily.[51] The *Sententia libri Ethicorum*, composed a few years after *De malo* and apparently more or less contemporaneously with the *Summa theologiae*, is a simple exposition where Aquinas hardly ever takes a stand against Aristotle. Actions, he states there, quoting the text, are concerned with particulars *(singularia)*, and in the particular circumstances obtaining at the time, mixed acts, such as that of the captain who jettisons cargo, are voluntary. They can even be said to be properly and truly *(proprie et vere)* voluntary, but Aquinas does not yet state that they are *simpliciter* voluntary. On the contrary, such acts are *simpliciter* involuntary, that is, involuntary "considered in general," "absolutely and universally," "in themselves," etc.[52]

In the *Secunda secundae* of the *Summa theologiae*, under the heading

---

[49] *Ethica*, III,1,4: 198–9.
[50] *De malo*, II,3: XXIII,36–7.
[51] III,12: XXIII,92.
[52] *Sententia libri Ethicorum*, III,1–2: XLVII,119–20; 123.

"Of fear" *(De timore)*, Aquinas once more considers the question whether fear excuses from sin. He replies (rather more sensibly than some contemporary theologians) that one's sin would be somewhat extenuated if done through fear, for a frightened man acts under a certain necessity. Hence the Philosopher says that things done through fear are not *simpliciter* voluntary but a mixture of the voluntary and involuntary.[53] In an earlier question, however, in the *Prima secundae*, Aquinas had rejected this terminology. The context is highly relevant; the author addresses the subject of the voluntary and the involuntary directly, and in one article asks whether fear *(metus)* causes involuntariness *simpliciter*. Aquinas reports briefly on the opinions of Aristotle and Gregory of Nyssa (i.e., Nemesius of Emesa apud Burgundio of Pisa), then proceeds to reverse the application of Grosseteste's key term. Rightly considered, acts performed through fear are voluntary *simpliciter* and involuntary merely "in a certain respect" (*secundum quid* – introducing in this discussion the corresponding term for contingency in Aristotelian logic, κατά τι).

Something is said to be *simpliciter* according as it is in act, but according as it is in apprehension only, it is not *simpliciter* but *secundum quid*. But that which is done through fear is in act insofar as it is done. For since acts are concerned with particulars, and the particular, as such, is here and now, that which is done is in act insofar as it is here and now and under other individuating circumstances. Thus, that which is done through fear is voluntary, inasmuch as it is here and now, preventing, as it does under the circumstances, a greater evil which was feared; such as throwing merchandise into the sea becomes voluntary in a storm, because of the fear of peril. Therefore it is clear that it is *simpliciter* voluntary. Hence also the mode of the voluntary accords with it, in that its principle is internal. But as to interpreting that which is done through fear, as something outside this event, and repugnant to the will, this is nothing but a contemplation. Hence it is involuntary *secundum quid*, that is, according as it is considered outside the actual event.[54]

Supported by the great authority of its author, this rather surprising contradiction of Grosseteste naturally gained a foothold among the theologians and was copied throughout the scholastic tradition. The argument and conclusion of the *Summa theologiae* are to be found, for instance, nearly verbatim in the influential mid-fifteenth-century work with the same title, by Antonino of Florence.[55] Returning now to the commentary tradition on the *Nicomachean Ethics*, we find that the different interpretations by Albert the Great and Thomas Aquinas were

[53] *Sum. theol.*, II–II,125,4: X,46.
[54] I–II,6,6: VI,61.
[55] *Sum. theol.*, I,4,3,4: cols. 247–8.

variously received in the decades that followed. The philosophical program of the Paris Averroists, namely, to establish an integral interpretation of Aristotle and to defend it against what was seen as a falsification at the hands of the Mendicants, finds expression in some anonymous collections of questions on the *Ethics*, though there are traces of Aquinas's *Sententia* in them as well. As the Philosopher says in the preface to the *Metaphysics*, actions are concerned with the particular.[56] Acts done through fear are absolutely involuntary, yet they are the results of choice and are voluntary at the time of choice. They are therefore more voluntary than involuntary, for that which is in act is more voluntary than that which is in potency.[57]

Henry of Friemar sometimes copies Averroist material, along with other sources, for his long commentary on the *Nicomachean Ethics*. For his analysis and solution of the question of compulsion and the will, however, he relies entirely on Aquinas in the *Summa theologiae*. A thing ought to be called *simpliciter* according as it is in act and *secundum quid* as consisting only in an apprehension. Therefore, mixed acts, which are done through fear, are *simpliciter* voluntary and *secundum quid* involuntary.[58] A briefer paraphrase on the same source, with the same conclusion, is to be found in one of Guido Terreni's questions on the *Ethics*.[59] The textual commentary by another faithful Thomist, Walter Burley, however, is a mere elaboration of the *Sententia*.[60] Gerald Odonis and Jean Buridan, in characteristic fourteenth-century scholastic fashion, merely take the opportunity to distinguish a number of different senses of *"simpliciter."*[61] With these authors, we are firmly entrenched in the logic and semantics of moral philosophy, rather than its substance. It is unnecessary to pursue the tradition of the *Ethics* commentaries beyond this point. By the time of Buridan, the case of the captain who throws away his cargo was established as a classic example of forced choice in scholastic economic literature. We shall pick it up again and record its further use in that context in later chapters.

---

[56] *Metaph.*, I,1: 981a16–17.
[57] Vat.lat. 832, f.18rb–va; cp. Paris BN lat. 15106, f.18va.
[58] Basel UB F.I.14, f.57vb; Toulouse BMun 242, f.230vb.
[59] Bologna BU 1625, f.18vb.
[60] *Exp. Eth.*, III,1: f.42ra–b.
[61] Odonis, *Sent. Eth.*, III,1: f.88va–b; Buridan, *Quaest. Eth.*, III,8: f.46rb–va.

CHAPTER 2

The Roman law tradition

2.1 The legal approach

Medieval Latin Aristotle commentators, discussing acts done through fear, would alternate between Grosseteste's *timor* and the technical term *metus* of Roman law. Albert the Great and Thomas Aquinas, as well as such later commentators as Buridan, would distinguish between different degrees of external compulsion, one decisive criterion being whether the threat was such as to frighten a "courageous man," a "man of character" *(vir constans)*. This man of character is a Roman law exemplar. When the new translation of the *Nicomachean Ethics* appeared in the middle of the thirteenth century, law was a firmly established academic discipline, just like theology, and the interchange of terms and ideas with Aristotelian philosophy started to flow immediately. It is particularly striking in the writings of Albert the Great, the *doctor universalis*. In his first commentary, *Super Ethica*, there is a series of replies to objections drawn from legal texts against Aristotle's concept of a mixed will. They are mostly of a terminological character, but one of them goes to the substantive core of the two disciplines, whose ideas about compulsion and the voluntary are to be the subjects of this and the following chapter. It can serve as an introduction to the present one and as a preview of the next.

According to law, Albert remarks, force and fear *(vis et metus)* excuse completely, for (quoting the *Digest*) that which is done through force or fear will not be upheld in law. If such acts are similar to voluntary acts (as Aristotle claims), however, there is no excuse; hence it seems that Aristotle is in error. To this, Albert replies that fear remits all loss but not all shame. The judge considers both parties to a case. Because it is not right that he who applies compulsion should profit from the loss of him on whom it is applied, the legislator absolves the latter from all loss, but as regards shameful moral behavior, only the one who is guilty of it is considered. Because his action is improper insofar as it has something of the voluntary about it, it is not excused, but some, if not all, of its shamefulness remains. Therefore, it is taught in theology that no fear can fully excuse from sin.[1] Albert's description of legal principles regarding *metus* is a little biased. He refers to one of the praetorian edicts that provided remedies in cases of *metus* and not to the principal doctrine that made such remedies relevant and that were, in fact, influenced by Greek legal philosophy. Albert the Great nevertheless makes a most important point.

The theology to which Albert refers is that of the patristic-canonistic tradition, the main origin of which is to be found in the works of St. Augustine. Augustine's approach to the problem of compulsion and the will is, like that of Aristotle, almost entirely unilateral. It goes without saying that the application of many kinds of force in many different situations is blameworthy, but it seems less relevant to discuss whether one who applies force acts voluntarily or not. When the question of the voluntary is raised in the Augustinian tradition, the focus remains strictly on the person who is subjected to the threat and on his duty to withstand it. The main difference is the notion of sin, which was foreign to Aristotle, and the new existential gravity that it brought to the problem. Aristotle remarks in the *Ethics* that there are certain acts so base that a man ought rather to die than to yield to the threat. To the early Christians, this was not an academic point but a real choice. All too many had been threatened with torture and death unless they forsook their faith and denounced their God. In Augustine's theology of the will, the torturer is as much a foreign figure as the tyrant of *Ethics*, III, or the mindless sea.

The question of responsibility for acts done under compulsion may be relevant to civil and criminal law as well as to ethics. One approach to Aristotle's doctrine, not pursued in this study, is from the point of view of classical Greek jurisprudence.[2] By the same token, one of the main fields of application of Augustine's doctrine on this subject is in medieval canon law, but the body of law to which Albert the Great refers is clearly the Roman law of contract. In matters of contract, the approach is necessarily bilateral. Moreover, as Albert indicates, the context is often economic. Both parties are present in the picture. The judge considers the nature and amount of pressure put by one of them upon the other, and how reasonable it is for the latter to fear the threat of the former, and rules accordingly, often shifting *profit and loss* between the parties. It might seem natural, in a study like the present one, to say what little there is to be said about compulsion and the voluntary in the theological tradition and then to proceed via the

---

[1] *Super Ethica*, III,1: 140–1.
[2] For literary references, cp. Irwin, 1980, n. 4.

legal tradition to our discussion of economics in the second, main part of the study. I have nevertheless chosen to reverse the order of chapters in this first part, not mainly because the Roman law tradition is historically the older one (which can be disputed), but because the influence between these traditions flew almost exclusively in the opposite direction. The early medieval canonists and theologians borrowed part of their terminology from Roman law. When they began systematically to develop a doctrine of economic ethics, they stated it mainly as the Romanists would, in terms of justice. In the *Sentences* of Peter Lombard, the main textbook of theology in the Schools, the question of usury was raised in a chapter on theft, which is a legal as well as a moral offense.[3] It caused the usurer's sin to be regarded as primarily a sin against justice. The Lincoln translation of the *Ethics* presented the scholastics with a fascinating formula stating the correct terms of exchange of goods and services. It is to be found in Book V, on justice.[4] In neither of these fundamental texts are the questions of compulsion and the will originally coupled with that of justice. They came to be so coupled under the influence of Roman law, where they are fully integrated.

2.2   The *Corpus Iuris Civilis* and its sources

In order to understand the nature of the influence exerted by Roman law on medieval thought, it is necessary to recall that it was transmitted almost entirely through the collection made in the sixth century under the auspices of the Emperor Justinian and later known as the *Corpus Iuris Civilis*. The original parts of this huge body of civil law, the *Institutes*, the *Digest* (or *Pandects*), and the *Code*, are made up of individual laws as well as of legal opinions, edicts, and ordinances, which originated over an extended period of time. Sometimes contradicting one another, they are also frequently obscured by alterations, modifications, and additions, some made by the compilers themselves, and some by pre-Justinian authors. The task of reducing the elemental texts to their pristine forms, and thus of reconstructing the legal systems that they were originally designed to codify and explain, is still going on and is still encountering problems that divide the specialists.[5] The problems

---

[3] *Sent.*, III,37,5; see section 4.1.
[4] EN,V,5; see sections 5.2 and 7.3.
[5] The classic study of compulsion in Roman private law is that of
  Schliemann, 1861. Schulz, 1922, refuted some of Schliemann's opinions
  and supplemented his work with the results of more recent research. These

and opportunities that presented themselves to the medieval Romanists were of a different nature. They had to accept Justinian's *Corpus* as such, in the form in which it had been handed down to them, and try to make sense of it as a whole.

A fundamental principle of European legal philosophy makes will a sufficient condition of justice. It is of Greek origin. Aristotle asserts that "no one is voluntarily treated unjustly."[6] Some of the leading Roman jurists confirmed it. Thus, Ulpian states that "that is no injury, which is done to the willing."[7] Similarly, according to Paul, "one who was ever willing cannot be seen to suffer an injury."[8] Large parts of Roman law deal with property, its acquisition and exchange, and a number of different contracts are distinguished. In Roman classical private law, some important classes of economic contracts, including that of buying and selling, belonged in the category of consensual contracts. This means that they required no specific deed or formula in order to be valid, no symbolic act or real transaction. All that was required was consent between the parties. Several other economic contracts were in this category as well, but not the important loan contract *(mutuum)*, which, besides consent, depended on the thing being delivered or the money counted in order to be completed. Such additional formalities need not concern us here. Focus may be placed on the factors that are incompatible with consent and thus, according to Roman law, constitute relevant bases for an action of annulment or damages.

It is clear that error or misunderstanding as to the subject matter of the exchange violates the conditions of consent. If it is deliberately induced on the seller's or the buyer's part, this becomes a case of wilful fraud *(dolus malus)*. Consent in relation to knowledge and understanding, as well as the different shades of the concept of deceit, are given close attention in Roman law, and the extensive medieval literature on fraud in economic transactions, as to substance, quantity, or quality of merchandise, depends to a great extent on Roman law terminology and principles. An important distinction was observed between wilful fraud,

---

conflicting interpretations are recorded and analyzed, and some novel ideas suggested, by Hartkamp, 1971. The present sketch is based, when possible, on the consensus of these three authors and otherwise mostly on Schulz.

[6] EN, V,11: 1138a12, in Grosseteste's translation, ". . . iniustum patitur autem nullus, volens."

[7] D.47,10,1,5: ". . . nulla iniuria est, quae in volentem fiat."

[8] D.39,3,9,1: ". . . nullam enim potest videri iniuriam accipere, qui semel voluit."

which invalidates contracts, and higgling and bargaining, which is part and parcel of most commercial deals. It should be noted, however, that the concept of *laesio enormis*, which permits buyer and seller to outwit, or "deceive," each other within, but not beyond, the limits of one-half above or below the just price, is a postclassical construction. So is, in fact, the concept of a *iustum pretium* itself. Classical Roman law, just like modern classical and neoclassical economic theory, recognized no such thing as a just price.

Fraud being incompatible with consent, what about compulsion? The operative words here are *vis* (force, violence) and *metus* (fear), as well as forms of the verb *cogere* (to compel). Both the *Digest* and the *Code* have titles devoted specifically to this question.[9] In the *Digest*, the jurist Paul defines *vis* as "an attack by some overpowering agency such as cannot be withstood."[10] A definition of *metus* is included in an important statement by Ulpian. It is "mental trepidation on the ground of urgent or apprehended danger."[11] *Dolus* and *metus* often appear as twin terms in Roman legal texts, but their implications as regards consent are not identical. There is no question but that a party to a contract could sometimes claim duress or compulsion as a ground for annulment. In the course of the centuries, however, legal thought and practice in this area had undergone considerable development, which provided material for the Justinian compilation, and it is difficult to construct a coherent theory of the pertinent paragraphs reproduced there. Moreover, those texts which seem to say something definite about compulsion and consent seldom relate directly to economic contracts and can be applied to such contracts only by analogy, which in law is usually a hazardous undertaking.

The essential point is that classical private Roman law did *not* in general consider the subjection to compulsion to be incompatible with consent. The key statement of this position is due to Paul and is to be found in the *Digest*. The paragraph in question, which refers to the law of inheritance, contains the following phrase, ". . . although I should not have willed if I were free; still, being forced, I have willed" *(quamvis si liberum esset noluissem, tamen coactus volui)*.[12] The

---

[9] D.4,2, *Quod metus causa gestum erit*; C.2,19, *De his quae vi metusve causa gesta sunt.*

[10] D.4,2,2: "Vis autem est maioris rei impetus, qui repelli non potest." The English translation in the text is that of Monro, which I usually quote here, when available (D.1–15).

[11] D.4,2,1: ". . . instantis vel futuri periculi causa mentis trepidatio."

[12] D.4,2,21,5. Monro translates, less literally, ". . . although I should have

kinship of this statement with Aristotle's conclusion in our quotations from *Ethics*, III, is evident, and an actual influence is most likely. The idea is that compulsion does not rule out will; it rather influences the person compelled to will something else. Though inheritance is not a formless contract, analogous applications to buying and selling and other contracts in the economic sphere were freely made by authors less strictly bound by legal formalities. Considering this development, *coactus volui* is, without question, one of the most fateful sayings in the history of economic thought. As to its authenticity, there used to be a school of legal historians who rejected the theory of the validity of forced consent in classical Roman law, insisting on an interpolation in the Pauline text, but the current majority opinion seems to be that a transaction agreed to through threat was indeed valid, taking this as the very starting point of the further development of Roman law.[13] Several other fragments incorporated in the *Digest* confirm this interpretation.[14]

Proponents of the validity theory, however, have to contend with other texts, which contradict Paul. Most explicit is the following statement, attributed by Justinian's compilers to Ulpian: "Nothing is as contrary to consent . . . as force and fear" *(Nihil consensui tam contrarium est . . . quam vis atque metus).*[15] The mention of *metus* here along with *vis* makes it clear that the author has in mind something more than actual physical force, that is, what in Romanist terminology came to be known as *vis absoluta*. Limiting the statement to such force would reduce it to a truism. It is meaningful and disputable only if extended to include the fear of violence, the force implied in a threat, that is, *vis compulsiva* in Romanist terminology.[16] There is

---

declined if I had had liberty of action, still, being compelled, I had the will to do it."

[13] Cp. Schulz, 1922, 174: "Der Ausgangspunkt der römischen Rechtsentwicklung war der Satz: 'das erzwungene Rechtsgeschäft ist gültig; nicht einmal eine Anfechtungsmöglichkeit ist gegeben.' "

[14] Thus D.23,2,22 (Celsus, on matrimony); D.29,2,85 (Papinian, on inheritance); D.40,9,17, pr (Paul, on manumission). Cp. Hartkamp, 1971, 88–101.

[15] D.50,17,116.

[16] The analogy between this distinction and that of Aristotle is obvious. The person who is "carried somewhere by . . . men who have him in their power" is subjected to *vis absoluta*; "mixed" acts are performed under *vis compulsiva*. The origin of these terms is uncertain. They are not classical. Kuttner, 1935, 303, suggests that they may not be of Romanist origin at all, but due to the medieval canonists. See section 3.2.

thus no avoiding the conclusion that two conflicting opinions about the relation between compulsion and consent find expression in the *Digest*, namely, Paul's *coactus volui*, and the one just quoted. Some legal historians explain this contradiction by declaring the latter statement to be a postclassical interpolation; Ulpian could not have written one word of it.[17] The issue, however, is not resolved. Recent research has also witnessed attempts to vindicate the traditional view that the words are those of Ulpian, that Ulpian here makes himself the spokesman for the widely held opinion that threats can rule out will, and that there was thus also in the classical period a difference of opinion on this crucial issue.[18]

As regards the interpretation of the inherited body of Justinian law in the Middle Ages, which is our only concern here, the confusion caused by these contradictory fragments is compounded by several other texts that state the legal remedies available to those having consented to something under the threat of violence. In the immediate continuation of the passage containing the phrase *"coatus volui,"* the speaker adds, "I ought to get an order of restitution from the praetor" *(per praetorem restituendus sum)*. From early on, several actions were possible. The second-century so-called *Edictum perpetuum Hadriani*[19] distinguishes between the *actio (quod) metus causa*, the *in integrum restitutio propter metus*, and the *exceptio metus*. The first of these seems to have originated with the praetor Octavian as a penal action. In postclassical and Justinian law, the first and second actions tended to merge, the exclusively penal character of the former no longer being maintained. The opening chapter of the title on *metus* in the *Digest* copies Ulpian, quoting the latter edict as well as briefly recording its history and explaining its present form:

The praetor says: "Where an act is done through fear I will not uphold it." *(Quod metus causa gestum erit, ratum non habebo.)* The old terms of the Edict were "through force or fear" *(vi metusve)*. The word "force" was introduced to express compulsion applied in opposition to the party's will; "fear" was held to mean mental trepidation on the ground of urgent or apprehended danger. But afterward the mention of force was left out for the reason that anything which is done by unmitigated force may be held to be done through fear too.[20]

---

[17] Schulz, 1922, 210.

[18] Hartkamp 83. Confirmation of this interpretation is sought in another Ulpian fragment that (admittedly much revised) found its way into the *Corpus Iuris Civilis* at D.29,2,6,7.

[19] Thus named after the emperor, but sometimes also after Julian, its codifier.

[20] D.4,2,1.

A number of other statements on the subjects of force[21] and fear are recorded in the same title. Thus, again, Ulpian on the same text: "This clause therefore comprises both force and fear *(et vim, et metum)*, and where a man has done any act under forcible compulsion *(vi compulsus)*, he can get restitution by this Edict."[22] These legal actions were praetorian creations and had no basis in classical civil law. It is, in fact, possible to view them as supporting, rather than opposing, the validity interpretation of the latter, because they would have been unnecessary if the basic premise had not been that contracts obtained by compelled consent were valid in the absence of further legal action.

The same can be said of some of the numerous ordinances and rescripts recorded in the *Code* of Justinian. Taken as a whole, they demonstrate the dominance of *coatus volui* in the later classical period.[23] In the postclassical period, a reversal set in under the influence of popular law. The invalidity principle won through, according to which consent was extended as a condition to all legal transactions, and force and fear came to be seen as incompatible with consent. A majority of legal historians subscribe to the view that Justinian deliberately turned back on this development and sought to restore the validity principle of the old civil law. Such evidence to the contrary as appears in the *Corpus Iuris* is taken by these scholars to be postclassical remnants. The reverse picture, however, finds favor among a minority of historians, who consider Justinian an adherent of the postclassical invalidity theory and regard contrary texts in the compilation as remnants of a classical position long since abandoned.

The question as to what amounts to actionable fear was much more clearly stated in the law. Most of the evidence is to be found in the titles on *metus* in the *Digest* and the *Code*. Some of these texts focus on the kind of compulsion envisaged and some on the kind of person affected by it, but these two aspects are, of course, closely linked. Some persons are more easily frightened than others; they cannot therefore count on legal redress. The standard criterion was that the threat must be such as to scare a *vir constans*. Gaius states with reference to the *Edictum provinciale*: "The fear which we must hold to be referred to in

---

[21] As regards force, the doctrine, as well as the phrases copied, appear also in nonlegal Roman sources; cp. Cicero, *De officiis*: ". . . quod per vim hostium esset actum, ratum esse non debuit" (III,28: LCL 30, 380); ". . . non debuit ratum esse, quod erat actum per vim" (III,30: 388).

[22] D.4,2,3,pr. Monro renders *metum* as "intimidation."

[23] Thus, C.2,4,13,pr; C.2,19,3–10 (some of which deal with buying and selling); C.4,44,1 (also on buying and selling); etc.

this Edict is not the fear felt by a weak-minded man, but such as might reasonably occur even in the case of a man of thorough firmness of character *(non vani hominis, sed qui merito et in hominem constantissimum cadat).*"[24]

What kind of fear is this? According to Labeo, as reported by Ulpian, "not simply any apprehension whatever, but fear of some evil of exceptional severity" *(non quemlibet timorem, sed maioris malitatis).*[25] A number of other statements are more explicit. In one of the following titles of the *Digest*, there occurs another standard phrase, "fear of death or bodily torture" *(timor mortis vel cruciatus corporis).* It appears repeatedly in the *Code.*[26] Elsewhere, mentions are made of fear for one's health, terror of a beating, fear of rape, of enslavement, of imprisonment, etc.[27] The compulsion implied by these various threats, if used to obtain an economic advantage, are cases of what would now be called extortion, but they are all of a physical character; the extorter is envisaged as threatening to use corporal violence.

2.3   The medieval Romanists

With the *Corpus Iuris Civilis* of Justinian, the medieval world thus received a set of doctrines on compulsion and the will, clearly influenced to some extent by Aristotle and presenting a dialectic option very similar to the one inherent in the concept of "mixed" acts. To an author intent on proving will and thus responsibility or culpability on the part of the threatened party, or the justice of a contract made between two parties, reference could be had to *coactus volui.* To one intent on exonerating a person from blame or sin, or on proving injustice, the legal remedies provided by praetorian law offered at least equally weighty authority. This option could also be exercised in nonjuridical work by authors drawing on Roman law principles for extraneous support. Such uses of the law, along with Aristotle and other sources, for one or the other argumentative purpose, are regularly in evidence in scholastic moral and theological literature addressing economic problems. It is not an approach to the law that would present itself naturally to the medieval glossators and commentators on the *Corpus Iuris Civilis* itself. The medieval Romanists nevertheless deserve to be spoken of briefly

---

[24] D.4,2,6.
[25] D.4,2,5.
[26] D.4,6,3; cp. C.2,19,4; C.2,19,7; C.4,44,8.
[27] D.4,2,3,1; D.4,2,4; D.4,2,7,1; D.4,2,8,1–2; D.4,2,22; D.4,2,23,1; C.2,4,13,pr; etc.

here, for two reasons: first, because they developed and accentuated some aspects of the doctrines in question: second, because it was largely by them, directly or via canon law, that these doctrines were brought to the attention of scholastic authors.

The classification of force in *vis absoluta* and *vis compulsiva*, if not of Romanist origin, was made the subject of further specification at the hands of the Romanists. Thus Odofredus, inspired by Placentinus and Azo, distinguishes between five different kinds of *vis*, four of which *(vis expulsiva, ablativa, turbativa, inquietiva)* leave no room for the voluntary, as against *vis compulsiva*, which is the same as *metus* and which "has the will in it, albeit forced" *(habet in se voluntatem, licet coactam)*.[28] In spite of the ambiguity of the allegedly classical fragments, it was thus generally recognized that compulsion does not, eo ipso, rule out will. The principle of *coactus volui* appeared in the *Glossa ordinaria* of Accursius in the form of a dictum, "forced will is will" *(coacta voluntas voluntas est)*.[29] This is already found in the *Summa Codicis* of Placentinus.[30] In commentaries on the *Digest*, it reappears in those of Odofredus[31] and Bartolus.[32] Long before this, the maxim was cited in canon law commentaries. Recognition of the contingency of *coactus volui*, expressed in praetorian law, is fully documented as well. In the words of Baldus of Perugia, next to Bartolus the leading figure among the fourteenth-century civilians, "fraud or fear does not by the law itself render a contract null, but annullable."[33]

As to the kind of threat that was considered to cause actionable *metus*, the Romanists did not notably extend the narrow interpretation of Justinian's law. Rogerius, who taught at Bologna in the twelfth century and composed a *Summa* on the *Code*, declares a contract to be valid provided there is will, even if forced *(voluntas quamvis coacta)*, the question being whether will can be said to be present under fear of death or physical torture.[34] This phrase was often repeated.[35] Odofredus sug-

---

[28] Odofredus, *In primam Codicis partem*, to C.2,19,1: f.95va; cp. Placentinus, *Summa Codicis*, loc. cit. in note 30; Azo, *Summa*, ibid.: col. 103.

[29] To D.4,2,21,5, as well as to D.50,17,4.

[30] *Summa*, to C.2,20 (for 2,19): p. 65.

[31] *Super Digesto veteri*, to D.4,2,21,5: f.U₃ra.

[32] *In primam Digesti veteris partem*, to D.4,2,21,5: p. 415.

[33] *In Codicem*, to C.8,38,5: III, f.175rb: "Dolus vel metus non reddit contractum ipso iure nullum, sed annullandum."

[34] *Summa Codicis*, II,11: 30–1.

[35] Azo, *Summa*, loc. cit: col. 104; Odofredus, *Super Digesto veteri*, to D.4,2,3: f.T₃vb; and to D.4,2,6: f.T₄rb; and frequently in later commentators.

gests some examples: fear of death, as when someone holds a sword over your head, saying, unless you sell me this thing, you are dead; fear of torture, as by a flogging.[36] He adds that a threat may sometimes involve what amounts to almost a fear of death, as when someone threatens to burn the written evidence of one's status (*instrumenta status*).[37] This example, which here occurs in a context of buying and selling, of a threat that does not involve immediate violence to the person, is to be found in the middle of the preceding century as well, namely, in the *Summa Trecensis*, at one time erroneously attributed to the great Irnerius.[38] The threat, nevertheless, is physical enough; it refers to enslavement. Where it occurs in the *Digest*, the *Glossa* notes that "slavery is similar to death."[39] Bartolus sums up the main doctrine regarding actionable fear as follows: "That fear is understood which occurs in the case of a man of firm character (*qui cadit in constantem virum*), such as the fear of death, or bodily torture, or slavery, or shame; it is otherwise in the case of some slight annoyance or disgrace."[40] Against Odofredus's drastic example, Bartolus points out that it is not necessary that a sword is actually being held above one's head.[41] On the other hand, a verbal threat is not always actionable, for some men talk a lot but do less.[42]

Some examples of how these principles would be applied in economic case discussions are provided by the thirteenth-century collection attributed to Chiaro of Florence. Chiaro is said to have been penitentiary to Pope Alexander IV and to have determined his cases in the Curia. If thus not exclusively a Romanist, he had studied law at Bologna and frequently drew on his expertise in that field. In reply to one question, Chiaro suggests that mutual consent validates a sales contract even if the price agreed upon is beyond the legal limits of one-half above or below the just price. "If you say that it is bought at a low price, I answer that if he knowingly sells [it], not coerced nor defrauded, but knowing and of a free will (*non coactus neque circumventus, sed sciens et spontaneus*), he has no right to reclaim it."[43]

---

[36] *In primam Codicis partem*, to C.2,19,4: f.96va; cp. to C.2,19,1: f.95va.

[37] Loc. cit.: f.96va.

[38] *Summa Trecensis*, II,10: 38; cp. Rogerius, *Summa Codicis*, loc. cit.: 31, Placentinus, loc. cit: p. 66.

[39] To D.4,2,8,1.

[40] Op. cit., to D.4,2,5: pp. 406–7.

[41] *In primam Codicis partem*, to C.2,19,7: p. 249.

[42] Op. cit., to C.2,19,9: p. 250.

[43] Q.21: Florence BNaz Conv. Soppr. F.VI.855, f.91ra.

A later question addresses the subject of *metus* directly. It is asked whether someone can be said to possess a thing by just title if, by means of fraud, fear, or allurements, he has induced the owner to sell it or give it to him. Chiaro replies:

If the thing is bought at a suitable price for as much as it is worth by a good measure, I may lawfully possess it and do penance for fraud or for the fear I caused. The reason is that forced will is will *(voluntas coacta voluntas est)*. However, if the thing is bought for less than what is due, because the other accepted less from fear, I am obliged to make a supplement up to the just price. But if a hundred pounds is obtained by means of fear or fraud, and this was fear which might have struck a man of firm character *(metus qui potuit cadere in constantem virum)*, it is robbery, and I am obliged to make full restitution, nor is there a contract according to law.[44]

The following case concerns a simulated sale with a resale agreement. When the time comes to reverse the sale, the buyer goes back on his promise. He wants to pay an equivalent price instead. This, however, is not a lawful sale:

Because it was fictitious, and made for no other reason, such a sale was in no way voluntary according to the will of the seller *(voluntaria voluntate venditoris)*. He neither willed it simply nor consented under compulsion but was always unwilling *(neque simpliciter voluit neque coactus consensit sed semper fuit involuntarius)*. Therefore, the payment of a just price does not make the sale lawful.[45]

Chiaro of Florence was a near contemporary of Odofredus. Commenting on the *Code*, Odofredus observes that *metus* cannot be inferred from the bare fact that someone has concluded a transaction on unfavorable terms.[46] Bartolus confirmed this,[47] and it remained the basic premise of the Romanists. There must be a reason for the unequal terms, and it must be attributable to the kinds of force and fear recognized by the law. Chiaro of Florence does not say what kinds of compulsion are envisaged in his cases, except for the one allusion to the power of resistance of the *vir constans*, which naturally recalls the various physical threats specified in the law and the commentaries. Suppose, then, that there is no question of fraud or of physical compulsion in this legal sense. Why should anyone, as Odofredus and Bartolus implicitly assume, conclude a transaction on unfavorable terms? The readiest answer is that he lacks firmness of character and is easily frightened or that he is simpleminded or careless. These are pertinent phenomena

---

[44] Q.87: ff.98vb–99ra.
[45] Q.88: f.99ra.
[46] *In primam Codicis partem*, to 2.4,13: f.73va.
[47] *In primam Codicis partem*, ibid.: p. 175.

for ethical theory. In scholastic moral theology, they caused considerable extensions to be made to the legal concepts of fraud and force. The main answer, however, is that he may be the victim of economic compulsion rather than physical compulsion. One party to a contract may be ever so clearheaded and careful and free of threats from the opposite party and yet agree to poor terms because he finds himself in a situation of economic or financial distress. He may be in *need* of some good and have to pay a high price for it, or he may *need* money and have to either borrow at usury, or sell something at a low price, or take a job at a low wage. I can find no evidence in Romanist sources of an extension of *vis compulsiva* to include the force of economic need. This is the most significant extension of that concept, for which we must thank the medieval theologians.

CHAPTER 3

The Augustinian tradition

3.1   St. Augustine on compulsion, the will, and sin

In late antiquity, classical Greek thought on the subject of compulsion
and the voluntary spread through different channels and was developed
in other schools besides that of Roman legal philosophy. Thus, at the
hands of the Stoa, the rationalistic idealism of the Socratic tradition
shrank to a philosophy of detachment, according to which virtue becomes reconciliation to the inevitable. There may still be a strange echo
of Aristotle in some of these utterances of Epictetus: "Externals are not
under my control; moral choice is under my control."[1] A man has a
moral purpose free from constraint. A threat of death does not in itself
compel a man, but his will, the fact that he yields to the threat. Moral purpose compels moral purpose.[2] "There rises up no thief of his moral purpose, nor any tyrant over it."[3] The direct influence, however, of these
and other expressions of post-Aristotelian philosophy on medieval
thought on this subject pales in comparison to that which was received
through, or from, the Church Fathers and, above all, from St. Augustine.

Augustine's influence was conceptual as well as doctrinal. We shall
be concerned with those aspects of his thought on compulsion and the
voluntary that influenced medieval canonistic and theological doctrine
of sin and culpability. For this purpose, it is useful to place in evidence
some frequently quoted texts. Questions concerning the will – man's
will, God's will, and man's will in relation to God's will – so completely
pervade Augustine's thought that to quote him piecemeal and out of
context, as we must do here, is sometimes to risk misconception. We
shall proceed strictly in the footsteps of medieval authors and merely
extract what they found relevant to the particular problem at issue.
(Quotations are numbered for the purpose of subsequent reference.)

Augustine's brief and straightforward definition of "will" is to be
found in *De duabus animabus* and is confirmed in *Retractiones*:

---

[1] *Diss.*, II,5,4: LCL 131, 239.
[2] *Diss.*, I,17,21–8; cp. I,1,23; I,22,10: Ibid., 119–21; 13; 145.
[3] *Diss.*, III,22,105: LCL 218, 167. Verbatim translations by Oldfather.

1. Will is a movement of the spirit, by nothing compelled *(cogente nullo)*, toward not admitting something, or toward attaining it.[4]

This *cogente nullo*, however, proves to be too strong in Augustine's case as well. In a passage in *De spiritu et littera*, he presents his version of Aristotle's mixed acts and the Roman law's *coactus volui*:

2. If we pay more precise attention to it, also that which someone is forced against his will to do, he does voluntarily, if he does it *(quod quisque invitus facere cogitur, si facit, voluntate facit)*. But because he prefers something else, he is said to do it against his will, that is, involuntarily. Wishing to avoid or remove himself from some pressing evil, he does what he is compelled to do. Now, if his will was so strong that he would prefer not to do it rather than not suffer the other, without doubt he would resist the compulsion and not do it. And therefore, if he does it, it is not with a full and free will, but all the same he does not do it except voluntarily *(non quidem plena et libera voluntate, sed tamen non facit nisi voluntate)*.[5]

Sin presupposes will. From extensive discussions in a number of works, the medieval Augustinians extracted some brief maxims giving different forms to the essential relationship between sin and the will. Thus, in *De libero arbitrio*:

3. Will is the principal cause of sin.[6]

In *De duabus animabus*, repeated in *Retractiones*:

4. Sin is the will to retain or attain what justice forbids.[7]
5. It is not sinned except voluntarily.[8]

In *De vera religione*, also repeated in *Retractiones*:

6. It is in no way a sin, if it is not voluntary.[9]

---

[4] *De duab. animab.*, 10,14: PL 42, 104; cp. *Retract.*, I,15,3: PL 32, 609.

[5] *De spir. et litt.*, 31, 53: PL 44, 234.

[6] *De lib. arb.*, III,16,49: PL 32, 1295: "Voluntas est prima causa peccandi." Sometimes quoted in a briefer form at 48: 1294: "Voluntas est causa peccandi."

[7] *De duab. animab.*, 11, 15: PL 42, 105: "Peccatum est voluntas retinendi vel consequendi quod iustitia vetat." Cp. *Retract.*, I,15,4: PL 32, 609.

[8] *De duab. animab.*, 10, 14: PL 42, 104: "Non igitur nisi voluntate peccatur." Cp. *Retract.*, I,15,2: PL 32, 609.

[9] *De vera relig.*, 14, 27: PL 34, 133: "Nullo modo sit peccatum, si non sit voluntarium." Cp. *Retract.*, I,13,5: PL 32, 603.

When the latter proposition was reviewed in *Retractiones*, the question of the will in case of compulsion was briefly examined with a view to sin. Augustine concludes in accordance with his general analysis in *De spiritu et littera*:

> 7. Also those sins which, not unreasonably, are said to be non-voluntary *(non voluntaria)*, because they are committed by persons either ignorant or compelled *(vel a nescientibus, vel a coactis)*, cannot be said altogether to be committed without will.[10]

In Augustine's commentary on the Heptateuch, there is an extensive analysis substantiating this proposition. The text in question is Numbers 15. 24–9, which deals with atonement for sins committed through ignorance. The commentator takes this as a point of departure for a discussion of sin and compulsion:

> 8. With good reason it is asked which are the sins of the unwilling *(peccata nolentium)*, whether those which are committed by persons through ignorance, or can that also rightly be said to be a sin of the unwilling, which he is compelled to do? For that is also usually said to be against the will *(contra voluntatem)*. At least, he wills that, because of which he does it, as in the case of one who does not want to commit perjury and does it because he will live, if someone threatens him with death unless he does it. Thus he will do it because he will live, and therefore it is not because he desires it in itself that he swears falsely but because he desires, by swearing falsely, to live *(non per se ipsum appetit, ut falsum iuret, sed ut falsum iurando vivat)*. If it is like this, I do not know whether these can be said to be sins of the unwilling, for which atonement is here said to be made. If it is carefully examined, perhaps no one will sin but sins because of something else which he wills. But certainly all men who knowingly do what is unlawful, would that it be lawful, and to that extent, no one desires to sin for its own sake, but for the sake of that which results thereof. If that is how things are, there are no sins of the unwilling, unless unknowing *(non sunt peccata nolentium, nisi nescientium)*, which are distinguished from the sins of the willing *(a peccatis volentium)*.[11]

[10] *Retract.*, loc. cit.: 604.
[11] *In Hept.*, IV,24: PL 34: 727–8.

3.2   Gratian and the canonists

The important gestation period of Western medieval thought, from about the middle of the twelfth century to about the middle of the thirteenth, when knowledge of Roman law was spreading and Aristotle was gradually being made available in Latin dress, also saw the publication of most of the corpus of canon law. The collection commonly known as the *Decretum*, made about 1140 by the Bolognese monk Gratian, will be in the focus of our attention. Consisting of synodic and papal decisions, richly supplemented with excerpts of scriptural, patristic, and other material, it served through most of this early period as the main legal basis for the Church's regulation of private as well as public life. Moreover, a number of its chapters inspired general discussions of important issues, including the one which concerns us here. In the thirteenth century, the *Decretals* (or *Liber extra*) of Pope Gregory IX, promulgated in 1234, replaced Gratian's compilation as the principal textbook of canon law, both in practical applications and in the interest of academic canonists. One of the five compilations of papal decisions, which together supplied most of the material for the *Liber extra*, also contains some texts of interest for this study. They introduce Romanist terminology and canonize parts of the Roman law doctrine on *metus*.

Freedom of the human will to sin and to combat sin is a fundamental premise of Catholic theology. Canon law will therefore be concerned with the question of culpability in situations where a person is faced with either of the two factors that may impede the exercise of his will, namely, ignorance and compulsion. In that respect (as far as the analogy is relevant), it resembles Roman law and classical moral philosophy. Here, as before, we shall pass over the subject of ignorance, merely noting that medieval and early modern teaching regarding fraud in economic dealings also drew on canon law. Our present purpose is to provide an overview of canonistic doctrine on compulsion and culpability, extracting some main features from a huge volume of medieval glosses and commentaries. The locus in Gratian that inspired most of this literature is to be found at the beginning of Causa 15 and is compiled from the works of St. Augustine. The first question has a long preface (known by its incipit as *Quod autem*), which is a combination of some Biblical texts and quotations #1, #4, #6 – from both sources – and #7 of section 3.1. The first chapter *(Merito)* reproduces quotation #8, in full and with nothing added to it.[12]

---

[12] *Decretum*, II,15,1, pr–1: *Corpus Iuris Canonici*, ed. Friedberg, I,744–6.

The kinship between Augustine's analysis and that of Aristotle, as well as a significant difference, were established in the early thirteenth century by the *Glossa Palatina* (thus named after a Vatican manuscript), an *apparatus* or set of glosses to the *Decretum*. It is sometimes tentatively attributed to Laurence of Spain, a leading Bologna canonist. The author would seem to have had access to the *Ethica vetus*. To the word "nonvoluntary" in *Quod autem*, the following gloss occurs: "(nonvoluntary), understand *simpliciter*, but Aristotle in the *Ethics* contradicts this, because the activities of those who suffer compulsion are not *simpliciter* voluntary but *secundum quid* voluntary."[13] This is a most pertinent remark. Granted that Aristotle concludes that mixed acts are "more like voluntary acts," he takes pains to emphasize the sense in which they can be said to be involuntary, something that Augustine and Gratian, intent on stressing man's personal responsibility before God, are disinclined to do. Note also the glossator's use of the terminology that Aquinas, moved by the same sentiment, was to reverse in the *Summa theologiae*.

Similar distinctions regarding the nature of the voluntary had been made before the turn of the century by other Decretists, most likely without the aid of Aristotle. John of Faenza, a professor of canon law at Bologna, composed a *Summa* in the 1170s. To *Quod autem*, he points out that a sin, being voluntary, can be understood in either of two senses. Someone may want that for which he commits the sin in the first place, or he may want something else, from which the sin follows, the latter sense being illustrated by the case of a man who commits perjury under threat in order to save his life.[14] The anonymous author of the *Summa Parisiensis*, in comment on *Merito*, suggests that a sin that is committed under compulsion can be said to be *voluntarium* but not *voluntatis*, which can perhaps be translated "with will but not of the will." In the sequel, he confirms another essential point made by interpreters of Aristotle. The act of perjury is voluntary in the sense that it is chosen at the time: "He does not will it, but it is said to him, unless you commit perjury you are going to die, and so he chooses life and commits perjury *(ergo eligit vitam et peierat)*."[15]

These ideas were developed by Huguccio, the foremost canonist of

---

[13] Vat.Pal. lat. 658, f.55ra; Durham C.III.8, f.89vb: "... supple simpliciter, Aristoteles tamen contradicit in *Ethicis*, quia opera coactorum non sunt (Durham: sunt non) voluntaria simpliciter, voluntaria autem secundum quid."

[14] Bamberg SB Can. 37, f.59va.

[15] Ed. McLaughlin, p. 173.

the twelfth century, whose *Summa decretorum*, composed shortly before 1190, is the masterpiece of its genre and was highly influential. Discussing sins committed under compulsion in comment to *Quod autem*, Huguccio concludes: "Such sins therefore are voluntary because, although a person does not will them directly, he wills that for which he comes to commit them, as Augustine exemplifies in the following chapter, which means that another will adheres to it, albeit forced or concealed *(inhaeret alia voluntas licet coacta vel velata)*."[16]

To *Merito*: "It is argued that forced will is will *(voluntas coacta voluntas est)*, for by compulsion a person proceeds to voluntariness, and the voluntary is brought about *(per coactionem venit quis ad voluntatem et efficitur voluntarium)*."[17]

The origin of the maxim "forced will is will" is uncertain. It appeared roughly simultaneously in Roman law sources and in canon law sources.[18] After Huguccio, the canonists did not tire of quoting it. The anonymous *Summa Bambergensis* to the *Decretum*, composed in the first decade of the thirteenth century, is a work with a strong Romanist leaning. To *Quod autem*, the author declares that "forced will is will," arguing in Roman law terms that "being forced, he has willed" *(coactus voluit)*, and to *Merito* interprets Augustine to mean that compulsion does not excuse someone who perjures himself in order to save his life.[19] To the latter locus, something similar is to be found in the so-called *Apparatus 'Ius naturale'* by Laurence of Spain. The author states that "forced will is said to be will" and cites the Digest *(coactus tamen vult)*.[20] Shortly after 1215, Johannes Teutonicus composed the first version of the *Glossa ordinaria* to the *Decretum*, selecting among earlier sources and supplementing them. The dictum *coacta voluntas est voluntas* appears in a gloss to *Merito*.[21] It is also in the *Glossa Palatina* in the same place.[22] Bartolomeo of Brescia retained it when he revised the *Glossa ordinaria* and gave it the form in which it appears in the early printed editions of the *Decretum*.[23]

Because the example in *Merito* is a case of perjury, it is to be expected

---

[16] Paris BN lat. 3892, f.221rb. Kuttner, 1935, 48, who appears to have used a Vatican manuscript, has *aliqua* in the last line.

[17] Loc. cit.

[18] See section 2.3.

[19] Bamberg SB Can. 42, f.91rb.

[20] Paris BN lat. 15393, f.152va.

[21] Bamberg SB Can. 13, f.130vb.

[22] Loc. cit. in note 13.

[23] Basel 1512, f.222vb.

that the analysis of sin in connection with compulsion and the will should extend to comments on a text that deals specifically with perjury. In the fifth question of Causa 22, Gratian cites a number of papal decisions regarding false oaths made under compulsion.[24] The commentary tradition on this locus was initiated and greatly influenced by Rufinus of Bologna, who composed a voluminous *Summa decretorum* before 1160. Rufinus starts by distinguishing two degrees of compulsion (*coactio*). It is either *modica* or *violenta*. This is a matter of the fierceness or strength of the compelling force, but the level of distinction is set quite high: If someone threatens to burn down your house tomorrow, it is still *coactio modica*. Such moderate compulsion is never accepted as an excuse. If the action that the person compelled has promised to perform is lawful, he must stand by his promise; if it is unlawful, the sin is imputed to him. *Coactio violenta* is of two different kinds, *absoluta* or *conditionalis*. They can also be distinguished by the labels *passiva* and *activa*. The former kind (absolute, passive, violent compulsion) is defined by an external power totally usurping control over a person and forcing him to do something to which he in no way consents, reducing him to a passive object, as when his hand is forcibly placed on the altar of an idol. Such incidents are never imputed to the person compelled, unless his being reduced to such straits is his own fault. The latter kind of *coactio violenta* (conditional, active, violent compulsion) is defined by Rufinus as the instant exposure to a present or future perilous condition, as when someone in anger puts a sword to your throat and threatens to kill you unless you do what he wants. It still leaves the threatened person potentially active: If he complies, he acts. The kinship between these constructions and those of Aristotle and of Roman law is evident. They may have given rise to the Romanist expressions *vis absoluta* and *vis compulsiva*. Rufinus's discussion of culpability in cases of the latter kind of compulsion is colored by the particular context. His judgment is very severe. It is better to die than to swear falsely against one's conscience; albeit compelled, the perjurer sins criminally.[25]

John of Faenza confirms this harsh doctrine,[26] but later canonists tended to soften it. Huguccio does not follow Rufinus here but paraphrases him in comment on a chapter on baptism.[27] Reproducing Rufinus's elaborate classification of compulsions, Huguccio concludes a little differently. Persons who act under *coactio conditionalis*, he states,

---

[24] Friedberg, I,882–9.
[25] Rufinus, *Summa*, to II,22,5,1: ed. Singer, pp. 399–401.
[26] Loc. cit.: Bamberg SB Can. 37, f.70va–b.
[27] III,4,118: Friedberg, I,1398.

are not excused from sin but from graver punishment.[28] A similar phrase appears in comment on a chapter in Causa 15 that deals with extorted confession.[29] Huguccio here also distinguishes between *coactio absoluta* and *coactio conditionalis* and takes the opportunity to draw a parallel to Roman law terminology. The latter form of compulsion corresponds to the *metus* that may strike a *vir constans* and that involves danger to health or bodily torture. Huguccio then proceeds to cite the maxim that forced will is will, concluding that such compulsion does not excuse from sin altogether but calls for milder forms of punishment.[30] Less severe still is Sicard of Cremona, whose *Summa* predates that of Huguccio by a few years. Adopting the classification introduced by Rufinus, Sicard teaches that even moderate compulsion, to which a man of firm character will not yield, and consisting in mere damage to property, may call for alleviation of punishment though it does not entirely excuse a sinful act.[31] Sicard's background may be significant. Before being appointed bishop of his native Cremona, he had lived for a time in Mainz, where his *Summa* may have been composed.[32] In his youth he had studied at Bologna, but he never taught there and did not belong to the inner circle of professional canonists. His softening of culpability doctrine points beyond this circle's narrow frame of reference and toward the concern with safety in property relations, which is fundamental in subsequent economic applications of the ancient traditions on compulsion and the voluntary.

In the decades that followed the contributions of Huguccio and Sicard of Cremona, Rufinus's terminology, as well as that of Roman law, became general in canonistic text. As regards the *Decretum*, it is enough to mention the *Glossa ordinaria*, which, at places mentioned previously, employs both.[33] At this time, however, the interest of the canonists was turning toward a different body of material. The last decade of the twelfth century saw the publication of a new compilation of decretals,

---

[28] Paris BN lat. 3892, f.394rb.

[29] II,15,6,1: Friedberg, I,754–5.

[30] F.224ra–b.

[31] *Summa*, to II,22,5: Bamberg SB Can.38,f.99h.

[32] There is some internal evidence to support this, but the question is not settled. Cp. Schulte, I,144, and references in Kuttner, 1937, 151.

[33] To II,15,1,1; Bamberg SB Can. 13, f.130vb; Basel 1512, f.222vb: "Refert qualis sit coactio an absoluta vel conditionalis." To II,15,6,1; Bamberg SB Can. 13, f.132vb; Basel 1512, f.226ra: "Si quaeris qualis metus debeat cadere in constantem virum, dico quod talis qui contineat metum mortis vel cruciatum corporis."

later to be known as the *Compilatio prima*. It was to be followed by four others. The first three of these five compilations contain titles on *metus* with headings recalling Roman law, and this material was later to be incorporated under a similar heading in the definitive collection of Gregory IX, the *Liber extra (X)*.[34] The most interesting of these collections is the *Compilatio tertia*, which was issued by Innocent III in 1210. It refers to such *metus* as might occur in the case of a man of firm character[35] and defines this as fear of death or bodily torture.[36] The persons involved in the first of these instances are King John of England, who threatened the dean of Lincoln. In a gloss, Laurence of Spain declares such a threat to be punishable.[37] Tancred, another professor at Bologna and glossator, points out that one who yields to it is blameless, and that the outcome is invalid.[38]

3.3   Peter Lombard and the theologians

At the time when the interest of the canonists was being deflected from Gratian's *Decretum* to the more recent decretals, a tradition on the subjects examined in the preceding section was gathering momentum in theological circles. Shortly after the middle of the twelfth century, Peter Lombard published the four books of his *Sentences*. Drawing on scriptural and patristic sources, it gradually relegated previous compilations of this kind to obscurity and established itself as the main textbook in systematic theology in the Schools. In a *distinctio* in Book II, Peter discusses compulsion and the will with regard to sin and draws on the authority of St. Augustine in much the same places in his works as Gratian did, reproducing quotations #1, #3, #5, #6, and #7 of section 3.1.[39] Elsewhere, he treats of perjury and other specific subjects, which invited comments on compulsion and the will by the Decretists and did so by the theologians as well. The commentary literature on the *Sentences* is vast. The present review must be limited to the three most influential works antedating the *Summa theologiae* of Thomas Aquinas, namely, the *Summa aurea* of William of Auxerre, the *Summa theologica* of Alexander of Hales, and Bonaventura's commentary on the *Sentences*.

[34] Cp. *Quinque compilationes antiquae*, ed. Friedberg, 11;71;110; *Corpus Iuris Canonici*, II,218–22.
[35] *Comp. III*,I,23,1; *X*.I,40,4.
[36] *Comp. III*,I,23,3; *X*.I,40,6.
[37] Paris BN lat. 3932, f.128va.
[38] Paris BN lat. 3931A, f.148va–b.
[39] *Sent.*, II,41,3–6: I,564–6.

The two *summas* are, like that of Aquinas, not literal commentaries, but adhere, albeit less closely, to the themes and textual arrangements of the *Sentences*. The purpose of the present section, besides reporting on the views of these three authors, is to record the establishment of a new terminology, namely, that of absolute and conditional will. The terminology was never very precise, but was used in different senses. Moreover, it overlaps with other terminologies used by these authors. Because this is of some importance in order to understand what was subsequently to be meant by absolute and conditional will in connection with economic subjects, we have to look briefly at these alternative usages and terminologies as well.

The ideas first expressed by the distinction between absolute and conditional will can be traced quite a bit further back.[40] The terms themselves are documented in a work by Stephen Langton and are reported from the teaching of Peter of Corbeil, both men being active before William of Auxerre. In one of his *Quaestiones*, Langton distinguishes between *volo* ("I will") and *vellem* ("I should will"). This corresponds to absolute and conditional will. I do not will to sin, but I should will to sin "if my fear had permitted it"; "fear never controls the interior will to sin, for it does not control the spirit but the hand; it controls the absolute will to sin in the exterior act but it does not control the conditional will."[41] In his *Summa*, William of Auxerre records the opinion of "the archbishop of Sens." This reference must be to Peter of Corbeil, who taught at Paris in the twelfth century, but whose academic work is lost. Peter appears to have discussed the same subject and to have used some of the same terminology as Stephen Langton, though William does not explicitly attribute the distinction between *volo* and *vellem* to Peter: Fear may cause someone to abstain from sin, and he may therefore be said to will not to sin; however, "he wills to sin with his conditional will, that is, if there were no punishment, but with his absolute will he does not will to sin."[42] The condition of the conditional will, then, to these authors is a latent and absent condition, namely, the removal of punishment for sin. There is no question of this taking place, and hence the absolute will represents what is actual and present. Because such will is associated with fear, namely, the fear of punishment for sin, this is a bit confusing in view of Aristotle's analysis of *timor* and the will and the Roman law doctrine

---

[40] On this tradition, and on some of the alternative uses of the terminology, cp. Saarinen, 1994, as well as Knuuttila and Holopainen, 1993.
[41] Paris BN lat. 16385, f.16rb–va.
[42] Quoted in William, *Summa*, III,31,4: 613.

of *metus* and the will, though it should be noted that it is in harmony with Aquinas's subsequent reinterpretation of Aristotle.

William of Auxerre distinguishes between the sensual will and the rational will. The latter is in our power and is the same as consent.[43] William also developed the terminology of *volo* and *vellem. Velleitas,* or conditional will, is the promptitude to will something under a not-present condition. Thus the prophet Jeremiah willed *simpliciter* that Jerusalem be destroyed for the sins of the people, because this was God's will, but should will with his conditional will that the people be spared if they show penitence.[44] As regards external compulsion, William establishes a dichotomy that is clearly related to the lawyers' *vis absoluta* and *vis compulsiva.* Discussing the freedom of the will in general, he makes a distinction between *coactio sufficiens* and *coactio inducens.* The former has nothing to do with the will, but the will can be influenced by the latter. "And of this Augustine says that *coacta voluntas voluntas est.*"[45] Here, and twice elsewhere when William cites this maxim,[46] his recent editors refer to *De spiritu et littera* in the lines of quotation #2 of section 3.1. This must be merely as to the sense; the literal phrase is not to be found in St. Augustine.

From the freedom of the will, William of Auxerre proceeds to discuss sin and, among other things, examines it with regard to ignorance and compulsion. William knew the *Ethica vetus.* He confirms that all sins are voluntary, even those committed under compulsion, citing Aristotle as well as St. Augustine. Two objections to this conclusion, and William's replies to them, are of interest here. It is argued that the will cannot be forced; hence a forced act cannot be voluntary, and hence a sin committed under compulsion is not voluntary. For his reply to this, William reaches back to his general analysis of the freedom of the will. The will cannot be forced by *coactio sufficiens,* but it can be forced by *coactio efficiens* (cp. *coactio inducens* discussed previously). It is also argued that if someone is compelled to perform a sinful act, he acts *invitus,* that is, against his will in the sense of doing it reluctantly; this means that he acts *non voluntarie* and sins; therefore, not all sins are voluntary. William replies by once more distinguishing between two kinds of will, namely, absolute will and a will that is *collativa* or *determinata,* words that might be rendered in English as "mixed" or "qualified." If someone commits a sin under compulsion, he does it

[43] *Summa,* I,12,4,1:230; 3: 233; 6: 240.
[44] I,12,4,4: 235–6; cp. Jer., 28.5–6.
[45] II,10,4: 284.
[46] II,3,7,1: 69; IV,17,5,6: 447.

voluntarily in this latter sense but not in the absolute sense. "As Aristotle says, 'such actions are voluntary when they are done.' "[47] In short, when William of Auxerre analyzes an actual and present condition influencing the will, rather than a latent condition, he avoids using the words "comparative" or "conditional" to describe the will. This is worth noting, because William was one of the very first authors to use this terminology in connection with actual agreements reached under compulsion in the economic sense. William was well schooled in canon law and was familiar with Romanist terminology. In view of his economic teaching, the severity of his doctrine regarding forced oaths is also worth noting. Such oaths are morally binding. They may be rendered invalid in civil courts if the *metus* in question is such as might affect a *vir constans*, but the Lord told us "not to fear those who kill the body."[48]

The *Summa theologica* of Alexander of Hales[49] draws heavily on the works of William of Auxerre and earlier authors in the theological and canonistic traditions. Alexander is familiar with the distinction between *volo* and *vellem* in cases involving latent conditioning of the will,[50] but he is more often occupied with actual conditioning of the will and with the moral aspects of present compulsion. For his analyses of this subject he employs a varied terminology. He cites the title on *metus* in the *Decretals* of Gregory IX and declares that such fear as might affect a man of firm character is at least a partial excuse for a sinful act.[51] He distinguishes between *coactio sufficiens* and *coactio inducens*[52] and explains that St. Augustine should be understood to refer to the latter kind of compulsion when he states that "forced will is will."[53] Referring to Aristotle as well as to Augustine in *Retractiones* (cp. quotation #7 in

---

[47] II,18,2: 597–8.

[48] III,46,6,2: 896–7; cp. Matt. 10. 28.

[49] Or, rather, the compilation with this title, published in his name. I quote it in the standard Quaracchi edition. The systematic subdivision of this edition is almost prohibitively complex. I shall therefore refer to it by volume and page numbers only. Vols. I–IV correspond to Books I; II,1; II,2; and III. Book IV is posterior to Alexander of Hales. It is not included in the Quaracchi edition and is ignored here.

[50] *Sum. theol.*, IV,1048.

[51] III,695.

[52] I,435.

[53] IV,630. The editors of the *Summa* refer to *De spiritu et littera*, 31,53 (cp. quotation #2 in section 3.1), just as in the case of William of Auxerre. The maxim also occurs, with the same editors' reference, at IV,489, on forced oaths, where Alexander otherwise largely copies William.

section 3.1), he distinguishes between the *simpliciter* voluntary and the *secundum quid* voluntary, using these terms in the sense later to be reversed by Thomas Aquinas.[54] At one point, he identifies the *simpliciter* voluntary with the absolute will and refers to the will under actual and present compulsion as conditional, invoking John Damascene in *De fide orthodoxa*, paraphrasing *Ethics*, III,1.[55] Elsewhere, there is a careful definition of these important terms in the sense in which they were subsequently to be used in economic contexts:

> We speak of will in two different senses; there is absolute and simple will *(voluntas absoluta et simpliciter)*, and there is comparative and conditional will *(voluntas comparata et conditionalis)*. Comparative or conditional will is when we do not will a thing simply but under a condition, with the removal of which, we do not will it. And this can happen in two ways. The condition in question can have a pulling effect, as when someone who would not sin simply would sin because of some great profit. Or it can have a pushing effect, as when someone would sin in order to escape death, with the removal of which [threat], he would not sin. And thus there are two kinds of conditional will, pulling *(trahens)* and pushing *(impellens)*.[56]

Less than a decade after the death of Alexander of Hales, the young Bonaventura commented on the *Sentences* of Peter Lombard, drawing on his teacher Alexander and on William of Auxerre, and tying together the three traditions on compulsion and the will in early European thought. Bonaventura treats of absolute and conditional will in God,[57] and of *velleitas* in men, "as when someone should will that the dead were alive."[58] Regarding actual and present conditioning of the will, he distinguishes between *coactio sufficiens*, as when someone is bound hand and foot, and *coactio inducens*, which is in the nature of a threat.[59] It is the latter kind to which Augustine refers when he declares that forced will is will[60] and to which Aristotle and John Damascene

---

[54] III,80–1.

[55] IV,1003; cp. note 23 to Chapter 1. Alexander's allusion is correct enough as to the sense, but the literal expression is not to be found in Burgundio's Latin translation of *De fide orthodoxa*.

[56] I,434–5. Alexander goes on to specify three kinds of absolute will, but these refer to God's will rather than human will.

[57] *Comm. Sent.*, I,46,1:820; I,47,1–2:840–2.

[58] IV,16,1,1,1:384.

[59] IV,4,1,2,1:100–1; cp. also II,41,Dub.3:956.

[60] Loc. cit., as well as III,39,3,2:877 (on forced oaths), and IV,29,1:699 (on forced matrimony). The editors refer to *De spiritu et littera*, 31,53. (This is the earliest of the modern critical editions of the three works reported on in this section.)

refer when they speak of mixed acts. A person's free will cannot be forced, but it can be induced. These are very different things.[61]

Although inducement *(inductio)* seems to be a sort of compulsion *(coactio)* – particularly according to human law, which states, that that which is done because of fear, is not to be upheld, especially when this fear is such as may occur in the case of a man of firm character, because exterior acts are considered – in truth, however, this inducement is consistent with freedom of the will and is not opposed to it in every way, but is rather opposed to the fullness of desire and will. For a person does not as fully will that which he wills on condition *(ex conditione)* as that which he wills absolutely *(absolute)*, as is evident from the throwing of merchandise into the sea; but in this a kind of freedom and will is nevertheless preserved.[62]

[61] II,25,2,4:615–17.
[62] Loc. cit.:617.

PART II

Need as compulsion:
the scholastic paradigm

Ben è vivo, e sì soletto
mostrar li mi convien la valle buia:
necessità 'l ci 'nduce, e non diletto.

Dante, *Inferno*, XII, 85–7

CHAPTER 4

Loans and usury

4.1 Usury as robbery

It is one of the ironies of capitalism in a Christian world that the city of Milan, a commercial and financial center in the homeland of the Church, should claim as its patron saint the man who said that usury is robbery. In *De bono mortis* of St. Ambrose, the following plain statement occurs: "If someone takes usury, he commits robbery, he shall not live."[1] The final clause provides a certain scriptural authority for Ambrose and for the numerous theologians and canonists who quoted him on usury. The statement is not to be found in one of his sermons against economic misdeeds, but in a chapter on the eternal felicity that awaits the virtuous. The reference is to Ezekiel: "If a man be just, and [among numerous other sins listed] . . . hath not given forth upon usury, . . . he shall surely live, saith the Lord God. If he beget a son that is a robber, a shedder of blood, and . . . hath oppressed the poor and needy, hath spoiled by violence, . . . hath given forth upon usury, . . . he shall surely die. . . ."[2]

There is thus a collocation of usury and robbery in the Biblical source, but no textual basis for an identification. Prominent patristic authority, however, was almost as strong as Old Testament authority. From a certain point of view, it might even be stronger. It is difficult to imagine a more effective human weapon in the medieval campaign against usury than St. Ambrose's definition of usury as robbery.[3] It was placed in crucial positions in some of the most influential literary media of moral instruction. Gratian quoted the

---

[1] *De bono mortis*, 12,56: CSEL 32/1, 752: "Si quis usuram accipit, rapinam facit, vita non vivit."

[2] Ezek., 18.5–13; cp. 33.13–19. English quotations from the Bible are from the Authorized King James Version.

[3] The supreme weapon was Christ's own statement in the Sermon on the Mount according to Luke, "Lend, hoping for nothing again *(Mutuum date, nihil inde sperantes)*," which was read throughout the Middle Ages as a divine precept against usury. If all human authorities and arguments failed, Luke 6.35 remained incontrovertible.

line verbatim and made room for it as a separate chapter of the *Decretum*.[4] Peter Lombard, in his *Sentences*, expounding the seventh commandment, states: "Here also usury is prohibited, which is contained under robbery."[5] Raymond of Peñafort explains why he has chosen to discuss usury in prolongation of robbery in his *Summa* for confessors, the leading work of its genre: It is "because usury differs little, or not at all, from robbery."[6]

Usury, to these authors, usually meant a charge in excess of the principal of a loan of money *(mutuum)*. Theft and robbery are defined in the *Institutes* of Justinian. "Theft occurs when someone takes what belongs to another against the will of the owner."[7] Robbery *(rapina)* is doing so by force. Who, the lawmaker asks, takes a thing more against the owner's will, than he who robs it by force?[8] When, and by whom, the idea that usurious gain is extorted from the borrower against his will, as a form of robbery, first became coupled with the traditions on compulsion and the voluntary reviewed in Part I of this study, is not quite clear. The connection is made in two works composed, most likely, in the second decade of the thirteenth century, namely, the *Summa confessorum* of Thomas of Chobham and the *Summa aurea* of William of Auxerre. There is nothing to indicate a direct influence between these authors, in either direction. One of the works was composed in England, the other in France. Perhaps the authors, who studied at Paris in the closing years of the twelfth century, received the idea from a common teacher; if so, he is yet to be identified.[9] In a chapter treating briefly of a number of cases involving usury, Thomas of Chobham remarks that even though a borrower may state that he pays usury freely, he does not do so with an absolute will *(voluntate absoluta)* but only with a comparative will *(voluntate comparativa)*, because he will rather pay something than be without the loan.[10]

---

[4] II,14,4,10: Friedberg, I,738.

[5] *Sent.*, III,37,5: II,211: "Hic etiam usura prohibetur, quae sub rapina continetur."

[6] *Summa de poenitentia et matrimonio*, II,7,pr: p. 227: "Dictum est supra de rapina, sed quia usura parum, vel nihil distat a rapina, de ea consequenter est agendum."

[7] I.4,1,6: "Furtum autem fit . . . cum quis alienam rem invito domino contractat."

[8] I.4,2,pr: "Qui res alienas rapit, tenetur quidem etiam furti (quis enim magis alienam rem invito domino contrectat, quam qui vi rapit? . . .)."

[9] Peter of Corbeil is, of course, a possibility (cp. section 3.3.), but he is one among a number of early Paris masters who could fit the bill.

[10] *Summa confessorum*, 7,6,11,4: 508.

William of Auxerre's first use of this construction occurs in his reply to the objection that charging usury is not tantamount to taking what belongs to another against the owner's will (citing the legal definition of theft), for the borrower wants the lender to charge a moderate amount of usury and, in fact, greatly rejoices when he finds someone who charges no more than this. To which William replies by pointing out that there are two kinds of will, absolute will and "respective or comparative" will. With his absolute will, the borrower does not want to pay usury, merely with his comparative will, in that the usurer refuses to lend for nothing. Thus the usurer takes what belongs to another against his "absolute and discrete" will, which means that usury is theft.[11] I cannot point to any earlier use of this distinction in connection with a present and actual conditioning of the will. In Part I, it was recorded in a noneconomic context from the *Summa* of Alexander of Hales, but this work postdates those of Thomas and William.

All the ancient traditions on compulsion and the voluntary are in evidence in yet another *Summa*, composed a decade or two later, by Roland of Cremona. Roland was a theologian who had taught at Paris and now taught at Bologna and was familiar with legal terminology and principles. Like William of Auxerre, he discusses usury in a comment on Book III of the *Sentences* of Peter Lombard. Usury is sinful, for it is paid with a forced will *(voluntate coacta)*. It may be objected that forced will is will *(coacta voluntas est voluntas)*, "as Augustine and Aristotle say," and that the usurer therefore does not take what belongs to another against his will, but this objection confuses two senses of the expression "against the will" *(invito)*, says Roland. When theft and robbery are

---

[11] *Summa aurea*, III,48,1,2: pp. 913–14. In my study of the economic ideas of the early Paris theologians, I quoted William of Auxerre's argument verbatim (Langholm, 1992, 78) and emphasized its influence on subsequent thought. Since then, M. N. Rothbard, in an amazing "Austrian" reinterpretation of scholastic economics, has picked it up again, not only to dismiss it but to ridicule it as "surely one of the silliest arguments in the history of economic thought" (I,50). This was brought to my notice only when I had all but finished the present book, which is thus in no way a retort to Rothbard. In view of his likely influence on a younger generation of economists, at least in some areas of the United States, I nevertheless feel that I ought to take this opportunity to warn against not taking the argument in question seriously. By transposing the Aristotelian model from physical to economic categories, William of Auxerre (or whoever preceded him), rather than saying something silly, in fact introduced what has remained the core issue of economic ideological dispute ever since.

defined, what is said to be against one's will is that which is not done
with an absolute will, whereas the objection interprets what is said to
be against one's will as that which is not done voluntarily, regardless
of whether the will is forced or not.[12]

Subsequent contributors to the economic tradition on the voluntary
occasionally made a distinction between robbery and usury, in that the
robber takes what belongs to another against his will, whereas the usurer takes it against his absolute will,[13] but this distinction is not essential.
Roland of Cremona is obviously right in suggesting that robbery is also
sometimes made with the forced consent of the victim. In legal terms,
the robber need not always use physical violence (vis absoluta); he may
obtain his purpose by threats of physical violence (vis compulsiva). Moreover, this threat need not always serve to prevent the victim's intervention against the robbery. On the contrary, it may sometimes serve to
obtain the victim's participation (locating and handing over valuables).
Nevertheless, usury is clearly a marginal case of robbery in that it always
involves mere vis compulsiva and participation. In that respect, the borrower promising to pay usury resembles the captain who jettisons cargo.
The first author to refer explicitly to Aristotle's example may be Peter
of Tarentaise (the future Pope Innocent V), who commented on Book
III of the Sentences in the late 1250s. Still using the Ethica vetus, Peter
argues that the usurer takes what belongs to another against the
owner's will "insofar as his absolute will and pleasure are concerned,
though he may will it with a conditional and forced will, like him who
throws merchandise into the sea." Usury, therefore, is theft in a broad
sense of the word, albeit not in a narrow sense.[14]

4.2   The argument from compulsion

The authors quoted in section 4.1 represent the early stages in the
development of an *argument against usury from compulsion*. This argument forms part of what is sometimes called the scholastic "natural law
case" against usury. The wrongfulness or sinfulness of usury was partly
accepted by the medieval scholastics on scriptural, patristic, and canonistic authority. This resort to authority was supplemented with attempts to prove usury wrongful with arguments from natural reason.

---

[12] *Summa*, III, Q.397: pp. 1190, 1193.

[13] Cp. Peter of Tarentaise, *Quodl.* 11: p. 251; Bonaventura, loc. cit. in note 16;
Albert the Great, loc. cit. in note 17; most explicitly in Astesanus, *Summa*,
I,32,1: f.43ra; and occasionally in later authors.

[14] *Comm. Sent.*, III,37,3,4: p. 309.

Trust in such proofs was particularly strong in the thirteenth and four-teenth centuries. A number of distinct lines of argument were estab-lished. The main ones were a theological *argument from the sale of time* (the usurer sells time, which belongs to God), a legally inspired *argu-ment from ownership* (according to the definition of a *mutuum*, ownership of money borrowed passes to the borrower and any profit obtained with it belongs to him), the Thomistic *argument from consumptibility* (money is consumed in use and therefore has no use separate from its substance – and hence no use value), the Aristotelian *argument from the sterility of money* (somewhat questionably based on the reading of a phrase in the *Politics* to mean that metal cannot breed, but later developed so as to apply to money as a fungible rather than to money as an inanimate object),[15] as well as the argument from compulsion.

The latter argument was frequently included in the natural law case. Among the thirteenth-century theologians, John of La Rochelle, Alex-ander of Hales, and Bonaventura copied or paraphrased William of Auxerre.[16] Albert the Great was also influenced by this tradition but introduced Aristotelian terminology. To the argument that usury does not seem to be theft because it is paid "with will and consent," he replies that the payment of usury is *simpliciter* against the borrower's will and voluntary only *secundum quid*.[17] As will be recalled, Thomas Aquinas elsewhere in his *Summa theologiae* reverses these terms, but when discussing usury he keeps to the usage of his teacher Albert. Having stated the consumptibility argument to prove that the taking of usury is unjust in itself, Thomas replies to seven initial arguments to the contrary. The seventh argument is that the borrower pays usury voluntarily. Thomas replies that he does not pay voluntarily *simpliciter* but "under a certain necessity" *(cum quadam necessitate)*, in that he needs the money that the other declines to lend without usury.[18]

Thomas's reply can be read as a summary of a more extensive dis-cussion in his *De malo*, of a slightly earlier date (late 1260s). Here no less than twenty arguments are stated initially to prove that charging usury is not a mortal sin. The seventh and eighth arguments touch upon the question of the borrower's consent. For his solution, Thomas here as well relies on a careful statement of the argument from the

---

[15] On these arguments and their developments by scholastic authors, see Langholm, 1992.

[16] John of La Rochelle, *Summa de vitiis*: ff.34vb–35ra; Alexander of Hales, *Sum. theol.*, IV,914–15; Bonaventura, *Comm. Sent.*, III,37, Dub. 7:835.

[17] *Comm. Sent.*, III,37,13: 705; 707.

[18] *Sum. theol.*, II–II,78,1: IX,156.

consumptibility of money. He then proceeds to reply to the contrary arguments. Because there is no fraud or force involved (so the seventh argument runs), in that the borrower pays usury voluntarily, he suffers no injustice. The premise is true, says Thomas, as far as absolute force is concerned, yet the borrower is subject to a certain "mixed force" *(violentia mixta)*, in that "the necessity of having to accept the loan imposes a serious condition so that he returns more than he is given." As though in anticipation of this reply, his imaginary opponent cites Aristotle (eighth argument). Mixed force is present only when some necessity threatens, "as in the case of one who throws goods into the sea in order not to endanger the ship." Loans, however, are sometimes accepted at usury without any great need. Therefore, at least in such a case, to lend money at usury is not a mortal sin. Thomas's reply to this is fundamental, and somewhat unusual for this normally moderate author, in that he here adopts what can only be called an extreme position. According to Aristotle in the *Metaphysics*,[19] "necessary" can mean two things, either that without which one cannot exist, or that without which one can exist but not well and properly, and in that sense all useful things are necessary. One who accepts a loan always suffers necessity either in the first or in the second of these two senses.[20] If this is interpreted literally, it means that usury is always paid involuntarily, regardless of the purpose for which the money was intended, and that all usury is theft.

This idea was not often stated quite as bluntly,[21] but it is important to note the unanimity of scholastic opinion on the subject of usury and compulsion in the century following Aquinas. According to Richard of Middleton, the borrower does not pay usury freely, but "as though under a condition of compulsion."[22] An anonymous commentator on the *Politics* states: not voluntarily *simpliciter*, but like one who throws merchandise into the sea.[23] Furthermore, Astesanus, in his *Summa* for

---

[19] *Metaphysics*, V,5: 1015a20–6.

[20] *De malo*, XIII,4: XXIII,253; 256.

[21] Thomas Aquinas was mainly quoted on economic subjects in the *Summa theologiae* (as he still is). Remigio of Florence, one of the relatively few scholastic authors to draw on Aquinas in *De malo*, copies his discussion of usury in *De peccato usurae* (34: 656). Elsewhere (15: 636), Remigio quotes Aquinas in the *Summa theologiae* and cites the example of the ship in peril.

[22] *Comm. Sent.*, IV,15,5,5: p. 223.

[23] This statement occurs in Q.26 to *Politics*, I, in Bologna BU 1625, f.64ra. A similar analysis, but without the reference to the jettison of cargo, is to be found in Q.28 to the same book, in a closely related commentary in Paris BN lat. 16089, f.282rb–va.

confessors: against absolute not comparative will.[24] Raniero of Pisa: not voluntarily *simpliciter*, but as though forced.[25] Giles of Lessines: as though forced by the perversity of the lender, with a comparative will, like one who throws merchandise into the sea to avoid peril.[26] The persistence of the Aristotelian analogy is remarkable. Numerous authors, condemning usury, compare the borrower's situation to that of the captain who jettisons cargo.[27]

Gerald Odonis suggests a different analogy, and a more appropriate (albeit dramatic) one, in that the peril to be avoided issues from other people rather than from the elements. In his commentary on the *Nicomachean Ethics*, Odonis devotes a question in Book V to Aristotle's proposition that no one suffers injustice voluntarily. This is the general rule, the commentator observes, but there are certain exceptions to it, and one of these occurs in cases where the will is not absolute but conditional and mixed with the involuntary, as when usury is paid by one who needs money and cannot have it without charge.[28] At Aristotle's mention of usury in Book IV of the *Ethics*, Odonis considers the question whether usury is always sinful.[29] This question also appears in the author's commentary on the *Sentences*. It would seem that this question must be answered in the negative. Consider, for instance, a merchant who borrows money at usury and profits greatly with it. Such a contract is voluntary on the part of borrower and lender alike and beneficial to both. Neither proposition is true, says Odonis. The contract is not beneficial to the borrower, for he must pay back more than he received. As regards his will, it is mixed. Need forces him (*necessitas cogit eum*) to pay usury, says the author in his *Ethics* commentary.[30] In the *Sentences* commentary, he poses his dramatic analogy. The situation of the borrower who agrees to pay usury is like that of a prisoner who prefers to be ransomed rather than hanged.[31]

In the fifteenth century, the argument against usury from compul-

---

[24] *Summa*, III,11,3: f.131ra.

[25] *Pantheologia*: II,1210.

[26] *De usuris*, IX:424; XV:431.

[27] For some additional fourteenth-century examples, cp. Langholm, 1992, 425 (Francis of Meyronnes), 442–3 (Alexander of Alessandria), 534 (William of Rubio).

[28] *Sent. Eth.*, V, Q.18: ff.220rb–221ra.

[29] EN, IV,1: 1121b34.

[30] *Sent. Eth.*, IV, Q.20: ff.149ra–150ra. Much of this material was utilized by Jean Buridan in *Quaest. Eth.*, IV,6: ff.75ra–76rb.

[31] *Comm. Sent.*, IV,15,6: ff.42va–43ra.

sion appeared only sporadically, mainly in confessional literature, and very little was added that was new. Jean Gerson states firmly that usury is and remains evil; it amounts to taking what belongs to another against his will, as in the case of one who jettisons cargo to avoid imminent shipwreck, or like a man of character who consents to matrimony from fear of death.[32] In Italy, Antonino of Florence, quoting the lawyer Lorenzo Ridolfi, states that even one who merely pays usury from fear of not obtaining loans in the future does not pay it voluntarily but as though forced (*quasi coacte*).[33] Experience shows, says Antonino, that people in need tend to affirm and put in writing whatever the usurer demands.[34] Bernardino of Siena quotes St. Ambrose and medieval theologians. Usury is against the law of nature; the usurer takes what belongs to another against the owner's absolute will, if not against his conditional or comparative will.[35] Battista Trovamala, in his highly influential *Summa* for confessors, draws on Ridolfi as well, perhaps via Antonino.[36]

4.3   Is paying usury a sin?

Though the focus of the discussions recorded in the previous section is primarily on the borrower, whose need forces him to pay usury against his absolute will, the conclusion concerns the lender, who is a robber, and therefore a sinner, because he exploits the need of his neighbor. The analogy with the captain who jettisons cargo is inappropriate insofar as it lacks this element of personal confrontation. In a different respect, it is more appropriate than the analogy with the subject who commits a crime to save his family from the tyrant's threat upon their lives. As noted already, I have found no mention of this example in scholastic sources dealing with economic subjects. The reason for this is presumably the fact that it entirely lacks an economic element. The captain, on the other hand, makes a sort of economic sacrifice by abandoning his property in order not to drown. Similarly, some borrowers make an economic sacrifice by promising to pay usury in the future in order to obtain present cash with which to buy necessaries. Life may hang in the balance in both cases. The most appropriate analogy is that of the always perceptive Odonis. It contains both

---

[32] *De contractibus*, I,13: 392.
[33] Antonino, *Sum. theol.*, II,1,7,6: col. 92; cp. Ridolfi, *De usuris*: f.18ra.
[34] II,1,7,7: col. 93.
[35] *Quadr.*, Serm. 38,1,8: IV,251.
[36] *Summa Rosella*: f.247ra.

personal confrontation and the economic element. The prisoner makes an economic sacrifice by paying ransom to his captors in order to save his life.

Needless to say, not all potential borrowers risked death if the loan was declined. Some would manage well without and would borrow at usury merely in order to obtain funds for profitable investments. In the opinion of Odonis, as well as in the immensely influential opinion of Aquinas, the usurer sins, anyhow. This is to stretch the argument as well as the analogies, but it follows from the basic premise of usury doctrine. The core of the natural law case, from which all the other arguments can, in one way or another, be derived, was the idea that money is barren.[37] It means that *all* profit of economic activity involving capital is the fruit of human management of money and not of money as such. In terms of justice, the problem of usury was unique. Unlike buying and selling, or the hire of labor, there was no weighing of claims and counterclaims between the parties involved, in order to estimate the just balance. Any charge that was not attributable to cost or risk or some other extrinsic title to interest was inherently unjust. Any rate of usury was sinful on the part of the lender. It was a foregone conclusion. By contrast, two other important aspects of the problem of compulsion and the will, examined by scholastic authors in connection with usury, were open to dispute. One of them concerned the moral position of the borrower.

According to Christian moral theology, a person who consents to another person's sin also sins.[38] Because charging usury is sinful robbery, does not the borrower also sin who not only consents to the payment but most often is the one who takes the initiative by approaching the usurer with the request for a loan? It was generally agreed that the borrower was less to blame if he did not actually prevail upon the lender to lend with a promise of usury but merely agreed, reluctantly, to pay usury as a necessary condition of obtaining the loan. Assuming the latter to be the case, the question of culpability on the borrower's part might depend on the nature of his motivation in asking for the loan. This invited an examination of need as compulsion from a different point of view. Compulsion of the borrower condemns the lender who charges usury. Does it exonerate the borrower who pays it?

William of Auxerre states firmly that one who truly needs the loan and cannot have it for nothing pays usury against his proper will (*contra*

---

[37] This, at any rate, is one way to construe the internal logic of these arguments; see Langholm, 1992, 553–9; 586–9.

[38] E.g., Rom. 1.32.

voluntatem rectam), and so does not sin. He adds that paying usury when there is no need is sinful, but that only charity can decide the issue.[39] A number of prominent theologians accepted the incidence of need as the decisive factor. John of La Rochelle and Bonaventura draw on William of Auxerre.[40] According to Thomas Aquinas, one who pays usury in need does not sin, for he does not pay voluntarily, but as though forced by need *(quasi coactus necessitate).*[41] Beyond William of Auxerre's "charity," no further attempt was made by these thirteenth-century theologians to formulate an exact criterion. Albert the Great, with customary frankness, states that he does not want to commit him-self to an opinion as to the decisive degree of need because the prob-lem is too difficult.[42] Peter Olivi, copied much later by Bernardino of Siena, is vague as well: If a loan cannot be obtained without usury, a borrower who pays it "compelled by his own need" *(propria necessitate compulsus)* does not sin; one who pays it "without a moderate degree of need" *(absque rationabili necessitate)* sins.[43] In the early fourteenth century, the question was considered with particular reference to com-mercial capital by Durand of Saint-Pourçain: A merchant sins if he has enough on which to live adequately from other sources and, motivated solely by avarice, borrows money at usury in the hope of investing it profitably and thus accumulating superfluous wealth. It is different if he has no other adequate livelihood than trade. Then his need of com-mercial capital is a just need, and borrowing at usury is not sinful.[44] This analysis was confirmed in the fifteenth century by Antonino of Florence.[45]

In view of the severity of Augustinian culpability doctrine in connec-tion with compulsion and the will, in the early canonistic as well as theological traditions, this concession to need as an extenuating factor is remarkable. It demonstrates a phenomenon announced in Part I, namely, the adaptability of concepts like "mixed acts" and "condi-tional will" to dialectical purpose. In the course of the fourteenth and fifteenth centuries, acknowledgment of the impracticality of refusing

---

[39] *Summa,* III,48,2: 920; cp. (less explicitly), Stephen Langton, *Quaestiones:* f.108va.
[40] John, *Summa de vitiis:* f.35ra; Bonaventura, loc. cit. in note 16.
[41] *Comm. Sent.,* III,37,1,6: VII,439.
[42] *Comm. Sent.,* III,37,15: 711.
[43] Olivi, *De usuris:* 76; Bernardino, *Quadr.,* Serm. 36,3,12: IV,220.
[44] *Comm. Sent.,* III,37,4: f.181vb; cp. Peter of La Palu, *Comm. Sent.,* III,37,2: f.231ra.
[45] *Sum. theol.,* II,1,9,14: col. 153 (quoting Durand through Peter of La Palu).

money to be lent at interest was spreading in theological and legal circles. Scholastic discussions of the subject took a new direction. It focused on the concept and the catalogue of extrinsic titles, which were gradually extended, whereas the argument against usury from compulsion tended to be abandoned. At the same time and by the same token, the idea that a borrower should be condemned for taking advantage of an established institution was losing its plausibility. A decisive point was reached near the end of the fifteenth century, with the analogous application of Aquinas's extended definition of need. In his best-selling *Summa* for confessors, Angelo Carletti argues that a borrower's legitimate need of money is not limited to grave want but may include utility as well. In his treatise on contracts, he mentions the regular conduct of one's business as an example. From someone who is already prepared to lend at usury, it is not a mortal sin to borrow for such purposes.[46] In the following century, this conclusion was supported by Francisco de Vitoria, the Spanish theologian and commentator on Thomas Aquinas: If I should get the chance to buy some landed property to add to my estate and I lack sufficient funds but can borrow it from someone ready to lend at usury, it is lawful to accept the offer. If he charges usury, it is not in accordance with my will *(non est ex voluntate mea)*.[47]

4.4   The question of ownership

By this time, when the center of scholastic learning had completed its move from France via Italy and, with Vitoria, the founder of the School of Salamanca, was about to establish itself definitively in Spain, a sort of consensus had thus been reached as regards the moral positions of both parties to a usurious loan. Nearly all interest regarding compulsion and the will in relation to usury would now be focused on a third problem, also originally introduced in theological literature long ago by William of Auxerre. This was the question of the passage of ownership of usurious money to the usurer. If the usurer is a kind of robber, it would seem that he does not become owner of the money extorted from the borrower. This conclusion caused a dilemma to arise, because it might seem to follow that such money could not be used for tithes or alms. To the extent that this inference rested on the physical conception of money, on its association with specie, which was widespread in early scholastic thought, this dilemma was fictitious. Whether

[46] *Summa*: ff.307vb–308ra; *Tract.*, II,2: p. 150.
[47] *Comentarios*, to II–II,78,4: 239–40.

ownership passes to the usurer or not, it was universally agreed that he was morally obliged to make restitution, but restitution could be made in kind. Hence, provided that the usurer possessed sufficient clean money as well as money tainted by usury, he might well spend the latter on tithes or alms and use some of the former to make good whatever obligation remained to his erstwhile victim or victims. It is therefore to some extent a measure of the decline of late scholasticism into argument for argument's sake that so much energy should still be spent on the question of the passage of ownership of usurious money, even long after monetary theory had advanced beyond this primitive stage. We must nevertheless examine the literary tradition on this question on account of its extended use of the analytical concepts and principles that are our main concern.

This tradition is also rooted in early canonistic sources. In the chapter following St. Ambrose's identification of usury with robbery, Gratian in the *Decretum* accommodates some lines by St. Augustine on usury in one of his epistles. The quotation contains this line: "All that is wrongfully possessed is alien [property]."[48] Commenting on this, Huguccio explains: "Those things which are received by way of usury are alien because there ownership is not transferred."[49] This straightforward interpretation was not confirmed in the *Glossa ordinaria*, and, at adjacent points in the text, the *Glossa* questions Huguccio's position. The preceding chapter inspired the following remark: "If the usurer is a robber, ownership is not transferred to him, as neither to a simoniac; however, it may be conceded that ownership is transferred to him."[50] Another gloss, to a mention of alms of wrongful possessions in the prologue to the following question in the *Decretum*, contains these ambiguous lines: "If ownership of unlawfully acquired things is not transferred, or if it is transferred, with an obligation to make restitution, alms cannot be given of it, as in the case of usury."[51] The *Glossa ordi-*

---

[48] *Epistola* 153, 26: PL 33, 665; cp. Gratian, *Decretum*, II,14,4,11: Friedberg, I,738: "Omne igitur, quod male possidetur, alienum est."

[49] *Summa decretorum*: f.218vb: "Ea quae pro usura accipiuntur sunt aliena quia ibi non transfertur dominium." Cp. Simon of Bisignano, *Summa*, to *Decretum*, II,14,4,11: Bamberg SB Can. 38, f.29ra: "Per rapinam, furtum, simoniam et usuras non transfertur dominium."

[50] To II,14,4,10: Bamberg SB Can. 13, f.129ra; Basel 1512, f.220rb: "Si ergo usurarius est raptor, ergo in eum non transfertur dominium, sicut nec in simoniacum; potest tamen concedi quod transfertur dominium in eum."

[51] To II,14,5,pr: Bamberg SB Can. 13, f.129rb; Basel 1512: f.220va: "Si de illicite acquisitis non transfertur dominium, vel etiam transfertur sed competit repetitio, non potest inde fieri eleemosyna, ut in usura."

naria to the *Decretals* of Gregory IX mentions tithes as well as alms and likewise suggests that ownership of usurious money either does not pass to the usurer or passes with an obligation to make restitution but does not say which.[52] Most canonists, following Godfrey of Trani,[53] adopted the former position. Among the theologians, some argued or concluded in favor of the former and some in favor of the latter position.

William of Auxerre argues that ownership does not pass, because the borrower pays usury *necessitate coactus*; his motivation is like the fear that may strike a man of character.[54] Roland of Cremona similarly points to the absence of absolute will.[55] Alexander of Hales and Bonaventura also conclude against the passage of ownership.[56] Albert the Great appears to have undergone a change of opinion. In his commentary on the *Sentences*, he records the two conflicting views but favors that of his fellow theologians, citing lack of absolute will.[57] Having familiarized himself more thoroughly with the *Ethics* through his two commentaries on this work, he argues in Aristotelian terms to the opposite conclusion in his commentary on Luke. The will of the borrower is mixed, like that of one who throws cargo into the sea in time of peril. Such mixed or conditional will has more of the voluntary about it than the involuntary. This supports the conclusion that ownership passes. "And this I hold to be true," says Albert.[58] Thomas Aquinas was variously interpreted by later authors but cannot personally be taken in favor of either position.[59] Prominent theologians like Henry of Ghent and John Duns Scotus conclude for the passage of ownership.[60] Peter of La Palu does

---

[52] *Decretals* with *Glossa ordinaria* (by Bernard Botone of Parma), at X. III,30,23: f.192va.

[53] *Summa super titulis Decretalium*, to X. III,30: f.148ra.

[54] *Summa*, III,48,1,2: 916.

[55] *Summa*, III, Q.398: p. 1194.

[56] Alexander, *Sum. theol.*, IV,734;906; Bonaventura, *Comm. Sent.*, IV,15,2,2,1: 371.

[57] *Comm. Sent.*, III,37,14: 709–10.

[58] *Super Lucam*, to Luke 6. 35: 437.

[59] Aquinas cites the opinion of the lawyers in *Comm. Sent.*, IV,15,2,4: VII,723; but in *Sum. theol.*, II–II,78,3: IX,165, he refers to a usurer receiving payment in things whose use is not their consumption, *quarum alius est dominus*.

[60] Henry of Ghent, *Quodl.*, IV,27: Paris 1518, f.144v; Scotus: p. 325. Note, however, that Scotus elsewhere (p. 321), referring to EN, III,1, states that one who gives something "as though forced by need" does not give it freely because compulsion excludes voluntariness *simpliciter*, and he

so as well, invoking Roman law. A contract agreed to through fear of death is valid in law and certainly has no more of the voluntary about it than the agreement to pay usury in order to avoid a greater loss.[61]

A lengthy argument against the passage of ownership, countering legal principles, is put forward by Gerardo of Siena. It is true that ownership passes according to civil law, but even there, an action to have it restored is available to the borrower. But according to natural law, ownership does not pass at all. The adage that forced will is will may apply to one who perjures himself as taught by St. Augustine in *Merito*, but not to one who pays usury. Unlike that of the perjuror, the forced will of the debtor has more of the involuntary about it than the voluntary.[62] A subtler distinction is suggested and developed by two other fourteenth-century theologians. Arguing in Aristotelian terms, Godfrey of Fontaines concedes that the mixed will of the debtor who pays usury implies a certain consent, but what he consents to transfer to the usurer is not ownership but the bare possession *(nuda possessio)* of the money in question.[63] Henry of Hesse applies this reinterpretation to Aristotle's own much-used example. Forced will is will. One who pays usury does so voluntarily in the same sense in which one who jettisons cargo when in peril at sea can be said to act voluntarily, namely, in the sense that he prefers to lose his property rather than lose his life. He does not thereby intend, however, to renounce ownership of the goods in question; he hopes to recover them. If they are marked with his letters or sign, anyone who might discover them in the sea or on the seashore is obliged to return them to him as the rightful owner. By the same token, if someone in need or poverty prefers to pay usury rather than lack money, such "half-compelled" *(semicoacta)* will does not suffice for the passage of true ownership to the usurer, for the debtor does not intend to absolve the usurer of the obligation to make restitution.[64] It may be noted that Hesse's interpretation of Aristotle's example is in accordance with the Rhodian Law of Jettison, included in the *Digest.*[65]

---

proceeds to apply this to usury. His position is thus less clear, and he was interpreted both ways.

[61] *Comm. Sent.*, IV,15,2,5: f.66ra.

[62] *De usuris*, II,1: pp. 193–8.

[63] *Quodl.* XIII,15: LPB 5 (1935) 286–91.

[64] Henry of Hesse, *De contractibus*, I,34: f.199va; I,36: f.200rb–va. In a work with the same title, Henry of Oyta (Dub. 18: ff.284rb–249rb) states a similar argument and reaches the same conclusion.

[65] D.14,2,2,8: "What is thrown overboard (to save the ship) remains the

A number of Italian fourteenth-, fifteenth-, and early-sixteenth-century authors of *summas* for confessors examined the question of the ownership of money paid as usury and referred to forced will or to conditional or comparative will. The majority of these (including Bartolomeo of San Concordio, Battista Trovamala, and Giovanni Cagnazzo) considered such will sufficient for the transfer of ownership to the usurer,[66] whereas one of the earliest and one of the latest (Astesanus, Silvester Mazzolini) considered it insufficient and concluded against.[67] Thomas de Vio (Cardinal Cajetan), the commentator on Aquinas, agreed.[68] So did Angelo Carletti. He notes the opinion that forced will may be sufficient for ownership to pass, but in the case of usury there is merely a question of giving up possession of what the usurer demands. "By the bare handing over of a thing ownership is not transferred."[69]

In the sixteenth century, these ideas were kept alive in the Spanish tradition centered on the University of Salamanca. The question of the passage of ownership to the usurer of money paid as usury was discussed repeatedly, sometimes at great length, with reviews of previous arguments and authorities, for and against. Francisco de Vitoria concluded against.[70] Domingo de Soto, cofounder with Vitoria of the School of Salamanca, refers to the Roman law doctrine on *metus* and associates it with Aristotle's seafaring merchant *(maritimus mercator)*, who, in fear *(metu)* of shipwreck, jettisons cargo. Granted that it is mixed with the involuntary, this act is nevertheless *simpliciter* voluntary, says Soto, but this does not mean that the merchant thereby gives up ownership of his goods. They are legally his if recovered. Similarly, what one who borrows at usury consents to is the bare handing over *(nuda traditio)* of what he must pay for the loan, not the transfer of ownership.[71] Soto's example, discussion, and conclusions are repeated by Domingo de Bañez.[72] Leonard Lessius states the same idea in different terms. The payment of usury is voluntary *absolute*, though involuntary

property of the owner, and does not vest in anyone who gets possession of it, for it is not considered to have been abandoned."

[66] Bartolomeo, *Summa*: f.468rb; Trovamala, *Summa*: f.259rb; Cagnazzo, *Summa*: f.483vb.

[67] Astesanus, *Summa*, III,11,3: f.131ra; Mazzolini, *Summa*: II,440.

[68] *De usura*, Q.1: f.86ra–b (referring to the jettison of cargo).

[69] *Summa*: f.309va.

[70] *Comentarios*, to II–II,78,3: 236–8.

[71] *De iustitia et iure*, VI, 1,4: f.188r–v.

[72] *Decisiones*, to II–II,78,3: pp. 395–6.

secundum quid, but the debtor does not thereby intend that the usurer should obtain ownership *absolute.*[73] An interesting addition to the argument in favor of this position was suggested by Miguel Salón, who commented on Aquinas's *Summa theologiae* toward the end of the sixteenth century. Whether motivated by true need or by such need as a merchant may experience who requires money for some profitable investment, the borrower pays usury with a mixed will and forced by need *(necessitate compulsus).* This is shown by the fact that he gives up as little as he can, which is the "sole and bare passing over of the thing, without conferring ownership." It is the same with him who throws merchandise overboard when in a storm at sea. He throws away no more than is necessary to save his ship and does not relinquish ownership. If the merchandise is salvaged, he can reclaim it.[74]

4.5   The breakdown of scholastic doctrine

One of the most influential Spanish authors on economic subjects in the sixteenth century was Luís de Molina, theologian and lawyer. He discusses the question of the transfer of ownership along the same lines as well, referring to Roman law and to Aristotle on the voluntary. Molina is prepared to make a distinction between money obtained by usury that is kept separate on the usurer's hand and money thus obtained that is mingled with nonusurious money and thus not physically identifiable. Ownership of the latter kind of usurious money, but not of the former kind, may be said to have passed to the usurer. Molina concedes, with Soto, that the borrower pays usury *simpliciter* voluntary and *secundum quid* involuntary, rather than vice versa (as Aristotle has it), but this is not sufficient for a just transfer to take place, for, however the question of the will is determined, the debtor pays a price for something that is not worth any price, which is unjust. Molina thus relieves the argument from compulsion of the burden of proof and places it elsewhere in the natural law case or perhaps, in the final analysis, on the divine precept to lend without charge.[75] With authors like Salón and Molina, however, the scholastic tradition on usury was on its last leg. In the seventeenth century, the greatest economic thinker trained at Salamanca was Juan de Lugo, who taught and wrote in Italy. According to Lugo, there can be no question but that the ownership of money paid as usury passes to the usurer. Whether the coins in question

---

[73] *De iustitia et iure,* II,20,18: p. 265.
[74] *Controversiae,* to ibid.: Vol. II, pp. 379–89.
[75] *De contractibus,* Disp. 326: cols. 435–43.

are mingled with other coins or not is irrelevant. This as well as other aspects of his theory of usury are directed against Molina. Lugo makes two important observations, with which I propose to close this chapter. Both are devastating to the scholastic doctrine and point forward to another era, already dawning elsewhere in Europe.

Lugo points to the sort of will with which a debtor pays a sum of money to which the creditor has a lawful claim and compares it with the will with which he pays usury. According to scholastic doctrine, all repayment in excess of the principal of a loan was not usurious. The four centuries that separate Lugo from William of Auxerre had seen a gradual extension of the acknowledged set of *extrinsic titles to interest*. Even in the early thirteenth century, it was generally agreed that a creditor could sometimes claim compensation for loss suffered because of failure on the borrower's part to repay the loan on time. From such loss because of delay, the basis of the claim for compensation was extended to a creditor's loss on account of the loan within the loan period itself, and the concept of a loss was extended from a loss actually sustained *(damnum emergens)* to a loss in the relative sense of a missed profit opportunity *(lucrum cessans)*. In the seventeenth century, it was generally agreed that if a lender had need of his own money or could have used it profitably but lent it to someone else instead, he could claim *interesse* under either of these two titles. This was not usury. But was it paid voluntarily by the debtor? Lugo writes:

Although the will [to pay usury] is mixed with something of the involuntary, it is *simpliciter* free, nor does this *secundum quid* involuntary prevent it from being effective, for a borrower does not in fact pay a just interest as *damnum emergens* less involuntarily than a usurious profit; therefore this defect of the voluntary does not impede the effectiveness of the transfer of ownership.[76]

From a purely logical point of view, this observation robs the Aristotelian model of most of its meaning as an instrument of economic analysis. It can be readily generalized from moneylending to other forms of economic exchange. Just as anyone can be said to choose freely within a restricted set of economic alternatives, his choice can be said to be involuntary because of this restriction, regardless of how narrowly, or with what justification, it is established. This does not render the concept of economic compulsion irrelevant from a moral point of view, as long as it is patently evident that people in need and distress sometimes pay rates of usury or comply with other exorbitant terms of contract that they would not otherwise have tolerated. To distinguish between compulsion in this sense and a reasonable balance of eco-

[76] *De iustitia et iure*, Disp. 25,11: Part II, p. 292.

nomic interests is a matter of judgment, and judgment is what scholastic economic ethics frequently fell back upon.

By choosing to overlook this and to focus on the logical flaw, Lugo is at one with the most notorious anti-Aristotelian of his age, Thomas Hobbes. This kinship is even more evident a few lines farther on. There, Lugo comments on Molina's proposition that a just transfer of ownership does not take place because the borrower pays a price for something that is not worth a price. This may well be true, but to Lugo it is irrelevant:

Because the borrower well knows that he has no obligation according to justice, nor the usurer any right, the former's intention cannot be to pay what is the latter's due according to justice; that would be to intend something which is impossible. His intention is merely to pay what is the other's due according to human faithfulness and because he promised to transfer ownership, not, however, for nothing, but for the loan and the benefit received. Granted that this is not worth a price, he will give a higher value for what was worth less, because he promised it.[77]

Lugo's treatise *De iustitia et iure* appeared in 1642. The very same year saw the publication of Hobbes's *De cive*. In this work, a novel idea of natural law finds expression. Decisively breaking with Aristotle, one of its main tenets is that men fulfill their promises, even when proceeding from fear, for justice pertains to the keeping of covenants, not to their terms.

[77] Loc. cit.

CHAPTER 5

Price and market manipulation

5.1   Value as power

When Thomas Aquinas in *De malo* pleads *violentia mixta* on the part of a needy borrower paying usury, he adds that the position of such a borrower is similar to that of a buyer in need to whom a thing is sold at an excessive price.[1] It is a sign of the analytic genius of Aquinas that he was able, in these simple terms, to anticipate the generalization of this central scholastic economic paradigm. More than a century was to pass before the captain who jettisons cargo became a current figure in discussions of price and before the fear that strikes a man of character became commonly associated with a buyer or a seller in economic need. In the late thirteenth century, theologians and canonists intent on defending their notion of justice in pricing were mainly occupied with a different, if related, theoretical issue. For some time to come, this tended to deflect their attention from the Romanists' *coactus volui* and the Aristotelians' interpretation of forced acts as being "more like voluntary acts." Rather than arguing against the voluntary nature of forced choice in economics, they had to counter a doctrine that seemed to legitimize economic power in general, and so, by implication, to condone the application of economic compulsion. This doctrine gave rise to an extensive scholastic literary tradition. It was couched partly in general terms and partly in terms of some specific forms of market manipulation whereby economic power might be obtained, such as speculation, collusion, and monopoly. In this chapter, we shall trace the several branches of this broad tradition until they merged with the traditions presented in the preceding chapters. Gradually, through this process, economic need came to be analyzed with reference to conditional will also in cases of buying and selling.

One of the most deep-seated premises that postscholastic economic thought purported to have inherited from Roman law, and against which scholasticism fought a long-drawn-out losing battle, was the idea

---

[1] *De malo*, XIII,4: XXIII,256.

of absolute domination over material resources, the idea that the right of legal owners to use and dispose of their possessions at will and on their own terms was complete and inviolate. "Anyone is moderator and arbiter of his own thing."[2] This famous dictum, actually an excerpt from an ordinance of the Emperor Constantine incorporated in the *Code*, was made to sound, out of context, rather more categorical than was intended. In the commentary tradition on the law, it nevertheless inspired an inference that, unlike the dictum itself, is entirely of an economic character, namely, that the value of any possession, to its owner, is the highest price at which it can be transferred, or disposed of, to someone else. As one of several ways to assess the merit of an object or a service, this is, of course, a much older idea. Thus Seneca, in one of his moral essays, discussing the obligation to pay for benefits received, asks, ". . . what difference does it make what they are really worth, since the seller and the buyer have agreed upon their price? . . . ; they are worth only the highest price at which they can be sold."[3] An early, and still unidentified, medieval Romanist crystallized this idea in the form of the pithy maxim that appears in at least six different places (sometimes, it is true, with modifying clauses) in the *Glossa ordinaria* to the *Digest*: "A thing is worth as much as it can be sold for" *(Res tantum valet quantum vendi potest).*[4]

This is precisely how value in exchange was later to be defined in classical and neoclassical economics. According to Alfred Marshall, the "value, that is the exchange value, of one thing in terms of another at any place and time, is the amount of that second thing which can be got there and then in exchange for the first."[5] This is still a current definition. In modern professional usage, value in exchange is (at least allegedly) a descriptive term, but it is heavily value-laden. When such a term appears in a legal gloss, this valuational content is intentional, because legal statements are, by their very nature, prescriptive within the domain of the law. To proclaim that a thing is worth as much as it can be sold for means that it may, in the given domain, be thus priced.

---

[2] C.4,35,21; cp. also C.4,38,14.
[3] *De beneficiis*, VI,xv,4: LCL 210, 393–5 (J. W. Basore's translation).
[4] In this naked form, the gloss appears at D.13,1,14,pr; D.36,1,1,16; and D.47,2,52,29. As a legal gloss, it predates the compilation of the *Glossa ordinaria* by Accursius. Its earliest appearance known to me is at D.36,1,1,16 in Bamberg SB Jur. 15, f.136va (in a slightly different form). In this manuscript, a number of pre-Accursian glossators have been identified by ascriptions, but the gloss in question is unfortunately anonymous.
[5] *Principles of Economics*, II,ii,6: 61.

If this were to be extended to the moral law, it would follow that no
sin or blame attaches to a seller who sells as dear as he can (or to a
buyer who buys as cheap as he can). Two related corollaries are readily
inferred. In its naked form, the legal value maxim makes nought of the
concept of a just price. By the same token, it legitimizes an unlimited
use of economic power. This is perhaps less immediately evident in
English than in the Latin languages, where "can" is a word on the
same stem as "power": *potest/potentia; puo/potenza, peut/puissance*, etc.
But it is occasionally stated explicitly in English as well. Thus Ricardo:
"By exchangeable value is meant the power which a commodity has of
commanding any given quantity of another commodity."[6]

When knowledge of law spread in the theological schools of the
thirteenth century, it is not difficult to imagine the consternation
caused by this scandalizing conception of value. Running directly
counter to the codes of ethics with which the spirit of profit had to be
tempered in a period of economic growth, it had to be neutralized in
some way. In principle, it was countered on two fronts, by being rewritten and by being modified. Henry of Ghent was instrumental in
setting in motion both these lines of attack. In an early *quodlibet* question, Henry suggested that the value maxim could be rewritten by replacing its key term. The proposition that a thing is worth as much as
it *can be* sold for should not be understood to refer to what is actually
possible in fact but to what is possible according to natural law, that is,
for as much as it *ought to be* sold for. Some years later, Henry commented on the maxim once more. What a thing can be sold for is not
to be understood in terms of absolute power but in terms of right reason.[7] In the early fourteenth century, the Aristotelian Gerald Odonis,
in his treatise on contracts, rewrote the maxim in terms of just equality. A thing is worth as much as it lawfully can be sold for, equality being preserved.[8]

Substituting "ought" for "can," and postulating Aristotelian justice,
for the scholastics amounted to much the same thing. A principle of
power is replaced by one of obligation. A number of prominent authors
rewrote the maxim in similar terms (though often in addition to modifying it more specifically as well). A thing is worth as much as it can
be sold for "if so permitted" (Antonino of Florence), "if sold at a just
price" (Battista Trovamala), "justly and reasonably" (Gabriel Biel),
"lawfully" (Conrad Summenhart), "lawfully and reasonably" (Juan de

---

[6] *Works*, ed. Sraffa, IV,398.
[7] *Quodl.* I,40: *Opera Omnia*, V,222; *Quodl.* XIV,14: Paris 1518, f.570v.
[8] *De contr.*, Q.4: f.81v.

Medina), "within the limits of just estimation" (Leonard Lessius), etc.[9] Henry of Ghent was a much-used and highly regarded authority in the schools of the Augustinian friars. Martin Luther may have drawn fairly directly on the original source when he thunders against contemporary German merchants: "It should not be thus, 'I may sell my wares as dear as I can or will *(kan odder wil),*' but thus, 'I may sell my wares as dear as I ought to or as is right and fair.' For your sale ought not to be an activity freely in your power and will *(macht und willen)*, without any law or measure, as though you were a god, obliged to no one."[10] Not long after Luther, however, the Spanish Dominican Domingo de Soto rejected all this as merely begging the question at issue. If someone asks you how much he can sell for, and you answer, "What justice dictates," you tell him nothing that he did not already know.[11]

Soto, however, did not leave the matter there, nor had Henry of Ghent done so. In the course of the centuries that separate them, a different line of attack on the libertarian ethos suggested by the maxim in its naked form was pursued as well. Rather than substitute "ought" for "can" or call on justice in general, the idea was to neutralize the maxim by the addition of modifying clauses ruling out those specific elements of an exchange that would render its terms unjust. In this, the theologians were initially aided by the Romanists. The lawyers would not, of course, accept the "can" without question, either. The Roman law of sale observed strict conditions of valid contract as well. Some of them found expression as addenda to the maxim where it appears in glosses and commentaries on the *Digest.* For one thing, there must be no fraud. At one point, the *Glossa ordinaria* states that a thing is worth as much as it can be sold for, provided that its condition is known.[12] This was extended by later Romanists to include understanding as well as knowledge of the objects and conditions of the exchange.[13] Scholastic authors with a legal bent would sometimes copy this.[14] It inspired others to state the maxim in a modified form explicitly ruling out fraud. Thus, as early as the middle of the thirteenth century,

---

[9] Antonino, *Sum. theol.*, II,1,8,3, and 5: cols. 130; 132; Trovamala, *Summa:* f.255ra; Biel: p. 201; Summenhart, *De contr.*, III, Q,57: p. 270; Medina, *Cod. rest.*, Q.32: p. 204; Lessius, *De iustitia et iure,* II,21,3: p. 276.

[10] *Von Kaufshandlung und Wucher:* p. 295.

[11] *De iustitia et iure*, VI,2,3: f.196r.

[12] Apparently due to Accursius at D.39,6,18,3, and frequently copied throughout the law by subsequent commentators.

[13] Cp. Alexander Tartagni, *Comm. Infort.*, to D.36,1,1,16: f.239rb.

[14] Ariosto, *De usuris*, III: pp. 76–7; Trovamala, *Summa:* f.255rb.

Roland of Cremona explained it to mean that a thing is worth as much as it can be sold for *sine fraude;*[15] similarly, Giles of Lessines;[16] and much later, Thomas de Vio: *absque dolo et fraude.*[17]

Occasionally, this tradition would be tied in with Aristotle on the voluntary and with the Roman law tradition on *metus.* Gerson, in a pithy paragraph, notes that the value maxim of the lawyers is not accepted in its naked form by the theologians. He quotes one of the legal rules listed at the end of Pope Boniface VIII's addition to the *Decretals* of Gregory IX. It echoes a principle with twin roots in Aristotle's *Ethics* and in classical Roman law[18]: "No injury nor fraud is done to one who knows and consents."[19] This is true, says Gerson, but only if his consent is absolute and not merely conditional and *secundum quid,* as when cargo is jettisoned, nor extorted by fear of death, nor induced by fraud, for ignorance causes involuntariness, in full or in part.[20]

Once more, we may pass over further mention of the subject of fraud. The reference to prices obtained through fear of death suggests a modification of the value maxim with regard to compulsion. Having rejected the general reference to justice, Soto states the maxim in what he considers to be its true sense. It means that a thing is worth as much as it can be sold for in the absence of force, fraud, and deceit, by which the will is removed in the buyer *(seclusa vi, fraude, et dolo, quibus in emptore tollitur voluntarium).*[21]

In the middle of the sixteenth century, when this was written, it is perhaps safe to assume that the *vis,* to which Soto refers as an additional factor invalidating the maxim, is meant to include economic compulsion as well as physical compulsion. He does not say this in so many words but indicates it in the following lines by limiting this restriction to necessaries, leaving luxuries free to find their own prices (a subject on which more follows). A thing is not worth what it can only be sold for to someone in need, for need is a form of compulsion. Earlier theologians had made this abundantly clear. The lines preceding those where Henry of Ghent replaces the civilians' "can" with an "ought" run as follows:

---

[15] *Summa,* III, Q.406: p. 1215.

[16] *De usuris,* IX: 424.

[17] *Summa de peccatis,* art. *Emptio:* f.55v.

[18] See section 2.2.

[19] *Liber sextus Decretalium,* V,12, *De regulis iuris,* Regula 27 (Friedberg, II,1122): "Scienti et consentienti non fit iniuria neque dolus."

[20] *De contractibus,* II,11: 401.

[21] Loc. cit. in note 11.

In accordance with the equity of natural justice, a thing ought to be sold and bought for as much as it is worth, and if someone wittingly sells it for more than it is worth at the time and place, or buys it for less, this is unequal and it is unjust even if he is permitted to do so and his neighbor, with whom he deals, does not oppose it, either because he does not know or because need compels him to accept what is unjust.[22]

Shortly afterward, and most likely under the influence of Henry, another prominent late-thirteenth-century theologian, Peter Olivi, squarely faces the legal value maxim in the opening question of his treatise on buying and selling. One of the arguments he sets out to counter sounds surprisingly familiar. It is the libertarian take-it-or-leave-it proposition:

No law compels me to give or exchange my goods except at a price agreeable to me and established by me in advance, just as, on the other hand, no one is obliged to buy another's goods above a price which pleases him. If therefore a contract of selling and buying is purely voluntary, it follows that price determination of goods in exchange will be voluntary as well, . . . according to the common saying, "A thing is worth as much as it can be sold for."

To which Olivi replies that albeit a person may not be obliged to sell, he is obliged to observe justice once his goods are offered for sale. In the body of the question, he is more specific. Consider a sales contract where the buyer is charged an excessive price. Is such a contract valid?

Just as someone may give a thing for no price at all, he may give it for a hundredth part of its value, nor is thereby any injustice done him unless, perhaps, his consent should happen to proceed, expressly or supposedly, from such a degree of fickleness and defect of will that it ought to have none or insufficient force of law or justice. Or if he acted compelled by such poverty or other need that his consent should not be considered to issue from a wholly free and spontaneous will.[23]

5.2   The role of the market

Need, then, is not to be exploited in buying and selling, because the needy consent against their true will. Before proceeding with the broad tradition thus launched by these clear signals from Henry of Ghent and Peter Olivi, it is necessary to untangle a complication caused by a different role assigned to need in the simultaneous and highly influential Latin commentary tradition on Aristotle's *Ethics*. In *Ethics*, V,5, there is a formula that was taken by the medieval commentators to state the general principles of justice in exchange. A cast of characters repre-

---

[22] *Quodl.* I,40: loc. cit. in note 7.
[23] *De emptione et venditione*, Q.1: ed. Spicciani, 253–7.

senting different occupations is presented: a builder, a shoemaker, a farmer, a doctor, who mutually exchange their products or services. "The number of shoes exchanged for a house (or for a given amount of food) must therefore correspond to the ratio of builder to shoemaker." What could this mean? What determines the ratio between exchangers? According to Aristotle, the cause of exchange, the reason why men exchange, is χρεία ("need"). Grosseteste rendered this word as *opus* in some places, elsewhere as *necessitas*. Because *opus* appears in the same chapter in a different meaning as well, rendering ἔργον ("work"), *opus* rendering χρεία was altered in the revised version of the Latin *Ethics* to *indigentia*. Struggling with the meaning of Aristotle's enigmatic formula, the early commentators (Albert the Great, who used the revised version for his second commentary, and Thomas Aquinas) suggested, as one interpretation, that *indigentia* was not only the cause of exchange, it was a measure of the just value of goods in exchange as well.[24] Aristotle could hardly have meant this, but it became firmly established scholastic opinion. Most modern English translators render χρεία in *Ethics*, V,5, either as "need" or as "demand." The latter choice of word is unfortunate in that it may invite anachronistic associations with the modern concept. Both, however, are fair translations of the scholastics' *indigentia*. The question then is this: How could this Aristotelian tradition be reconciled with the tradition from Henry of Ghent and Peter Olivi? How can *indigentia* be a just measure of value in exchange if need is not to be exploited?

The problem was solved by a distinction between individual and common, or collective, need. It was a matter of aggregation. Henry of Friemar, commenting on the *Ethics* in the early fourteenth century, explains that "human need *(indigentia humana)*, if it is to serve as a measure of goods in exchange, ought not to be taken partially with regard to this or that person, but universally, with regard to the whole community."[25]

According to Peter of La Palu in his commentary on the *Sentences* of Peter Lombard, a price may be lawfully increased because of the common need of men *(propter communem hominum indigentiam)*, but not because of the "pitiable need of a single person" *(propter miserabilem indigentiam unius)*.[26] Buridan suggested that *indigentia* should be under-

---

[24] On Aristotle's discussion of justice in exchange at *Ethics*, V,5 (1132b21–1133b28), the problems of translation and the contributions of the early commentators, see also section 7.3. For a more detailed analysis of the Latin Aristotelian tradition on economic value, cp. Langholm, 1979.

[25] Basel UB F.I.14: f.134rb; Toulouse BMun 242: f.278ra.

[26] *Comm. Sent.*, IV,5,3,3: f.25rb.

stood to comprise, not only the wants of poor people, but also the luxury desires of the rich. Thus extended, the measure of value to him is "the common need *(indigentia communis)* of those who can exchange with each other."[27] Henry of Hesse quoted this and added, ". . . in any district, region or city."[28] This takes the Aristotelian concept to a point where it seems better to render it "demand" than "need," and indeed natural to associate the just value measure with the current, competitive market price.

This is confirmed by a parallel development in Romanist sources, where a similar result was reached at more or less the same time. It originated with a statement that occurs in almost identical wording in two fragments from the jurist Paul, inserted by Justinian's compilers in two different places in the *Digest*. It states that the value of things is based, not on the disposition or utility of single persons, but commonly *(non ex affectione nec utilitate singulorum, sed communiter)*. In both places, the *Glossa ordinaria* copies an older gloss attributed in a number of early manuscripts to Azo, who states the value maxim with an addition: "A thing is worth as much as it can be sold for, that is, commonly."[29] This interpretation was soon adopted in canonist circles. A combination of the value maxim and the quotation from Paul is to be found in a gloss by Laurence of Spain to a chapter in the title on usury in the *Decretals* of Gregory IX, having first appeared as a gloss in the earlier compilation from which this chapter was taken.[30] This was brought into the theological tradition by Godfrey of Fontaines.[31] In the centuries that followed, the identification of the just price with a common estimate became general. A number of authors, including such authorities as Antonino of Florence and Angelo Carletti, explicitly modified the value maxim by stipulating a common estimate.[32] What is a common estimate? Commenting on one of the places in the *Digest* where the *Glossa ordinaria* states the maxim in its naked form, Bartolus of Sassoferrato

---

[27] *Quaest. Eth.*, V,16: f.106ra–b.

[28] *De contractibus*, I,5: f.187va.

[29] To D.9,2,33,pr; and to D.35,2,63,pr. Attributed in the former locus to Azo in Paris BN lat. 4458, f.75va; Bamberg SB Jur. 13, f.128rb; and in other manuscripts.

[30] To *Comp. I*,V,15,8 in Bamberg SB Can. 19, f.70rb (in Tancred's *Apparatus*); to X.V,19,6 in Paris BN lat. 3967, f.189vb and in Paris BN lat. 3968, f.158ra (in Vincent of Spain's *Apparatus*); attributed to Laurence of Spain in these and other manuscripts.

[31] *Quodl.* V,14: LPB 3 (1914) 67.

[32] Antonino, *Sum. theol.*, II,1,16,4: col. 258; Carletti, *Summa*: f.107vb; cp. also Ariosto, loc. cit.; Cagnazzo, *Summa*: f.487rb; Mazzolini, *Summa*: I,294.

explains: "A thing is worth as much as it can be sold for, that is, commonly and in a public place, to many people, over several days." These are, of course, the characteristics of the regular, competitive market.[33]

Identifying the just price with the price obtaining in the market under certain conditions was not, in itself, a controversial issue in scholastic economics. The ideas recorded in the previous paragraphs from Aristotelian and legal sources found expression in theological texts as well. Long before Buridan and Bartolus, Albert the Great, in his commentary on the *Sentences*, defined the just price as that "which the goods sold can be valued at according to the estimation of the market at the time of the sale," a phrase frequently to be repeated in one form or another.[34] If there is a controversy, it concerns the modern interpretation of this doctrine. One of the trickiest problems in the history of value theory derives from the fact that the same proposition, namely, the justice of the market price, was upheld for many centuries in the course of which its ethical foundation, and the definition of its terms, subtly changed. Until a few decades ago, it was not uncommon in critical studies to encounter the suggestion that the medieval scholastics simply permitted the forces of the market to run their course and accepted the resultant "common estimate of the market" as the just price. More recently, this liberalistic interpretation has been challenged by a younger generation of scholars, with whose arguments, as far as they go, I fully agree.

The modern mechanistic conception of the market as a suprapersonal force setting the terms to which an individual exchanger must submit was foreign to the medieval masters. Their frame of reference was a moral universe that obliged any buyer or seller to act for the common good and agree to terms of exchange accordingly, regardless of the advantage granted him by the forces of the market. This means that the common estimate of the just price could not refer indiscriminately to whatever price might be obtainable under existent market conditions. It was only with the dissolution of the medieval paradigm, initiated by some of the late scholastics, that a freer play of market forces was permitted to influence the just price.[35] Granted this, which

---

[33] Bartolus, *In secundam Digesti veteris partem*, to D.13,1,14,pr: p. 207. Much later, more explicitly, the great Spanish theologian Domingo de Bañez, commenting on Aquinas's *Summa theologiae* (*Decisiones*, to II–II,77,1: 352), proclaims: "A thing is worth as much as it can be sold for according to the common estimate of the market *(secundum communem aestimationem fori)*."

[34] *Comm. Sent.*, IV,16,46: 638: "Iustum autem pretium est, quod secundum aestimationem fori illius temporis potest valere res vendita."

[35] The most prominent scholar urging this revision of the scholastic doctrine

I willingly do, what is to be made of the persistent reference in scholastic texts to the common estimate of the market as an expression of
justice? The interpretation that fits this textual evidence best is to assume that the market estimate of justice is limited to markets in a more
or less normal state. This is a rather loose concept, but it is supported
by further evidence to be presented in Chapter 6, insisting that the just
price cannot be fixed to a point. In other words, market prices may
vary somewhat from time to time with supply and demand, without
thereby violating the requirements of justice.

Two inferences can be made from this concept. First, it follows that
the market estimate is in a sense redundant when the market is, in fact,
operating normally, because the just price will then establish itself au-
tomatically. No scholastic author that I know of suggested, as a principle of justice (albeit perhaps sometimes as a matter of charity), that
a buyer or a seller actually operating in a competitive market under
normal conditions should be obliged to buy above, or sell below, the
current price. The second inference is equally important but seems to
me to be generally overlooked. It follows that when conditions notably
differ from what is assumed to be normal, the market estimate becomes
operative, as a guideline. In the Middle Ages, with its poor means of
communication, and with all the uncertainty and hazard associated with
the supply of necessaries, buyers and sellers would frequently meet under circumstances that permitted bargaining powers to be brought into
play to a much larger extent than when the market was working more
or less normally. The parties involved might still come to a reasonable
agreement about price, each perhaps yielding a little because their

of the common estimate is Gómez Camacho (1978, 96–101; 1981, 54–7),
who cites Dempsey, De Roover, and Grice-Hutchinson as representatives of
the conventional interpretation. In my view, a closer examination of these
authors will indicate that their respective positions are not all that
different. Anyhow, they all discuss the works of fifteenth- and sixteenth-
century scholastics. The objection to identifying the just price with
whatever price is obtainable in the market applies above all to the
medieval scholastics. As will be demonstrated with regard to monopoly at
the close of this chapter, the breakdown of the medieval paradigm at the
hands of some of the later Spanish scholastics involved, among others,
Molina, who is Camacho's main source. It is characteristic of all the three
main subjects discussed in this Part II that the School of Salamanca
represents a transitional stage, wherein the doctrines of the medieval
masters mingle with more liberalistic ideas about the role of the market,
frequently in one and the same author. As regards the subject of the just
price, this point is well made by Lapidus (cp., particularly, 41–5).

ideas about justice initially differed. This, as we shall see in Chapter 6, was one way to understand the "common estimate" as well. On the other hand, they might end up with patently unfair terms of exchange. The party taking advantage of the other might then be held to restitution by his confessor. Whatever the case, specific criteria of justice would be useful, and one such criterion was the normal market price, estimated on the basis of experience or by analogy.

This interpretation makes nought of another spurious controversy in the critical literature. There are still some historians who insist on placing a scholastic market interpretation of the just price in opposition to a cost interpretation, but this controversy is a reflection of a much later ideological conflict. Albert the Great and Thomas Aquinas alternatively explained Aristotle's formula in *Ethics*, V,5, in terms of labor and expenses, and there is an equally well-established scholastic tradition following this lead, both in the commentaries and in theological texts. Cost and market were complementary and mutually supporting criteria by which to reach a reasonable estimate of price by the parties involved, or by confessors and arbiters, when the need arose. Incidentally, there is thus no contradiction either, as sometimes assumed, between the just price as a market estimate and the just price as an estimate made by a "good man." What the good man needed were precisely such criteria as cost and market.[36]

My purpose in tracing the development of Aristotelian *indigentia* from individual need to market demand, as well as the development of the legal value maxim from its naked form to its modification in terms of a market estimate, is twofold. My secondary purpose is to clarify my position with respect to an ongoing scholarly dispute regarding the

---

[36] The unfortunate misconception referred to in this paragraph harks back to the nineteenth century but was boosted by Tawney's (36) interpretation of Aquinas as a labor theorist of value and of Marx as his descendant, the latter being thus "the last of the Schoolmen," and by a simplistic reading of Schumpeter (93–4) as an exponent of a contrary view, allegedly reducing scholastic value doctrine to a market theory. On the positions of Dempsey, De Roover, Grice-Hutchinson, and numerous other scholars on this issue, cp. Langholm, 1992, 190–1, n.73 (interpreting Albert the Great), and ibid., 412, n.32 (interpreting John Duns Scotus). On my own position, cp. further, ibid., 479–83, and references in note 24 to the present chapter. One can only hope that this pseudo-controversy will not be renourished by Rothbard's absurd notion (I, x–xi; 52; and passim) that the scholastics were "proto-Austrians" and that references to labor in connection with value on their part were mostly regrettable slips of the pen.

meaning of the "common estimate of the market." My primary purpose is to suggest what, in my opinion, made this market estimate appear reasonable in the eyes of the medieval scholastics. It might be
tempting to read into it a dawning recognition of the benefits of a free
market economy. This would be a grossly misleading anachronism. In
the medieval context, it makes more sense to interpret the market estimate of the just price, understood in the sense explained previously,
as a means to combat the exploitation of individual economic need.
The scholastic masters recognized that, by insisting on an estimate of
the price level that might have established itself in the regular competitive market under normal conditions (just as a normal cost estimate), it was possible, to an adequate extent, to reduce economic
compulsion, because competition between sellers protects buyers, and
vice versa. Confirmation of this interpretation is provided by scholastic
case discussions of unjust pricing. Fraud and physical compulsion apart,
the majority of these discussions concern cases of market manipulation,
whereby strong bargaining positions can be obtained, so that the opposite party (most often a buyer, but sometimes a seller) can be subjected to economic compulsion. This can be illustrated by tracing three
literary traditions, each of which drew a wealth of commentary along
these lines throughout the scholastic centuries. These traditions
reached the medieval theologians via Roman and canon law.

5.3   Speculation

In the chapter of the *Decretum* immediately preceding the one that cites
St. Ambrose's identification of usury with robbery, Gratian copied an
old injunction against speculation in foodstuffs, known by its incipit as
Quicumque. Erroneously attributed to Pope Julius I (fourth century), it
actually originated as a capitulary of Charlemagne, issued at Nijmegen
in 806. Somewhat abbreviated and slightly rewritten, it reads as follows
in Gratian's version: "Whoever, at time of harvest or vintage, not because of necessity but of cupidity, buys grain or wine, for instance, buys
a measure for two pennies and keeps it until it is sold for four pennies,
or six, or more, we say that [such a one acquires] filthy gain."[37]

Many of the early commentaries on this chapter by the Decretists
focused on economic activity on the part of the clergy. This need not
concern us here except for noting that buying something and later
selling it altered or improved at a higher price was to some extent

---

[37] *Decretum*, II,14,4,9; cp. *Capitulare missorum Niumagae datum*, C.17, in
    Capitularia Regum Francorum, ed. A. Boretius, Vol. I, p. 132.

permitted for the clergy (and generally for the laity) because such activity could be associated with that of a craftsman rather than a merchant. (This served as one of several roots of the labor criterion of the just price in scholastic literature.) As regards laymen, two important points of interpretation were provided by Rufinus and Huguccio, neither occurring *ad locum* but elsewhere in their respective *summas*. Both were in the nature of exceptions to the condemnation of profitable resale expressed in *Quicumque*. Rufinus taught that someone who bought necessaries for consumption might charge a higher going price if need, or utility, later made him decide to sell some of it. Sicard of Cremona and the author of the anonymous *Summa Monacensis* generalized this so as to comprise any sale of a surplus of necessaries bought for consumption.[38] Huguccio greatly liberalized this doctrine by applying it as well to goods originally bought for the purpose of profitable resale rather than consumption. Such activity was above reproach provided that it was not motivated by avarice but conducted with the intention of spending the profit on the support of oneself and one's dependants. Then it was permitted in the case of a layman, said Huguccio, "because commerce is granted him" *(ei concessa est negotiatio)*. This phrase was repeated at *Quicumque*.[39] For the theologians intent on laying the foundation of a scholastic economics in the thirteenth century, this provided most welcome authority with which to counter the negative attitude to commerce expressed by the Church Fathers.

Raymond of Peñafort and his glossator, William of Rennes, brought this modified tradition on *Quicumque* into the confessional literature and interpreted it in terms of a market criterion of the just price. It is lawful, Raymond teaches, to sell a surplus of necessaries "as it is commonly sold in the market" *(prout communiter venditur in foro)*. William, in a gloss, copies Huguccio's extension of this license to regular commerce not motivated by avarice. Raymond also commends the laying up of provisions if a general shortage is expected, citing the example of Joseph, who interpreted Pharaoh's dreams and gathered all the food of the seven years of plenty and stored them against the seven years of famine that followed. William notes that such stores must eventually be sold *secundum commune forum*. Those who engage in the kind of speculation condemned in *Quicumque*, however, inspired by nothing but avarice, were to be detested like abominable monsters, a phrase by Raymond to which William found nothing to add.[40]

---

[38] Rufinus, *Summa*, to II,14,3: p. 341; Sicard, *Summa*, to II,14,3–4: f.92v; *Summa Monacensis*, to II,14: f.23ra.

[39] *Summa*, to II,14,4,3: f.218rb; to II,14,4,9: f.218va.

[40] Raymond, *Summa*, with glosses, II,7,9: Rome 1603, pp. 235–6. William's

By stitching together text and glosses of the *Summa Raymundi*, Monaldus of Capodistria constructed a casuistry that was to reappear, with variations and elaborations, in scores of scholastic treatises leaning somewhat toward canon law, including nearly all the most important titles of the fifteenth and sixteenth centuries.[41] The authors would mention various forms of lawful and even meritorious economic exchange, then conclude by citing *Quicumque*, more or less verbatim, on the dirty business of speculating in foodstuffs for personal enrichment. Invariably, this activity would be characterized by a phrase originating in early canonistic literature and transmitted to the later scholastics by Raymond and Monaldus. It is to be found (as far as I can judge, for the first time) in the *Glossa Palatina*. Guido of Baiso routinely attributes it to Laurence of Spain. To the word "cupidity" in the text of *Quicumque*, the glossator explains, "eager for personal profit harmful to the community, in that dearth is induced *(caristia inducatur)*."[42] "Inducing dearth" became a catchword describing the way illicit gains could be obtained through market manipulation.

An explicit reference to compulsion was established in the tradition of *Quicumque* by an author who has not figured much in histories of economic thought but who exerted great influence from the late thirteenth century, namely, Ulrich of Strasbourg. Having discussed the cases of various other economic operators, including Joseph the dream interpreter, he proceeds to explain that profitable buying and selling

may be conducted according to commutative justice as merchants do, and these may lawfully receive a profit for their work by which to support themselves, provided that they do not intend to induce dearth *(caristiam inducere)*. Or it may be conducted from avarice, in such a way that someone gathers so much [of a certain kind of victual] that all are compelled *(compelluntur)* to buy from him at his pleasure and he therefore sells it as dear as he wishes. And it is evident that such people sin enormously, not only against their neighbor, but also against the community of neighbors.[43]

A closely related summary, concluding with the same two cases but using another word for "compelled" (*coguntur* rather than *compellun-*

---

reference to resale *secundum commune forum* is rendered *secundum communem formam* in this edition and is corrected here from manuscript, cp. Munich SB Clm 9663, p. 201.

[41] Monaldus, *Summa*, art. *Usura*: f.290ra–b.

[42] *Glossa Palatina*, to II,14,4,9: Vat. Pal. lat. 658, f.54rb; Durham C.III.8, f.88va; cp. Guido of Baiso, *Rosarium*, to ibid.: f.140ra.

[43] *De summo bono*, VI,3,4: Erlangen UB Lat. 530/2, ff.105v–106r.

tur), is to be found in the *Summa Pisana* of Bartolomeo of San Con-cordio.[44] Following one or the other of these early models, reaping a profit by inducing dearth was represented as a form of compulsion by prominent authors like Raniero of Pisa, Henry of Hesse, Antonino of Florence, Alexander Ariosto, Angelo Carletti, Battista Trovamala, Sil-vester Mazzolini, and Gabriel Biel.[45] Someone buys up all the supplies of a certain necessary, and others are *forced* to buy from him at the price that it pleases him to charge. Many others stated this in less ex-plicit terms. It may be noted that some authors, like Johannes Nider in his guide for merchants, and Bernardino of Siena in his confessional manual, also condemn those who, motivated by greed, merely expect or hope for (rather than cause) a future shortage by which to make a profit.[46] Conrad Summenhart, in the course of a prolonged discussion, insists that it is not sufficient not to intend to induce dearth; the mer-chant is blameless only if his forestalling does not in fact induce dearth.[47] Motivation, however, was normally considered to be an im-portant factor.

5.4   Price discrimination and collusion

The idea of one person buying up all the supplies and controlling the price would naturally tie "inducing dearth" in with the fight against mo-nopoly, and this association is frequently to be observed in scholastic texts. In late Spanish scholasticism, many references to *Quicumque* are to be found in chapters or treatises on monopoly. Owing to the main liter-ary channel through which the word "monopoly" reached the scholas-tics, however, they would conceive of it both in terms of several merchants conspiring to raise prices and in terms of a single merchant achieving this on his own. The two practices would be discussed under the same heading. Before turning to the subject of monopoly, it will therefore be useful to trace briefly another tradition on collusion be-tween sellers, which was sometimes associated by scholastic authors with the tradition recorded in section 5.3, as well as with the tradition on mo-nopoly. As in the case of *Quicumque*, its textual basis harks back to Caro-

---

[44] *Summa*: ff.482vb–483ra.
[45] Raniero, *Pantheologia*: II,1156–7; Hesse, *De contr.*, I,42: f.203rb; Antonino, *Sum. theol.*, II,1,23,16: col. 327; III, 8,3,4: col. 306; Ariosto, *De usuris*, III: pp. 94–5; Carletti, *Summa*: f.306vb; *Tract.*, II,3: p. 183; Trovamala, *Summa*: f.256vb; Mazzolini, *Summa*: I,295; Biel: p. 195.
[46] Nider, *De contr.*, III, Regula 19: f.15v; Bernardino, *Confessionale*, 28: p. 173.
[47] *De contractibus*, III, Q.65: p. 299.

lingian price regulation. In 884, Carloman, King of the West Franks, issued a capitulary prohibiting price discrimination of transients. Known by its incipit as *Placuit*, it was included, in somewhat abbreviated form, in the *Compilatio prima* and passed from there into the *Decretals* of Gregory IX, where it reads as follows: "It was decreed that priests admonish people to be hospitable and not sell dearer to those who pass through than they sell for in the market; otherwise transients should report to a priest so that, by his order, they sell to them with kindness."[48] Among other things, this capitulary would obviously serve as a strong confirmation of the market criterion of the just price. The most explicit modifications of the Romanist value maxim in this respect are to be found in comments on *Placuit*. Thus, in the late fourteenth century, Antonio of Budrio, commenting on *Placuit*, writes, "A thing is worth as much as it can be sold for, that is, as much as it can be sold for in the market *(in mercato)*, or where it is usually sold."[49]

In terms of column space, however, most of the canonistic commentary material on *Placuit* is occupied with the questions of the extent of the power of local authority to regulate prices and of when and on what kinds of merchandise it should be exercised. We cannot go into this important discussion in detail. Briefly, Vincent of Spain's *Apparatus* to the *Decretals* contains a gloss to *Placuit* stating that no one is compelled to sell if either price or measure displeases him.[50] This triggered a controversy that the great canonist Andreae resolved by limiting the proposition to goods not yet offered for sale. Moreover, a particular person is not to be compelled, but a general price may be stipulated for all who offer for sale certain goods such as meat, grain, and wine. In the case of other goods, anyone is moderator and arbiter of his own thing, as the Roman law proclaims.[51]

In the fifteenth century, another highly influential canonist, Nicola de' Tedeschi (archbishop of Palermo: Panormitanus), paraphrased and enlarged on Andreae's analysis and established a general distinction

---

[48] *Comp. I*, III,15,2; X.III,17,1; cp. *Karolomanni Capitulare Vernense*, C.13, in *Capitularia Regum Francorum*, Vol.II, p. 375.

[49] *Super tertio Decretalium*, to III,17,1: f.75va.

[50] Paris BN lat. 3967, f.129va; lat. 3968, f.107vb. The former manuscript attributes the gloss to Tancred; however, it contains a direct quotation from D.18,1,71. Contributions to the ensuing discussion were made both by Romanists commenting on this locus and by canonists commenting on *Placuit*.

[51] *Super tertio Decretalium*, to III,17,1: ff.51vb–52ra.

between necessaries and luxuries.[52] Some of his readers composed works for the forum of conscience and provided additional examples. Thus, Angelo Carletti lists some necessaries deserving protection: grain, medicine, wine, clothes, dwellings.[53] Battista Trovamala focuses on the opposite category: On playthings and objects sought only for pomp and ornament, a seller may set his price at will.[54] Vitoria brought this doctrine into the Spanish schools, and his successors compiled veritable catalogues of conspicuous consumption articles on which the forces of supply and demand might play freely: precious stones, pearls and jewels, antique statues, exotic dogs, monkeys, falcons and elegant horses, musical and comical entertainment.[55] In the absence of fraud, such things may be sold, Soto indicates, for as much as it is possible to wring out *(extorquere)*.[56] Salón relates this to the value maxim and makes an explicit distinction between physical and economic compulsion. Regarding luxuries, "a thing is worth as much as the seller, short of force *(vis)* and fraud, can extort from the buyer."[57] As far as exploitation of the buyer is concerned, scholastic doctrine was limited entirely to necessaries. (The case is, of course, different if someone *sells* a luxury object because he is in need of money, money being then a necessary.)

The commonest needs of travelers are food and shelter. They can be exploited if local suppliers agree not to underbid each other. The theologians, rather than the canonists, emphasized the collusion aspect of *Placuit* and gave it a name. It seems to have originated with Alexander of Hales. Since early on, the medieval theologians had adopted the position (against some of the Church Fathers) that commerce was not blameworthy in itself but could be rendered so under certain circumstances. Drawing on the *Summa Raymundi*, the *Summa Alexandri* lists sinful commerce *ex circumstantia personae* (engaged in by a cleric), *causae* (motivated by avarice), *modi* (conducted by means of falsehood and perjury), *temporis* (on Sundays and holidays), *loci* (in a place of divine

---

[52] *Super tertio Decretalium*, to III,17,1: f.82ra–b.
[53] *Summa*: f.81ra.
[54] *Summa*: f.75ra
[55] Vitoria, *Comentarios*, to II–II,77,1: 122–4; Domingo de Bañez, *Decisiones*, to ibid.: p. 350; Luís López; *Instructorium*, I,13: p. 40; Juan Azor, *Inst. mor.*, III,8, (1),21: col. 688; Gregorio de Valencia, *Comm. theol.*, III,5,20,2: col. 1429; Valère Regnault, *Praxis fori poenitentialis*, XXV,16: Vol. II, p. 413; Pedro de Navarra, *De ablatorum restitutione*, III,2: Vol. II, pp. 147–8.
[56] *De iustitia et iure*, VI,2,3: f.196r.
[57] *Controversiae*, to II–II,77,1: Vol. II, p. 19.

worship), and then adds, *ex circumstantia consortii*, quoting *Placuit*.[58] Lists like this proliferated in subsequent scholastic literature and the forming of "consortiums" for the purpose of raising prices often figured in them. Some authors writing in the textual tradition from Alexander of Hales would tend to keep strictly to *Placuit* and visualize these combinations as means of putting economic pressure on transients.[59] But generalizations and tie-ins with other literary traditions also occur. Bernardino of Siena, in his vernacular sermons, spoke against every kind of price discrimination.[60] Antonino of Florence associated Alexander's consortiums with collusion to establish monopolistic power.[61] Angelo Carletti, followed by Silvester Mazzolini, related the tradition from Alexander of Hales on *Placuit* to the tradition from *Quicumque*.[62] In the latest phases of scholasticism, these various literary traditions tended to blend. Monopoly became the key word.

5.5   Monopoly

The scholastic tradition on monopoly has two literary roots, but only one of them grew to notable fruition. In the *Politics*, Aristotle recounts the story of Thales, the philosopher, who rented all the olive presses of Miletus and Chios and let them out at a large profit when the season arrived. The medieval Latin translator called this *monopolia*, rendering the Greek word literally. Aristotle adds a second example, where a successful monopolist (in iron) was expelled from Syracuse for interference with the tyrant's affairs, for monopolies are favored means of raising revenue for the government.[63] The Latin commentators all mention these state monopolies. Giles of Rome explains that monopolies are profitable because the single seller "determines the price by the judgment of his own will" *(taxat pretium pro suae voluntatis arbitrio)*.[64]

---

[58] *Sum. theol.*, IV,723; cp. Raymond, *Summa*, II,8,1–3: pp. 244–7.

[59] Raniero: II,1152; Biel: p. 195.

[60] *Prediche volgari* (Florence 1424), ed. Cannarozzi, Serm. 7: Vol. I, pp. 102–3: "che compagno si fa, cioè non che debbi vendere una medesima mercatanzia più a uno che a un altro." *Prediche volgari* (Siena 1427), ed. Delcorno, Serm. 38: Vol. II, p. 1130: "consorzio – debbi essere amaestrato di vendare . . . tanto a uno quanto a un altro." In the written Latin sermons, Bernardino quotes Alexander of Hales and refers to transients, cp. *Quadr.*, Serm. 33,2,5: IV,148.

[61] *Sum. theol.*, II,1,16,2: col. 252.

[62] Carletti, *Summa*: f.213ra; Mazzolini, *Summa*: II,204.

[63] *Politics*, I,4: 1259a.

[64] *De regimine principum*, II,iii,12: f.224r.

This phrase recalls one quoted from Ulrich of Strasbourg and the one by which I summarized the tradition of *Quicumque*. Something more must be said about its meaning later on. As regards private monopolies in particular, Albert the Great, commenting on the main example, emphasizes Aristotle's intention: Taunted on account of his poverty, Thales merely wished to demonstrate the practical insight that philosophers possess and might well have used had they cared about wealth. Thomas Aquinas joins in; what Thales did should be attributed to wisdom, not to avarice.[65] These remarks tended to deflect the censure that this text might be expected to invite. In consequence, Aristotle on monopoly all but disappeared from scholastic discussions of compulsion and the misuse of economic power.

Albert, however, makes a remark that suggests a familiarity with a different tradition on monopoly. He suggests that the Sicilian monopolist was expelled because his activity was harmful to the community. Therefore, Albert notes, monopolies are prohibited by law. This is almost certainly a reference to the Roman law. In the late Empire, agreements and grants in restraint of trade had reached such proportions that the Emperor Zeno, in 483, issued a decree against them, which Justinian's compilers, less than a century later, included as a separate title *De monopoliis* in the *Code*. It states that no one is to "exercise a monopoly" in food or clothing or any other useful thing, nor are several persons to "combine or agree" about a minimum price of any merchandise, and this is extended to all crafts and professions.[66] The medieval glossators and early commentators were rather sparing in their comments on this title. What mainly occupied them was the etymology of the word "monopoly." Odofredus, the most voluble and colorful of the thirteenth-century Romanists, points forward to the late scholastic tradition and may well have inspired it. I am fully aware, says Odofredus, that Azo explains this title in the *Code* in terms of singular sellers, but the law also mentions conspiracies and forbids them especially, and this is not something of the past, for such practices still flourish in "almost all trades and crafts in this city of Bologna."[67]

At approximately the same time, the canonist Henry of Susa (cardinal-bishop of Ostia: Hostiensis) quoted the *Code* on monopoly in his

---

[65] Albert, *Politica*, I,8: 68–9; Thomas, *Sent. Pol.*, I,9: XLVIII,111.
[66] C.4,59.
[67] Odofredus, *In primam Codicis partem*, to 4,59: f.255vb; cp. Azo, *Summa*, to ibid.: col. 461.

Summa on the *Decretals*, focusing on the conspiracy aspect.[68] In the penitential tradition, the subject was broached by Astesanus. A monopoly, he explains, is "a body or society of monopolists."[69] Bartolomeo of San Concordio quoted Hostiensis,[70] as many subsequent authors were to do. The real flourishing of literature inspired by the legal texts in question can be dated only from the middle of the fifteenth century. Drawing on Hostiensis, Antonino of Florence, in his *Summa*, distinguishes between two different purposes of collusion or conspiracy between sellers, namely, either to establish a monopoly properly so called (by leaving all sales to one within the group) or to create a cartel (by agreeing on a common price).[71] Admonishments against monopoly and/or collusion between sellers for one or both of these purposes are to be found in all the major Italian *summas* and handbooks for confessors until the middle of the sixteenth century.[72] After that, this literary tradition was continued in Spanish economic treatises and found some of its fullest expressions there.

Except when exercised for a praiseworthy purpose, for instance, to secure supply or to prevent a rise in prices, monopolies are sinful because they involve compulsion. In one of his confessional manuals, Antonino of Florence warns merchants against making pacts whereby their customers are forced to buy at an excessive price *(cogantur emere caro pretio)*.[73] In his almost equally influential *Summa*, Thomas de Vio (Cajetan) points out that a government grant or concession is not a sufficient excuse if the purpose of the monopoly is to raise prices, for governments are not permitted to commit robbery *(rapina)* either. A monopoly is harmful to private individuals and "offensive to common liberty" *(communis libertatis offensivum)*. The statement encountered in the tradition of *Quicumque*, that the seller can set his price at will and force others to buy at his pleasure, should not lead one to believe that the scholastics misunderstood the nature of compulsion involved in monopoly. Buyers are forced to buy that much dearer from a monopolist because they cannot buy elsewhere, said Cajetan. Our authors cer-

---

[68] *Summa aurea*, to *X*.I,39: f.65va.
[69] *Summa*, III,8,12: f.128va.
[70] *Summa*: f.128ra–b.
[71] *Sum. theol.*, II,1,16,2: col. 252.
[72] Ariosto, *Enchir.*: f.116rb; Pacifico of Novara, *Summa*, Ch. 17: f.111v; Bartolomeo Caimi, *Confessionale*, art. *A mercatoribus*: f.115v; Trovamala, *Summa*: f.76ra–b; Carletti, *Summa*: f.82rb; Cagnazzo, *Summa*: f.167va–b; Bartolomeo Fumo, *Summa*: p. 286; p. 645; Mazzolini, *Summa*: I,295.
[73] *Confessionale (Defecerunt)*, art. *De mercatoribus*: f.92r.

tainly understood that one who controls supply cannot set whatever price he pleases and force everybody to accept it; what he can do is choose a price above what would otherwise have been the competitive market price and force some people to accept it, because they are in need and can afford it. (Worst off are those who are in need but cannot pay the price.) "The more the price is increased, the more iniquitous the monopoly."[74]

Commerce can be rendered unlawful *ex monopolio*, says Juan de Medina, as when someone strives to become the only seller of a certain commodity, or when several merchants agree among themselves not to sell certain goods below a certain price. Because the citizens need these goods, they would be forced *(cogerentur)* to buy from this single seller or from one of those who made the pact, and they would be compelled *(compellerentur)* to pay the price asked. This is prejudicial to the buyers, who would have obtained these goods at a much lower price in the absence of monopoly.[75] Discussions of monopoly and of monopolizing conspiracies, thus interpreted, and often in conjunction with the forms of market manipulation prohibited by canon law, are standard in works by authors belonging to the School of Salamanca or influenced by that school.[76] There is often an emphasis on economic compulsion. In the words of Luís López, "There is a certain unspoken violence involved in monopolies" *(Violentia quaedam tacita interveniat in monopoliis)*.[77] The old value maxim of the Romanists was modified with a view to this. For Soto's "force" *(vis)*, read "monopoly." "A thing is worth as much as it can be sold for in the absence of every monopoly, fraud and deceit" *(Res tantum valet quantum vendi potest, cessent omne monopolium, fraus et*

---

[74] *Summa de peccatis*, art. *Venditio:* f.229r.

[75] *Cod. rest.*, Q.30: p. 194.

[76] Soto, *De iustitia et iure*, VI,2,3: f.196r; Bañez, *Decisiones*, loc. cit.; Molina, *De contractibus*, Disp. 345: cols. 552–8; Martín de Azpilcueta, *Enchiridion*, XXIII,91–2: pp. 582–3; Azor, *Inst. mor.*, III,8,(1),28: cols. 709–10; Gregorio de Valencia, loc. cit.: col. 1427; Lugo, *De iustitia et iure*, Disp, 26,12: Part II, pp. 341–3; Lessius, *De iustitia et iure*, II,21,21: pp. 294–5; Regnault, *Praxis*, XXV,22: Vol. II, pp. 422–3; Paul Laymann, *Theologia moralis*, III,iv,17: pp. 432–3; Hermann Busenbaum, *De contractibus*, Dub. 8: pp. 318–9. Luther on monopoly (op. cit., pp. 305–7) is in this tradition as well.

[77] *Instructorium negotiantium*, I,42: p. 152. Chafuen, 1986, 112, citing Francisco García, a sixteenth-century author who wrote in the vernacular, notes that monopoly and cornering the market could be regarded as a sort of "implicit violence"; however, he does not pursue this aspect of late scholastic thought, emphasizing rather its anticipation of classical liberalism.

dolus).[78] The Spanish scholastics also inherited a tradition regarding collusion on the part of buyers, for the purpose of reducing prices.[79] This was normally condemned if exercised for private gain, with one striking exception. "When the sellers form a monopoly," Domingo de Soto teaches, "the buyers may likewise justly use their prudence in the opposite direction, as though driving back force with force *(quasi vim vi repellentes)*"[80] – an early expression of the principle of countervailing power.

Under this heading, however, a rather more fundamental reconsideration of the practices discussed in this chapter found expression in the works of some prominent later representatives of the Spanish scholastic tradition. It reflects the breakdown of the scholastic paradigm to be examined in more general terms in Chapter 6. Its most explicit spokesman was the Belgian Leonard Lessius, but his ideas were to some extent anticipated by Bañes and by Molina (whom he quotes), and they were subsequently endorsed by Lugo. Lessius agrees with those who deem sellers' conspiracies unjust if their purpose is to force buyers to pay prices above a *lawful* level, but the traditional doctrine about "inducing dearth" is only one way of looking at the purchase and subsequent profitable resale of a necessary like grain by a single merchant or a group of merchants. To condemn such practices as sinful is a probable conclusion, but the contrary conclusion is not improbable, either. Consider the following argument:

[The merchants] have not sinned against justice in buying, assuming, as we do, that they bought at the current price. Nor does it matter that dearth is induced *(inducta sit caritas)* in this way, for the presence of a multitude of buyers also induces dearth. Hence, they do not sin against justice in buying, for the act, from which dearth follows, is not against justice. Nor do they sin by holding back the goods or by not selling them, for they are not obliged by justice to sell, since they have not obliged themselves to do so by any contract *(cum nullo pacto ad hoc obligarint)*. They could have kept the goods for another time or brought them to another place, or even destroyed them, without injury to anyone, because they had absolute ownership of them. Nor would the citizens have

---

[78] Azpilcueta, *Enchir.*, XXIII,80: p. 577. Similarly, López, op. cit., I,13: p. 40; Salón, *Controversiae*, to II–II,77,1: Vol. II, p. 17.

[79] The Romanists referred to this; cp. Odofredus, loc. cit. Mazzolini mentions it in *Summa*: II,200. Vitoria introduced it in the Salamanca tradition (*Comentarios*, to II–II,77,1: 121), and it was subsequently touched upon by most authors along with monopoly proper and sellers' conspiracies.

[80] Loc. cit.; as well as other authors referred to in note 76. Alternatively, Martin Bonacina, *De contractibus*, II,v,3: p. 403: "like a nail being driven back by a nail."

any title in justice to buy them, unless they wanted to sell; otherwise one would have to say that they were sinners against justice if they threw their possessions into a river.[81]

Two ideas, already encountered, reappear in this quotation. First, and fundamental to the argument, there is the ancient idea cited at the opening of this chapter, namely, that anyone is moderator and arbiter of his own thing, exercising absolute domination. Second, there is the new idea, quoted from Lugo on usury at the close of Chapter 4 and soon to gain ascendancy in the natural law tradition, namely, that justice is primarily a matter of *keeping* contracts. Both these ideas tend to undermine the scholastic paradigm. Commenting on these lines in Lessius, Gordon, in his study of preclassical economics, remarks that the merchants in question, unlike the conspirators previously mentioned, "have not attempted to sell above the just (market) price. They have given and taken what, objectively, the market would bear. They, themselves, however, have been a force in determining the level of the market price. They have been part of that consensus termed 'common estimation.' "[82] In the context of the present study, this is a most pertinent observation. Taking the common estimate as one criterion of justice, the medieval scholastics, early on, conceded that this estimate, insofar as it referred to the market, would vary to some extent with supply and demand. They would not thereby, at first, permit economic actors to disclaim *subjective, personal* moral responsibility for their own use of economic power. This was something that happened gradually with the increasing *objectivization* (to use Gordon's term) or (as I shall call it when we encounter it again in the chapters that follow) *depersonalization* of the idea of the market. More than anything else, it signals the breakdown of the medieval scholastic approach to economic ethics.

[81] Loc. cit., p. 295.
[82] Gordon, 1975, 270.

CHAPTER 6

Need and the will
in buying and selling

6.1   The principle of mutual benefit

In scholastic terminology, for instance as quoted from Alexander of
Hales in section 5.4, the traditions on speculation, price discrimination,
collusion, and monopoly can be viewed as elaborations of the circumstances under which commerce is morally blameworthy. It is true that
Alexander lists *circumstantia consortii* as a separate item, but the various
forms of market manipulation may equally well be related, either to
circumstantia modi or to *circumstantia causae*. That is, they can be seen
as unacceptable modes of doing business, or, as frequently pointed out
by the authors themselves, they may be expected to have been inspired
by morally suspect motivations. By the same token, conformity with a
current market-price estimate may serve as a guarantee that these circumstances are absent. These criteria, however, are not easily applica-
ble. When buyer and seller do not actually meet in a competitive
market (which would have made the market criterion redundant), the
just market price is a most elusive quantity. Moreover, there are all
kinds of markets in all kinds of states, and market manipulation is a
relative concept. Some scholastics, in all earnestness, recommended
that the government fix prices of all necessaries. To leave them to the
decision of the parties themselves, said Henry of Hesse, is to loosen the
rein on cupidity, which excites almost all sellers to a quest for excessive
gain.[1] Comprehensive price regulation, however, was not a practicable
policy. Introducing the exchange model in *Ethics*, V, Albert the Great
revived a distinction suggested by Cicero. There are three ways in which
ratios of exchange can be determined, according to Albert, namely,
either by *par* (that is, by Aristotelian just equality, soon to be identified
with the competitive market price), by *pactum* (that is, by agreement
reached by the exchangers), or by *iudicatum* (that is, by government
decree).[2] The former being difficult to pinpoint and the latter not being available, the ethics of most exchanges had to be judged on the

---

[1] *De contractibus*, I,11: f.111vb.
[2] *Ethica*, V,2,9: 355; cp. Cicero, *De inventione*, II,liv,162: LCL 386, 328–30.

basis of the attitudes of the parties themselves to the terms of their own agreements, by considering the nature of their own consent and their satisfaction. Throughout the scholastic era, aspects of this general question were discussed in a broad literary tradition that ran parallel to the ones on specific business practices.

The purpose of the present chapter is to trace this general tradition. Our emphasis will be on its treatment of economic need and the will. These subjects were in the focus of our attention in the preceding chapter as well. Though there is considerable overlap in scholastic sources between this general analysis and the discussion of particular cases, in order not to start on the wrong foot, it is necessary here to bring into evidence a feature of the scholastic conception of economic exchange that was totally absent in Chapter 5. There, it was presented as a matter of confrontation, one powerful party immorally exploiting a weaker one. This is, of course, the main theme of the present book, but (at least as regards buying and selling, that is, the exchange of commodities) it was always balanced in European thought by a conception of economic exchange as a matter of cooperation between the parties. The farmer needs not only shoes, but also the aid of the shoemaker. The shoemaker needs food, but also, and therefore, the aid of the farmer. Division of occupations is the reason and the everyday sign of such mutual needs of reciprocal services. This is the Socratic view. Adopted by Aristotle from Plato, it is most fully expressed in the *Politics*, but it is in evidence in the *Ethics* as well. On this note, the concept of reciprocity is launched in the opening lines of *Ethics*, V,5. Services rendered by others should be repaid, and the initiative taken in rendering services to others. In order to remind the citizens of this, a prominent place in the city is given to the temple of the Graces.[3] This last line inspired Albert the Great to the most charming characterization of exchange in all of economic literature: It is "a flowing back and forth of graces" (*fluxus et refluxus gratiarum*).[4]

Reciprocity to Aristotle implies justice, and commutative justice implies equality between what is given and received in exchange, but this is not something that can be defined to an exact point. The early Aristotelians hastened to emphasize this. It is merely in the nature of an estimate.[5] Granted that such estimates can be made with reference to some market (or to cost), it must normally be left to the parties themselves to reach an agreement. Henry of Ghent describes how this comes

---

[3] EN, V,5: 1132b33–1133a5.
[4] Loc. cit.: 356.
[5] Thus Thomas Aquinas, *Sum. theol.*, II–II,77,1: IX,148; frequently repeated.

about. At the start, the seller will place a higher value on the commodity than the buyer. A bargaining process is then initiated, the seller gradually lowering his bid, the buyer raising his, until – without any compulsion and deceit (*sine omni coactione et deceptione*) – they arrive at an intermediate value to which both consent and which both take to be average and equal. This, according to Henry, is what a common estimate amounts to. This is how one should understand the maxim that states that a thing is worth as much as it can be sold for, in that the prices of things are not to be estimated on the basis of the affection of singular individuals, but commonly.[6] This alternative interpretation of the common estimate opens the avenue that is to be explored in the present chapter. It does not take "common" in the sense of "usual" or in the sense of "joint" if this is meant to refer to the whole community, as in the case of the competitive market estimate. Rather, it takes "common" to mean that which is established jointly, or in common, by the two parties actually involved in the given exchange.

Peter Olivi asks himself whether prices based on common consent, thus understood, are not in fact to be preferred to a just price fixed to a point. The latter would not serve the common good, for it would be impossible to hit upon it exactly in practice, and it would therefore necessarily lead to sin. Moreover, it involves an illusion, for value is not punctual but conjectural; it permits of some latitude, and different people estimate it differently. Olivi replies that, granted that our estimation of value cannot be fixed to a point, it must be measured within probable and reasonable limits. Within these limits, however, prices based on the common consent of the parties involved are indeed to be preferred, provided that "the consent of both parties to this price and this estimate cannot be considered involuntary owing to ignorance and inexperience or owing to some need somehow forcing [either of them] to accept it (*ratione alicuius necessitatis ad hoc quodammodo compellentis*)."[7]

These arguments led John Duns Scotus to state his famous doctrine of economic exchange as involving an element of gift. The premise of all economic theory is that each party to a given exchange benefits by it in a certain sense, for otherwise he would not have chosen to exchange. Once the seller's bid has reached its lowest limit, and the buyer after all decides to buy, it is because he thinks himself better off by doing so than by declining the offer, and vice versa. Aristotelian just equality therefore cannot refer to utilities. Both parties experience a utility surplus. This principle was frequently and firmly stated by scho-

[6] *Quodl.* III,28: Paris 1518, f.88r–v.
[7] *De emptione et venditione*, Q.1: 253–7.

lastic authors before Scotus.[8] The question whether, this being so, an objective just price can be defined at all is not raised by him. His point of departure (quoting Olivi) is that it permits of some latitude. What this latitude is, and how far it extends, is sometimes known from custom and sometimes from positive law.

Sometimes, however, it is left to the contracting parties themselves, namely, when in view of mutual needs they both consider that they give and receive from one another equal value. Exchange between men would be difficult if the parties did not intend reciprocally to remit some of that rigorous justice, so that, insofar as they do, a gift may be said to accompany every contract. And if this is the way that contracts are concluded, as though founded on the law of nature which says, "Do to another what you would have done to yourself," it is sufficiently probable that the parties, if they are mutually satisfied, intend to mutually remit the difference if something is lacking from the justice which they seek.[9]

The idea that the just price permits of a certain latitude, an interval on the value scale within which the exchangers are free to reach their own agreement, went some way toward reconciling the traditional patristic (and recently discovered Aristotelian) requirement of strict justice, with the Roman law principle of *laesio enormis*. According to the latter, buyers and sellers were allowed to outwit or "deceive" one another within the limits of one-half below and above the just price.[10] Originally restricted to the sale of landed property, there was a tendency in the Middle Ages to generalize this principle and apply it to most kinds of economic contracts. The "deception" in question did not include regular fraud, though some of those who opposed it may have misunderstood it on this point. Short of fraud, however, each party could use his wit and his bargaining position to his own advantage. The early theologians would have nothing of this. Thomas Aquinas expressed the common sentiment. Human law accepts this principle for practical reasons, but divine law leaves nothing unpunished that is contrary to virtue, and it insists on just equality.[11] The interval between one-half below and one-half above the just price is clearly a considerable one in relative terms. Scotus's "latitude" could be interpreted as a compromise. In the fifteenth century, it was sug-

---

[8] Most explicitly by Richard of Middleton, a confrère and immediate precursor of Scotus and (allegedly) one of his teachers; cp. *Comm. Sent.*, III,33,3,4: pp. 389–90; *Quodl.* II,23: Vat. Borgh. 361, ff.98va–101vb.

[9] Op. cit., pp. 283–4.

[10] C.4,44,2; cp., for instance, Odofredus, *In primam Codicis partem*, to C.4,44,8: f.247rb.

[11] *Sum. theol.*, loc. cit.

gested that the just price has three levels: a lower (*pius*), a middle (*discretus*), and a higher (*rigidus*) level.[12] Numerical examples prove this to define a much narrower interval. Originally intended to make room for price differentials between cash and credit sales, it would also be used to justify buying and reselling at a profit. It was widely accepted.

The idea that a price agreement could incorporate a gift element became a commonplace as well. The lines quoted from Scotus were copied by Odonis and Nider in their treatises on contracts, by Bernardino of Siena in one of his Latin sermons, and by Antonino of Florence in his *Summa*.[13] Directly, or through any of these intermediaries, Scotus's suggestion was adopted by later German authors, by some of the leading exponents of the Italian penitential tradition, and by numerous members of the School of Salamanca. It was often tied in with the tradition from Olivi and Henry of Ghent, which was transmitted through the same channels. As a pure ideal, it is one of the noblest bequests of the scholastics to economic thought. In a spirit of mutual benevolence, buyer and seller can come to terms that are just because they satisfy both. With time, however, it came to be realized that it was a difficult, not to say dangerous, principle in practical application. A gift need not be limited to the interval between the pious and the rigid levels of the just price, nor indeed to the interval defining *laesio enormis*. As pointed out by Olivi, just as a person can give a thing entirely free of recompense, he can give it for a very small part of its value.[14] But this is charity. It is not what one would think of as a gift in connection with a regular economic contract, as the final outcome of a bargaining process. As such, the "gift" would merely serve to close the gap between somewhat different estimates of just value.

Like that of consent, the gift principle can then be reduced to a tautology: whenever a price is agreed upon there is, eo ipso, consent and a gift. A true gift, however, just like true consent, is voluntary. The agreement is therefore morally subject to the same condition regarding the gift, as regarding consent. The gift is effective and the contract valid only in the absence of the factors specified in the quotations from Peter Olivi in this section and in the opening section of Chapter 5: fickleness and poverty, ignorance, inexperience, and compelling need. At the close of the scholastic era, the general consensus reached on

[12] Bernardino of Siena, *Quadr.*, Serm. 34,3,1: IV,183; Antonino of Florence, *Sum. theol.*, II,1,8,1: col. 126.

[13] Odonis, *De contr.*, Q.3: f.81r; Nider, *De contr.*, II: f.12r; Bernardino, op. cit., Serm. 35,1,2: IV,193; Antonino, op cit., II,1,16,3: col. 257.

[14] See section 5.1.

this issue was summed up by Paul Laymann: A price should not be increased or decreased on account of the buyer's or the seller's need, unless a gift is involved, "which, however, in case of need cannot be readily taken for granted."[15] Martin Bonacina phrases it a little differently: A seller cannot be presumed to donate the discrepancy when need compels him to sell at a lower price because he is unable to obtain a higher one. It is probable that there is a gift on the part of the buyer, if he buys at an excessive price, knowing its value, and not being compelled to buy because of need, or fraud, or fear, or any other similar circumstance.[16] In the scholastic tradition on need and the will, there was a tendency to view the position of the seller as somewhat different from that of the buyer. In this chapter, a section is devoted to each position, with a joint concluding section.

6.2   Need and the will: the buyer

The overall tendency in early economic ethics is to regard the seller as the more powerful party to an exchange relationship and to focus on the buyer as the needy party, the nature of whose will is therefore in question. This bias was very marked in Chapter 5, which was concerned, with but some minor digressions, with sellers manipulating the market. Part of the reason for this bias may be literary. In principle, the problem of the just rate of exchange is symmetrical, and some of the sources that fueled scholastic dispute on this issue approached it as such, most notably the exchange model in *Ethics*, V, which is mostly stated in terms of barter. The legal value maxim, on the other hand, may perhaps be said to invite an emphasis on the power of the seller rather than the buyer. That is how most later authors would interpret the influential comments on this maxim by Henry of Ghent and Peter Oliv:. The decisive reason for the bias, however, was empirical rather than literal. Bargaining power will usually be on the side of the professional merchant. Though the merchant may do business with the nonprofessional producer-seller as well as with the nonprofessional buyer-consumer, the greatest imbalance of bargaining strengths will usually occur in this latter phase of the commercial cycle, which is also the more visible phase. The merchant will control the resources and will normally need money less than his customers will need his goods. This, at any rate, is true in the case of necessaries, which were the main concern of scholastic economics.

---

[15] *Theol. mor.*, III,iv,17: p. 423.
[16] *De contr.*, II,iv,23: p. 401.

It was only in the early fifteenth century that the principles developed in academic circles found systematic expression in advice and exhortations addressed directly to the merchants themselves. In Chapter II of his treatise on commercial contracts, Nider states his version of the modified value maxim, most likely drawing directly on Henry of Ghent: "A thing is worth as much as it can be sold for, that is, according to how much buyers can be made to pay for it, who, it must be noted, buy freely and by choice, and are not fools, in distress *(artati)*, or deceived."[17] In one of the twenty-four rules formulated in Chapter III of Nider's treatise, by which merchants can judge whether their dealings are safe from sin, these conditions are repeated, and the second condition is clarified by reference to the Aristotelian concept of a mixed will:

Twelfth Rule. Just as a thing, whose true assessment is unknown, can be sold with a safer conscience and trust, when sold to a man of experience who is not straitened by any need *(artatus aliqua necessitate)*, has no inordinate desire for it, and is not cheated or induced by any trick, by way of words, acts or signs, to buy it dearer than he would have bought it without this trick, so, without doubt, [the merchant] is less certain to be in good faith, but is rather suspect of bad faith, in three cases. First, when he sells to someone simple-minded or inexperienced. Second, when the buyer is in need *(quando emens est necessitatus)*. Third, when by means of clever signs, acts, or words, even if they are true, he induces the buyer to buy at a higher price than he otherwise would. The first. . . . As to the second, it is well known that someone in distress readily buys dearer, not voluntarily simply, but voluntarily in a mixed sense *(non voluntarie simpliciter sed voluntarie mixte)*, and yet, because of the distress of the buyer, the seller ought not to receive more but ought rather to deal mercifully with him. As to the third. . . . [18]

In Italy, Bernardino of Siena relaunched the ideas of Peter Olivi. Bernardino discovered a manuscript of Olivi and used it occasionally when preaching in the vernacular.[19] In his Latin sermons, he quotes Olivi extensively. Not unlike Nider in the case of Henry of Ghent, Bernardino ties Olivi's doctrine on compulsion in with that of Aristotle on the voluntary. In the forum of conscience, a contract is invalid if obtained on account of ignorance or fickleness or some great poverty or other compelling need, "even though such a contract appears to proceed from the consent of both parties, because, according to Aristotle in *Ethics*, III, ignorance and any kind of compulsion excludes the will *(ignorantia et aliqualis coactio excludit voluntarium)*."[20] Whereas Nider at-

---

[17] *De contr.*, II: f.9v.
[18] Op. cit., III: f.14v.
[19] Siena BCom U.V.6, with marginal notes in Bernardino's hand.
[20] Op. cit., Serm. 33,2,7: IV, 157. Bernardino's paraphrase of Olivi combines

tributes a mixed will to a buyer in need, Bernardino thus invites the interpretation that a buyer in straitened circumstances pays a higher price wholly against his will. In Aristotle's own terms, "mixed acts" are not "more like voluntary acts": They are involuntary acts.

This stern doctrine reappears in later Italian authors. Angelo Carletti, in his treatise on contracts, quotes Bernardino verbatim, citing *Ethics*, III.[21] In his *Summa* for confessors, Carletti seeks additional support from Roman law. The value maxim is modified with reference to *metus*. A thing may be sold for as much as the seller can get for it, under certain conditions, one of which is free will. Prices obtained through such need as excludes the will are sinful. How to judge whether such is the case? First, check if the goods in question are food or some other necessary.[22] Second, check if consent is given in order to avoid some great damage, "for such need and all fear which affects a man of character exclude the freedom of the will."[23] He adds that it is different in case of some minor fear. Pacifico of Novara, Bartolomeo Caimi, Silvester Mazzolini, Bartolomeo Fumo, and other authors of confessional works also draw on Olivi through Bernardino and confirm the latter's teaching.[24] It should be noted, in order to balance the picture, that several of them also apply the principle of need and the will by analogy to the position of the seller, following a different line of tradition from Olivi (see section 6.3). They emphasize, as Carletti does as well, that truly voluntary consent validates the contract. The rule of the sixth book of the *Decretals* is quoted repeatedly: "No injury nor fraud is done to one who knows and consents."[25]

Some of these works for the confessional were widely disseminated. Further developed in them, and mainly spread through them, Bernardino's interpretation of Olivi was met with response outside Italy as well. Discussing the gift element in sales contracts, Gabriel Biel quotes Angelo Carletti, with an addition: Need and all fear affecting a man of character exclude the freedom of the will, "which is required of a gift."[26] Summenhart draws on Olivi along with later sources, notably

elements of the passages quoted in this and the preceding chapter. Cp. also Serm. 35,1,3: IV, 195.

[21] *Tract.*, I,1: p. 11; cp. p. 23.
[22] See section 5.4.
[23] *Summa*: ff.80vb–81ra.
[24] Pacifico, *Summa*, Ch. 17: f.112r; Caimi, *Confessionale*, art. *A mercatoribus*: f.116v; Mazzolini, *Summa*: I,294; Fumo, *Summa*: pp. 283–4.
[25] See section 5.1 with notes 18 and 19.
[26] Op. cit., p. 200.

Gerson. Frequently reverting to the subject of need and the will in the course of his lengthy discussion of exchange and value, Summenhart freely varies his terminology and his references, but his message remains firm. A sale is unjust if the buyer is deceived, or straitened by need, or driven by some inordinate affection. It is true that he who consents suffers no injustice, but only if his consent is absolute and not merely conditional and *secundum quid*, as Aristotle says about throwing merchandise into the sea and about consent extorted by fear of death. Need invalidates a sale; the price must be paid freely, without any element of the involuntary being mixed with its payment. The seller sins by taking a higher price from someone in straitened circumstances. Ownership of such money does not pass to him; its payment is not voluntary, but mixed with the involuntary, for also conditional compulsion reduces its voluntary nature.[27]

In Spain, the reception of these ideas was more problematical. By the time of the foundation of the School of Salamanca, a reaction to them had already set in. Vitoria, however, who quarreled with Carletti regarding other factors invalidating a contract, agrees with him about compulsion on the part of the buyer, at least by implication (being more explicit about this factor in the case of a needy seller).[28] Medina embraces Summenhart's teaching, voicing certain reservations that rather tend to underscore the lack of will in the case of need.[29] Molina supports him in this. He quotes Gerson (through Summenhart) to the effect that overcharging a consenting buyer is no sin against justice because (in Molina's words) "no injury is done to him who wills and consents" (*volenti et consentienti non fit iniuria*), but he emphasizes that this is true only in the case of consent that is wholly voluntary and not of the mixed kind.[30]

Gregorio de Valencia quotes some of this and cites an analogy familiar from usury doctrine. A buyer compelled by need to pay an excessive price does not will to give up ownership of the excess amount but merely wills the exterior act of handing over the money in order thus to relieve his need. His position is much like that of someone compelled to give money to a thief in order to save his life; he performs the exterior act but does not give up his right to recover his money. Thus also, he who throws merchandise into the sea would not will (*non vellet*) to cede his right to his goods if recovered but merely wills the

---

[27] *De contr.*, III, Q.56: p. 261; Q.57: p. 270; pp. 273–4.
[28] *Comentarios*, to II–II,77,1: 122–4.
[29] *Cod. rest.*, Q.32: pp. 206–7.
[30] *De contractibus*, Disp. 350: cols. 579, 582.

exterior act of jettison, for this, which he is compelled to do, is precisely what is sufficient to get him out of his predicament.[31] A similar distinction between paying what is necessary and disclaiming ownership to it is made by López.[32] Other late scholastic authors also contributed to keeping this tradition alive by examining the proposition that the willing man is not injured and rejecting it in case of need. The final word here may be given to Pedro de Navarra, who discusses this question in the context of the Scotist doctrine of the gift. It is difficult to determine whether a gift is present in a given exchange, but it is clear that if there is true need, there is no valid gift. Just as usury is not a gift, even if the debtor declares that it is, because he is compelled by need to pay usury in order to obtain the loan, so also in the case of buying and selling. A buyer who is compelled by the need of food to pay an excessive price for it pays it with a mixed will. That which he seeks to avoid strikes him with the kind of fear that may affect a man of character. It is different if he buys for profit or pleasure; then his lack of will is trivial and minimal.[33]

6.3   Need and the will: the seller

Pedro de Navarra extends his analysis from a buyer in need being overcharged to a seller in need being underpaid. In one respect, the analogy with a borrower agreeing to pay usury suits the case of the seller better. The need that forces each of them to accept unfavorable terms is the need of money. In a market economy, this predicament is ubiquitous and open to exploitation in many forms. It is experienced by anyone to whom money is a necessity, not as such, but as a means of satisfying a pressing want. What he offers in exchange may be a promise to pay it back with usury, or it may be some material possession, ranking anywhere on the scale from luxuries to what is also relatively necessary at the moment but less so than money. It may also be his own labor. While a parallel can thus be drawn from this section to Chapter 4, on usury, another parallel can be drawn to Chapter 7, on wages. In Chapter 5, need on the part of the seller was only mentioned once or twice in passing, but it is an underlying feature in most of the forms of market manipulation discussed there. A merchant or a group of merchants are able to control the supply of food and other necessaries and sell them dear only by buying them cheap in advance and usually keeping them in store for a while.

[31] *Comm. theol.*, III,5,20,2: cols. 1428–9.
[32] *Instructorium*, I,13: p. 42.
[33] *De ablatorum restitutione*, III,2: Vol. II, pp. 153–4.

Powerful people, Godfrey of Fontaines notes, can hold onto things until they are worth more; the poor are compelled by need (*indigentia compelluntur*) to sell earlier.[34] This is the reverse side of *Quicumque*. There is no moral objection to buying something at a low price if this price is accepted by the seller *simpliciter* voluntarily, Henry of Hesse teaches, but such is not the case if the seller is forced by necessity to accept it. It is therefore reprehensible and a grave sin to buy grain or wine at time of harvest or vintage from poor people compelled by a need of ready money to accept prices below a legal estimate, in order, driven by avarice, to store these staple necessaries in the normal expectation of a price increase.[35] Hesse's contemporary and colleague at Vienna, Henry of Oyta, elaborates on the case of the needy seller, using some familiar terms and drawing on a familiar analogy. In cases of this nature, the seller would have willed to (*vellet*) exchange at a just price and agrees to the terms offered merely because of need. His consent is voluntary only in the sense in which this can be said of one who jettisons cargo at sea in order to save his life: His is "a will mixed with a compelling force" (*voluntarium mixtum cum violentia cogente*).[36]

The proposition that a thing may be given for a very low price because it can be given without any recompense at all naturally led authors influenced by Olivi to examine the question of will on the part of the seller. Antonino of Florence was instrumental in turning the tradition in this direction. Whereas Bernardino, who unearthed Olivi, focused on the buyer, Antonino focused on the seller. Assuming the absence of other factors invalidating a sale, a price below what is normally considered to be just may or may not be valid.

Nor is there in this any injustice done on the part of the other, unless the seller should be forced to sell, being induced by some great need to do so (*nisi cogeretur venditor ad vendendum, aliqua magna necessitate ad hoc inducente*), seeing that he cannot otherwise provide for himself; he should certainly have willed (*vellet*) the just price, but cannot obtain it.[37]

Battista Trovamala follows Antonino in discussing the problem in terms of a depressed price but quotes Aristotle through Bernardino on compulsion and the will.[38] Most of the other late-fifteenth- and early-sixteenth-century books of instruction for confessors and penitents use some of this material, some focusing entirely on the plight of the needy

---

[34] *Quodl.* III,11: LPB 2 (1904) 220.
[35] *De contr.*, II,22: f.214rb–va.
[36] *De contr.*, Dub.8: f.242rb–va; cp. Dub.10: f.243va–b.
[37] *Sum. theol.*, II,1,16,3: col. 257; cp. also II,1,17,8: col. 269; II,2,1,12: col. 349.
[38] *Summa*: f.75ra.

seller, some viewing the problem of compulsion and the will from both angles. Angelo Carletti in his *Summa*[39] and all the other authors cited in the preceding section in the tradition from Olivi via Bernardino of Siena in the respective contexts refer to need and lack of will on the part of the seller as well.[40] Mazzolini elsewhere touches upon this subject in connection with barter, "as when someone in need exchanges a horse for bread."[41] Ariosto warns merchants against the sin of buying cheap because of the seller's need and defect of will (*vitium voluntatis*).[42] Of the leading contemporary German representatives of scholasticism, Biel (following Carletti) refers in passing to the needy seller,[43] whereas Summenhart devotes a separate chapter to him and concludes in complete analogy with the reverse case. If a seller is forced by need to accept a price that is too low, the buyer is obliged to make good the deficiency or make restitution. In a case like this, the seller's transfer of the merchandise to the buyer "will not be purely voluntary but will have something mixed in it of the involuntary" (*non erit illa datio mercis pure voluntaria sed mixta ex involuntario*). Ownership of the goods in question does not pass to the buyer because (repeating an unusual variant of a familiar phrase) "also conditional compulsion detracts from the nature of the voluntary" (*coactio etiam conditionalis diminuit de ratione voluntarii*).[44]

The form in which this doctrine was introduced in Spain by Francisco de Vitoria is worth quoting if only because it represents yet another variant of the terminology originally suggested by the early Latin commentators on Aristotle's *Ethics*. Having made the distinction between necessaries and luxuries and, as a first principle regarding the latter class of commodities, having endorsed freedom of bargaining because "no injury is done to the willing," Vitoria states two principles relating to compulsion suffered by the seller:

The second principle is this, that, for commutative justice to obtain in human exchange, it is not sufficient that it is simply voluntary (*simpliciter voluntarium*) from both sides; it is necessary that it has nothing of the involuntary mixed with it (*non habet aliquid admixtum de involuntario*), as is evident from the throwing of merchandise into the sea. Therefore, if someone should sell a house from fear of a beating or from ignorance or violence, that contract, albeit simply voluntary, is nevertheless not just because it has something of the involuntary

---

[39] *Summa*: f.81ra.
[40] See note 24.
[41] *Summa*: II,250.
[42] *Enchir.*: f.118ra; cp. *De usuris*, III: p. 78.
[43] Loc. cit. in note 26.
[44] *De contr.*, III, Q.58: p. 277.

mixed with it. The third principle is this, that that which is done because of need *(necessitate)*, albeit simply voluntary, has something of the involuntary mixed with it. Consequently, in the case of such an exchange it is not sufficient that it be simply voluntary; it is required that there be no need nor violence *(nulla sit necessitas nec violentia)*. For someone compelled by need *(coactus necessitate)* may simply will *(potest simpliciter velle)* to exchange some object, and in this there may yet be something of violence because of need *(aliquid de violentia propter necessitatem)*. Hence, if the person in question, compelled by need, should sell the house at a low price, the buyer would not buy it justly.[45]

Vitoria was commenting on the *Summa theologiae* of Thomas Aquinas and may conceivably have been influenced by the fact that Aquinas (though elsewhere in that work) reverses Aristotle's key terms.[46] Nevertheless, to argue against justice because of insufficient will and repeatedly to represent the absence of a mixed will as a stricter requirement than will *simpliciter* is unique in these sources (as far as my knowledge of them extends).[47] The line of argument traced in this section appears to have been more or less completely aborted after Vitoria's contribution. Such references to lack of will on the part of a seller in need, as can be found in later authors, mostly occur as side remarks along a different line of argument. Already established by the time of Vitoria, this approach caused the scholastic paradigm to recede and eventually to vanish.

6.4   The paradigm abandoned

The turnabout came with Cajetan, another commentator on Aquinas. The logical objection to traditional reasoning that seems to have motivated him is the one made much later by Lugo in connection with usury.[48] Not surprisingly, Conrad Summenhart is the first author on record to have given voice to it. Summenhart is something of an enigma among late scholastic authors. His mastery of the sources is amazing. He mostly concludes in accordance with safe, traditional teaching but sometimes only after lengthy discussions, in the course of which revolutionary new ideas are put forward and rather unconvincingly refuted. In consequence, there are some inconsistencies in his treatise. In the two preceding sections of this chapter, Summenhart was quoted on need and the will on the part of the buyer and the seller,

---

[45] *Comentarios*, to II–II,77,1: 123.
[46] See section 1.3.
[47] It is perhaps proper to note that Vitoria's lectures were edited from (sometimes rather rough) reports.
[48] See section 4.5.

respectively. These passages are to be found in questions dealing with the just price. Summenhart confirms established opinion, but in a much earlier question, he rejects it. This occurs in the course of a discussion of the passage of ownership to usurious money, which the author supports, and refers by analogy to buying and selling. It is true that the debtor pays usury involuntarily, but this, in itself, is not a valid argument against the passage of ownership. "A buyer often pays a just price not simply and purely voluntarily but would rather pay less; nevertheless the seller becomes the owner of the whole price."[49] In other words, injustice because of compulsion cannot logically be inferred from the incidence of conditional will alone, because the will of anyone who finds his highest wish excluded from his range of choices will be conditional.

Cajetan faced this dilemma and suggested how it might be resolved. He discussed the subject of the will in connection with economic exchange in several works, focusing mainly on the seller but occasionally on the buyer as well. Considerable space is devoted to it in his epoch-making commentary on the *Summa theologiae* of Thomas Aquinas. He also touches upon it (referring to the commentary for particulars) in his confessional text, the *Summa de peccatis*, a work equally outstanding and influential within its particular genre. There is finally a brief question and answer regarding this subject among his minor works. In order to come to grips with the problem of need and justice in exchange, it is necessary, according to Cajetan in his commentary on Aquinas, to make a distinction between *causa* and *modus*, that is, between the motivation that prompts a certain person to agree to certain terms of exchange and the way in which, or the circumstances under which, the exchange comes about. The just price is that which particular goods are usually and commonly sold for in a certain place *and in a certain way*. Things sold at auction and things sold through a middleman will fetch different prices. A person who offers a thing for sale must expect to get less for it than one who is approached by somebody else with a request to sell. Assuming absence of fraud and compulsion (in the physical sense), such price differentials are in the nature of things and legitimate. Each mode of exchange is governed by its own equality of justice, within reasonable limits of tolerance. This does not absolve those who create monopolies and charge whatever price they want; such activity is unjust in the highest degree, because monopolists force people to pay more than the commodity would commonly have been sold for in the absence

[49] *De contr.*, II, Q.23: p. 91.

of monopoly. One might say (though Cajetan does not state it explicitly) that monopoly is not a lawful *modus*.

If all depends on the mode of selling, however, the author asks himself in opposition, does it not follow that no injustice attaches to a purchase at a price far below what a thing is commonly sold for in a given location and accepted by the person who offers it for sale only because he is in need? Such a price does not appear to be just, because the exchange is not entirely voluntary (*omnino voluntaria*) but half-forced (*semiviolenta*), as when someone throws merchandise into the sea to avoid death. The author replies:

> Granted that this kind of sale has something of the involuntary mixed with it as regards the reason (*causa*) for the sale, it is nevertheless simply and absolutely voluntary (*simpliciter, et absolute voluntaria*). The rule is that if a thing is sold at a just price, the exchange is not harmed by the fact that the sale is involuntary as to its reason, as is evident from the case of him who, induced by the need of his poverty, sells land which he had from his ancestors, and from similar cases. Hence, if the price is just, as we said, such admixture to the voluntary (*admixtio voluntarii*) is no objection.[50]

In his penitential *Summa*, Cajetan explains about *causa* and *modus*, mentioning sales at auction or through brokers. Besides the tendency for a commodity to fetch a lower price when offered by the seller (rather than being sought by the buyer), there may be few buyers around at the time, or they may not need or much care for the commodity, or they may lack ready money. A person who buys it cheap for any of these reasons does not sin, for he simply pays what is being asked. Nor is the seller's motivation relevant. The author concludes in phrases reminiscent of Summenhart, applying them to the case of the needy seller:

> A price is not rendered unjust *ex causa*, for instance, if someone is led to sell by necessity and thus not voluntarily, for the want by which someone is forced to sell (*inopia qua cogitur quis ad vendendum*) does not render the sale involuntary, because otherwise also a sale made at the higher level of the just price (*rigido pretio*)[51] would be rendered involuntary, which is patently false.[52]

It is important to note that Cajetan does not claim that economic compulsion is irrelevant substantially, only that it is irrelevant analytically. Abuse can be arrested by a different criterion. This is made clear in reply to one of the *dubia* presented to him by a certain master and published among his *Opuscula*. It is true, he observes there, that acts

---

[50] *Comm. Sum. theol.*, to II–II,77,1: IX,148–50.

[51] See section 6.1.

[52] *Summa de peccatis*, art. *Emptio*: f.54v.

compelled by need are done with a mixed will, which is not to be exploited. To charge a much too high price, or to pay one which is much too low, on account of need on the part of the other party to the exchange, is sinful, but it is unnecessary to seek the origin of such a sin in anything but the inequality of thing to thing, that is, of price to thing bought; for in that the injustice consists, which is contrary to commutative justice.[53] To sum up this account of Cajetan's teaching in Aristotelian terms, what he suggests is, in effect, that the tradition from *Ethics*, III, on compulsion and the voluntary, is best abandoned in favor of the tradition from *Ethics*, V, on justice as equality.

Cajetan's ideas met with very wide acceptance. He was soon paraphrased or quoted by Fumo in Italy and by prominent authors like Vitoria, Soto, and Medina in Spain.[54] In the course of the following century, numerous authors writing in the Salamanca tradition would repeat after him that *modus* rather than *causa* determines the just price.[55] This principle has much to commend it. Internal factors like need and will do not make for a readily operational criterion. Even if they did, such a criterion might lead to unreasonable results. It would violate fundamental scholastic ideas of justice if identical objects, offered for sale in identical ways, as a matter of *justice* should be paid different prices, depending on the seller's motivation for the sale. If he happened to sell because he was in great need of money, to help him out would be a matter of charity, not justice. Cajetan can be read to say no more than that one should observe the possible effects of need on the price actually paid and arrest exploitation by means of external criteria, but this is not the only way to read him and most likely not what he meant. He does not simply embrace the traditional competitive market-price estimate of justice as a criterion supplementing, and in principle conforming with, the traditional cost criterion.

By specifying different modes of exchange, and by referring explicitly to the number of buyers and to other critical determinants of supply and demand (as his followers regularly did as well), Cajetan endorses (or invites the endorsement of) a freer play of bargaining power than the medieval scholastic masters were inclined to do. In view of the development of commercial techniques and institutions from the prim-

---

[53] *Responsio*, to Dub.3: f.66vb.

[54] Fumo, *Summa*: p. 282; Vitoria, loc. cit.: 118–19; Soto, *De iustitia et iure*, VI,2,3: f.196r; Medina, *Cod. rest.*, Q.31: pp. 197–9.

[55] Cp., among others, Lugo, *De iustitia et iure*, Disp. 26,4: Part. II, p. 313; Regnault, *Praxis*, XXV,16: Vol. II, p. 412; Bonacina, *De contr.*, II,iv,21: p. 401; Busenbaum, *De contr.*, Dub. 8: p. 316.

itive marketplace of the past, an acknowledgment of alternative ways of conducting business, with different normal rates of exchange ensuing, is natural and reasonable, but it inevitably points the further development of economic ethics in a certain direction. For all that Cajetan's followers spoke out against monopoly and similar practices, the distinction between legitimate and illegitimate *modi* would necessarily begin to blur. With the focus placed exclusively on external criteria, an important relationship between *causa* and *modus* might blur as well, namely, the fact that certain modes of exchange will be sought systematically by those with a certain motivation – for instance, their need. It is the needy who will implore others to buy and sell rather than await a better deal. If the *fact* that initiative to exchange will influence price is accepted as being in the *just* nature of things, protection of the needy will lose a significant part of its theoretical foundation. Though economic compulsion may have been meant to be merely analytically irrelevant, it is likely that it gradually will come to be regarded as substantially irrelevant as well.

Cajetan's doctrine represents a first step (deliberate or not) toward the depersonalization of economic ethics that characterizes postscholastic thought. The logical next step would be to condone a transaction even on terms that are known to be unjust, because the stronger party, on objective criteria, can disclaim responsibility for the plight that forces the weaker party to accept those terms. This ethical alienation between exchangers represents a decisive break with the ideals with which Christian economic philosophy had been infused since the times of the early Church Fathers. Three quarters of a century after Cajetan, Domingo de Bañez, another Dominican commenting on Aquinas, had taken this step:

If the offended party knows the just price, but is compelled by need to buy or sell, then the contract is valid in the court of conscience. This can be proved thus: For albeit knowing the just price, he nevertheless wishes to (*vult*) enter into this contract and suffer this loss, therefore the contract is simply voluntary (*simpliciter voluntarius*) and valid. . . . The contract itself is valid even though it is unfair. This can be shown by a simile. He who throws merchandise into sea when a storm springs up, throws it voluntarily, absolutely speaking (*simpliciter loquendo*), albeit involuntarily in a certain respect (*secundum quid*), because he would not have willed to throw it (*nollet proicere*); therefore such will suffices for a contract of buying and selling, because the offended party is in no way compelled by the other party to enter into the contract. . . . The party who is compelled to make the contract is not compelled by the other party but by something else, namely, by his want (*a sua egestate*).[56]

---

[56] *Decisiones*, to II–II,77,1: p. 354.

Even without insisting on Aquinas's reversal of Aristotle's dichotomy, and admitting that unjust terms of exchange are accepted by the needy with a will that is "mixed" or *secundum quid* and conditioned by circumstances, this novel doctrine can be maintained. Roman and canon law principles will carry the day. Giovanni Cagnazzo, the author of one of the last major Italian penitential *summas* predating Trent, was an admirer of Cajetan and dedicated his work to the cardinal. In articles on economic subjects, Cagnazzo repeatedly cites the rule that the knowing and consenting suffer no injury. In the article on buying and selling, he calls upon the authority of Panormitanus, who quotes the old adage that forced will is will, and goes on to proclaim, without mentioning justice at all, "Mutual agreement is essential to buying, and conditional will is sufficient" (*Mutuus consensus est de substantia emptionis, et voluntas conditionata sufficit*).[57]

---

[57] *Summa*: f.164vb; cp. Panormitanus, *Super tertio Decretalium*, to III, 17,3: f.83ra.

CHAPTER 7

Labor and wages

7.1   Scholastic approaches to labor

"The Law further ordains merciful conduct toward hired workmen because of their poverty. Their wages should be paid without delay, and they must not be wronged in any of their rights; they must receive their pay according to their work." These words, written in the late twelfth century, are those of Moses Maimonides in the *Guide for the Perplexed.*[1] There is an echo of them in the *Summa theologiae* of Thomas Aquinas: "Laborers who hire out their work are poor people who seek their sustenance from their daily toil, and therefore the law wisely ordains that their wages be paid promptly, lest they should lack food."[2] The remark is merely made by way of reply to an objection concerning the suitability of one of the judicial precepts of Leviticus.[3] The economic conditions of contemporary wage earners are not addressed for their own sake and the subject is not pursued further, but even such passing reference to it is rare in medieval scholastic sources. It was not until the fifteenth century that systematic attention began to be paid to the question of the just wage. The paucity of early source material on wages is all the more remarkable when compared with the wealth of thirteenth- and fourteenth-century literature on justice in the exchange of commodities and the lending of money. From the point of view of the present study, this is somewhat disappointing and may seem difficult to explain in view of the fact that there is probably no other class of economic contracts in which the relative bargaining powers of the parties tend to be less evenly balanced than in the case of the hire of manual labor.

One partial explanation, as well as a necessary point of departure of any account of scholastic economic doctrine relating to labor and wages, is that when labor was discussed, its economic aspect was fre-

---

[1] *Guide*, III,42: p. 351.
[2] *Sum. theol.*, I–II,105,2: VII,267.
[3] Lev. 19.13: "The wages of him that is hired shall not abide with thee all night until the morning."

quently not in the focus of attention at all. Men are doomed to labor in this life, and, in the Christian life, labor has many blessings. It serves to combat idleness, which is the source of much evil, to discipline the body, and to inflame devotion, as well as to provide necessary bodily sustenance. Such is the teaching of Bonaventura and Aquinas,[4] but a list of statements to this effect could be extended almost endlessly from medieval sources. As regards the writings of the mendicant friars, who form the great majority of scholastic authors, there would sometimes be an emphasis on the role played by labor, and increasingly by spiritual as opposed to manual labor, on the part of those within the religious orders. The friars, of course, worked without pay. There is no question but that their position and attitudes tended to reflect on what they taught about labor in secular society as well. This explanation, however, does not take us very far. The economic aspect of labor was not at all ignored by the medieval scholastics. On the contrary, whenever economic exchange was being discussed, one of the fundamental principles of scholastic ethics in the medieval period was that honest labor deserves its material reward. The adage repeatedly stated in the Bible that "the laborer is worthy of his hire," and other scriptural texts to this effect, interpreted in material terms, were commonplace.[5] Reward of labor was an important implicit factor in the doctrines on usury and price reviewed in preceding chapters of this study. The present chapter will serve to bring some of it into the open. In other words, there is no failure to discuss labor as such in our sources, either from an economic or from a noneconomic point of view, but rather a lack of interest, for quite some time, in the reward of labor in terms of wage, that is, in terms of a contract between employer and employee, or master and laborer, on the lines of a loan or a sales contract. Two further suggestions as to how this can be explained historically must be considered. They are based in two important medieval institutions, feudal bondage and the guilds.

Since William of Auxerre, who took his guidelines partly from canon law, the academic writings of the scholastic masters on the subject of economic ethics were based on the concept of justice and couched in terms of justice. Norms of ethics thus conceived and expressed had a limited field of application. Medieval political thought accepted slavery and various degrees of serfdom and villeinage as being in the order of things. The societies whose problems our authors addressed but whose

---

[4] Bonaventura, *Expos. reg.*, V,1: 419; Aquinas, *Sum. theol.*, II–II, 187,3: X,510–11; *Quodl.* VII,17: IX,565.

[5] Matt. 10.10; Luke 10.7; 1 Cor. 3.8; 1 Tim. 5.18.

fundamental structures they seldom questioned included a large class of laborers to whom justice in wage relations did not apply because justice, as understood in scholastic economic ethics, presumed an agreement between politically independent parties. (A fortiori, the question of the will, with which this study is primarily concerned, would not apply for those whose very position in the social system was one of bondage.) The feudal lord would have a duty to protect his dependants and to see to the supply of such needs and comforts as befitted their lowly status. Medieval preachers and authors of edifying and admonitory tracts would remind them of that duty and of the virtue of charity, just as they would encourage the dependants to accept their lot as God's will and remind them of the virtue of humility. The scholastic master, in his academic writings, would have no call to discuss the justice involved, as he would in the case of moneylending and in the case of buying and selling.

It can probably be argued that acceptance of this social structure also tended to blunt awareness of the plight of manual laborers in a weak bargaining position but politically free to choose their employment and make their own labor contracts. The reason most often given, however, for the lack of interest in the question of the just wage by the medieval scholastics is that it was to some extent solved, or rather taken out of their hands, by the guilds. This institution incorporated its individual members in a system that not only fixed the normal reward for their efforts but served as a safeguard against the kind of arbitrary events and fluctuations by which opportunities for exploitation mainly arose and called for moral guidelines. As long as this system worked, there was less need for ethics. There is, no doubt, something to say for this explanation. To my mind, it paints a much-too-rosy picture of medieval labor conditions. The medieval craft guilds were, after all, primarily associations of masters, that is, of employers, whose interest in the welfare of journeymen, apprentices, and other employees was at best indirect. The guilds, however, were established and officially acknowledged social institutions and therefore less immediately the objects of (and on the whole probably less deserving of) moral censure than occasional monopolies and "consortiums" seeking short-term profit by abuse of economic power. The lack of concern with the ethics of the guilds in the Middle Ages is nevertheless a phenomenon sometimes commented on by historians.[6] To judge by scholastic sources, domestic wage laborers were considered to be more precariously situated than artisan wage laborers, but it was only with the growth of an

---

[6] See the recent study by Epstein, with references.

urban proletariat that the question of the just wage was placed on the scholastic agenda in earnest. It is difficult to trace this question much further back than to Florence in the fifteenth century. By then, scholastic economic ethics had embarked on the new development recorded in previous chapters as regards usury and price doctrine. Its most significant feature was an increasing concession to the forces of supply and demand. This came to put its mark on late scholastic wage doctrine as well.

One additional factor deserves to be mentioned if only because it is frequently overlooked. A large portion of scholastic economic writing took the form of commentary on standard texts. In many of those texts that mention labor, whether deriving from Scripture, from the Church Fathers, or from canon law, the prototype is some artisan who sells the product of his own skilled labor. The occupation of the artisan, as an independent producer-seller, borders on that of the merchant, who uses his particular skills as well and supports himself on his profit margin. When scholastic authors turned to labor in the early thirteenth century, they were mainly concerned with the justification of commerce and commercial profit. For this purpose, the crafts served as a benchmark. The case of the artisan was unproblematical, precisely because he earned his livelihood from labor in the proper sense. The justice of his reward could be accepted as an axiom, theoretically from Scripture, factually from the guilds. It seemed reasonable to explain and justify commercial profit analogously, as well as profit on various kinds of financial transactions. When labor (or industry) was subsequently discussed, and the labor interpretation developed and modified, it was largely in this commercial context, and it was after this development, and in this modified version, that it was later brought back and applied to wages proper. This is one of the lines of tradition to be traced in this chapter. Another line concerns the crafts themselves. With the translation of Aristotle's *Ethics*, the scholastics were presented with a different model, one that rendered the simple artisan prototype problematical. Aristotle introduced a selection of different professionals and craftsmen who mutually barter their services or the products of their respective crafts. This text invited an examination of the question of price differentials per labor unit in exchange between persons possessing different skills, the result of which could, when called for, be applied by analogy to explain and justify wage differentials as well. These two lines of tradition did not run independently of each other, but it is convenient to devote a section to each, before turning to late scholastic wage doctrine and eventually to the question of the will of the needy wage earner.

7.2   Labor and value: commerce

The artisan prototype was established by Rufinus in his *Summa* on the *Decretum*. In Chapter 5, Rufinus was quoted on profitable resale of an unexpected surplus of a necessary originally bought for consumption. He refers to *Quicumque* and thereby introduces one of the kinds of market participation to which the sinful business of "inducing scarcity" was later frequently to be contrasted. The long and highly influential discussion in which this reference occurs is not to be found in comment on the question in the *Decretum* that contains *Quicumque* but on the preceding one. It deals with usury in a broad sense and is partly addressed to the clergy, but Rufinus takes this opportunity to clarify some points regarding different forms of economic activity on the part of the laity as well. Rather than being bought originally for consumption, a thing may be bought with the intention, from the start, of selling it again at a higher price. If such is the case, a distinction should be made whether or not something is spent on its improvement while in the possession of the buyer. "For if, with his labors and expenses, he has made the thing better, then making a profit on that thing is entirely lawful for laymen, as in the case of artisans."[7]

This was copied by John of Faenza and paraphrased by Sicard of Cremona.[8] Huguccio's version is an elaboration:

But if he buys something as material on which he exercises some craft and thus acquires some profit from it, this is lawful for laymen, and for clerics provided that the craft is suitable for clerics, nor is this to do business *(negotiari)*, as stated in Distinction 88, *Eiciens*, nor is profit here acquired from commerce *(negotiatio)* but from craftsmanship *(artificium)*, as did Paul.[9]

St. Paul was a tent maker. The *Glossa ordinaria* notes that even clerics may buy raw material *(rudis materia)* and work it up for a profit. The apostles were permitted to do this.[10]

The text to which Huguccio here refers, by its incipit, as *Eiciens*, is the first of three consecutive later additions *(paleae)* to a series of chapters in Part I of the *Decretum*, dealing with activities prohibited to the clergy.[11] These additions have no commentary tradition there, but it is interesting to note both the fact that Huguccio refers to one of them from Part II and the use that he makes of it. They were to

---

[7] *Summa*, to II,14,3: p. 341.

[8] John, *Summa*, to loc. cit.: f.58va; Sicard, *Summa*, to loc. cit.: f.92v.

[9] *Summa*, to II,14,3,pr: f.217va.

[10] To loc. cit.: Bamberg SB Can. 13, f.128va; Basel 1512, f.219va.

[11] *Decretum*, I,88,11 *(Eiciens)*; 12 *(Quoniam)*; 13 *(Quid est)*: Friedberg, I,308–10.

play an important part in the transfer of canonistic labor doctrine from craftsmanship to commerce. To this, the Decretists contributed very little. Huguccio, who, on the following page, notes that laymen are allowed to engage in commerce but does not relate this to labor,[12] in the present context even finds it necessary to reemphasize the difference between these activities. In the early thirteenth century, Thomas of Chobham notes that merchants may also charge for improvements made to the goods they buy and sell, but their main service to society is carrying goods from places of plenty to places of scarcity; therefore, they may also charge "the value of their labor and transport and expenses."[13] Shortly afterward, Alexander of Hales makes much clearer sense of this, basing his teaching on the three *paleae* of the *Decretum*. In *Eiciens*, a sequence taken from an anonymous commentary on Matthew, the traders evicted by Christ from the Temple are said to be those who buy things and resell them "whole and unaltered," as against craftsmen, who alter the things they buy by working on them.[14] In *Quoniam*, from Augustine's commentary on the Psalms, a merchant is quoted by the author claiming that he labors as well, bringing merchandise home from foreign parts.[15] *Quid est* is a much briefer extract from Cassiodorus on the Psalms, heaping abuse on the avarice of merchants, a prominent theme in the other texts as well.[16] Commenting on this material, Alexander of Hales points out that merchants do not always sell things "whole and unaltered." If they do not alter them as to substance, like artisans, they alter them as to place and time, by bringing goods to where they are needed and by storing them until they are needed. For this, they may lawfully seek recompense. Those whom the Fathers condemn are merchants who do business without labor and care, motivated only by a desire for endless wealth.[17]

Alexander of Hales laid the foundation on which scholastic doctrine on labor and value built until the end of the fifteenth century. Avarice was rampant in business and roundly condemned, but if the merchant observed due circumstances, his profession was honorable and his re-

---

[12] See section 5.3.

[13] *Summa confessorum*, 6,4,10: 301–2.

[14] *Opus imperfectum in Matthaeum*, to Matt. 21.12: PG 56, 839–40. This fifth-century homily, by an unknown author, was attributed in the Middle Ages to St. John Chrysostom.

[15] *Enarrationes in Psalmos*, to Psalm 70.17: PL 36, 836.

[16] *Expositio Psalmorum*, to Psalm 70.15; CCL 97, 634–5.

[17] *Sum. theol.*, IV,721–4.

muneration just. Thomas Aquinas granted the merchant a moderate profit, not as an end in itself but as a payment for his labor (*stipendium laboris* – a famous phrase).[18] Henry of Ghent pointed out that merchants are professional experts who may charge for their industry (*industria*), which is something more than simple labor.[19] Peter Olivi, following suit, justifies commercial profit computed on the basis of labors and expenses, risk, industry, and vigil.[20] John Duns Scotus lists similar factors: labor, industry, solicitude, risk.[21] These principles were frequently restated and confirmed,[22] until another observation made by Scotus in the same context was pointed out as questionable and caused the labor doctrine to be reconsidered. A parallel development in usury doctrine is worth noting as well. Because money is barren, profit on commercial ventures involving capital must be due to something else, and William of Auxerre suggested what this was, namely, human labor and industry.[23] A number of prominent early scholastic authors confirmed this, and it was repeated by virtually all those who discussed the subject as long as the sterility doctrine was maintained. This theory obviously lent support to the merchant's claim to have these factors covered in his prices, but it broke down when the principle of sterility was questioned.

This scholastic "labor theory" has been the cause of some controversy and misunderstanding, both as regards the just price of commodities and as regards its possible relevance to wages doctrine. Where Huguccio grants a layman the license to engage in commercial activity, he twice states the provision that this should be for the support "of himself and his own" (*sibi et suis*).[24] William of Rennes introduced this phrase in the confessional tradition in a gloss to Ray-

[18] *Sum. theol.*, II–II,77,4: IX,153–4.
[19] *Quodl.* I,40: *Opera Omnia*, V, 229.
[20] *De emptione et venditione*, Q.6: 266.
[21] *Op. cit.*, pp. 317–18.
[22] Odonis, *De contr.*, QQ.7–8: ff.85r–87v; Astesanus, *Summa*, III,8,10: f.126ra–vb; Bartolomeo of San Concordio, *Summa*: f.127va; f.279ra; Raniero, *Pantheologia*: II,1156; Bernardino, *Quadr.*, Serm. 33,2,2: IV,146; *Prediche volgari* (Florence 1424), Serm. 7: Vol. I, pp. 103–4; Nider, *De contr.*, II: f.11r–v; Antonino, *Sum.theol.*, II,1,16,2: col. 250; col. 252; Ariosto, *Enchir.*: f.116rb; *De usuris*, III: p. 82; Trovamala, *Summa*: f.75ra; f.170va; Carletti, *Tract.*, I,1: p. 13; p. 23; *Summa*: f.81ra; Cagnazzo, *Summa*: f.168ra; Mazzolini, *Summa*: I,295; II,204; 426; Biel: p. 191; pp. 197–8.
[23] *Summa*, III,48,4: 937.
[24] *Summa*, to II,14,4,3: f.218rb; to II,14,4,9: f.218va.

mond of Peñafort's *Summa*.[25] It was often repeated by scholastic authors relating labor to the just price, sometimes with a suggestive
addition. In conclusion to his explanation of the three *paleae* of the
Decretum summarized previously, Alexander of Hales states that commerce is lawful if conducted under due circumstances and for a necessary and pious purpose, for instance, so that the merchant "can
provide for himself and his family with necessaries" *(possit sibi et suae
familiae in necessariis providere)*.[26] Reference to the merchant's "family"
or "house" is a regular feature of subsequent discussions of this subject.[27] In connection with a well-known modern controversy, this has
led some critics to the conclusion that medieval scholasticism allowed
the merchant a "family wage." There is obviously some truth in this,
but only if interpreted in a rather narrowly restricted sense. The crucial point is that the canonists and theologians here address the case
of merchants who are frequently able to charge prices above a reasonable recompense for their labor and industry, expenses and risks.
The merchant, as a seller, was normally assumed to be in a strong
bargaining position in exchange with a buyer-consumer in a weaker
position. What must be kept in check was the merchant's avarice, the
boundless quest for gain, which so sorely tempts men who deal with
money. For this, certain guidelines were needed. Reasonable cost cov-
erage, including personal efforts, as in the case of artisans, was one
such guideline, but it does not follow that the merchant can always
count on a profit margin that pays him adequately for his labor and
industry and supports his family establishment. The principle sets an
upper limit, not a lower limit. This is evident if it is viewed in relation to the other main principle on which the idea of the just price
rested, namely, the common estimate of the market.

If our authors almost with one voice approved of the merchant's right
to cover cost and support his family with his labor, they were nearly unan-
imous in embracing the justice of the competitive market price as well.
The attempt to extend a modern ideological conflict between labor and
market back to medieval scholasticism must fail in the face of massive

---

[25] To *Summa Raimundi*, III,8,5: p. 248: ". . . ad sustentationem suam et
suorum."

[26] *Sum. theol.*, IV,723.

[27] Loc. cit. in note 22: Astesanus: f.126ra; Raniero: II,1152; Nider: f.11v;
Antonino: col. 251; Ariosto: f.116rb; p. 94; Trovamala: f.75ra; Carletti: p. 8;
Cagnazzo: f.168ra; Mazzolini: II,204; Biel: p. 194; as well as Thomas de Vio,
Comm. Sum. theol., to II–II,77,4: IX,154.

contrary textual evidence. In view of this, the two principles make sense only as complementary and mutually supporting criteria by which to reach a reasonable price estimate when there is not actually a competitive market in operation. As such, their purpose was to prevent speculation, discrimination, collusion, and all kinds of deliberate interference with the market mechanism.[28] This is problematical in cases where the labor and market estimates differ or where it is difficult to envisage a market in operation at all. This would not be at all unusual in the medieval context. In economies with imperfectly developed markets, sellers in favored positions can sometimes allow themselves quite liberal *stipendia* for their activities and keep their families and households in style without much danger of entry and competition. When there is actually a competitive market in operation, however, the labor criterion is overruled by the market criterion. The competitive market does not only prevent (or put a certain limit to) exploitation; it may also fail to recompense true, but inefficient, labor, just as, on the other hand, it may sometimes pay efficient labor more than Huguccio's principle was designed to do. It took some time for these relationships to be pointed out. When they found systematic expression in works by sixteenth-century Spanish authors, it is natural to relate this both to developments in the real economy and to a general tendency toward emancipation from the authority of the great medieval masters. Both these factors influenced the ideological shift witnessed in previous chapters. On the subject of the just price, it led to a wider acceptance of market forces at the cost of the ancient idea that labor deserves its reward.

An early indication of this new line of thought was given by Summenhart. Having explained that a merchant can normally count on a price that covers labor and expenses, this strange German eclectic makes a point of stressing "normally." In human estimation, which determines prices, commodities will sometimes fall below this level.[29] Vitoria conveyed these reflections to his Spanish audience.[30] Medina decisively influenced the course of subsequent discussion of the subject in the Salamanca tradition by drawing attention to an observation made long ago by John Duns Scotus in support of the merchant's right to a reasonable reward for his labors. Merchants perform a necessary and useful social service, transporting and conserving goods and making them available when needed. If no one did this on his own initiative, Scotus points out, the government would have to hire functionaries and

---

[28] See section 5.2, with references in note 36.
[29] *De contr.*, III, Q.56: p. 260.
[30] *Comentarios*, to II–II,77,1: 117–18.

to pay them adequately.[31] Medina interprets this to mean that merchants should in fact grant themselves a fixed salary covering labor and expenses. He objects to such an idea and proceeds to explain the difference between being a salaried government official and an independent merchant living on what he can earn and carrying his own risks.[32] His arguments were to be repeated and developed by many later Spanish authors and other authors in the Spanish tradition.[33]

This rule of Scotus, says Domingo de Bañez, is highly deceptive as a guideline. This can be shown, as follows:

First, because it often happens that the price of goods in exchange decreases after the merchants have made their purchases, either because there are few buyers or because of an abundance of goods arriving from elsewhere, and then it clearly would be unfair if such merchants should sell their goods even at the price at which they were bought. This is so because the just price then is that which is current according to the common estimate of the market, which in fact would then be much lower than the price at which they made their purchases, and therefore they can get nothing for their industry and labor. Vice versa it may happen that after these merchants bought their wares, the just price increases owing to a multitude of buyers or a scarcity of goods, and then the just price will be that which is current according to the common estimate of the market, even if much higher than the payment stipulated by government officials.

Second, Bañez points out, the idea of a fixed wage for merchants would lead to some strange results. It would mean, for instance, that the government must pay for goods lost at sea, or that those that were saved must be sold at a much higher price. A merchant profits justly only if he arrives with his goods intact.

Furthermore, if the relation between two merchants were such that one bought his wares much dearer than the other, either because they were brought from much further off or because the latter bought them wisely when there were few merchants around, it would follow that these merchants could sell their goods at the same time and in the same place at notably different prices. This is so because the one who bought them dearer would not obtain his full salary unless he sold them dearer than the other. In short, the conclusion is proved and the point of our doctrine is demonstrated, namely, the difference which exists between a mere government servant and a merchant who is the owner of his money and his goods. For all that pertains to the office of a servant is to carry

---

[31] Op. cit.: p. 318.

[32] *Cod. rest.*, Q.31: pp. 198–9.

[33] Thus Soto, *De iustitia et iure*, VI,2,2: f.194v; Salón, *Contr.*: Vol. II, p. 16; Valencia, *Comm. theol.*, III,5,20,2: col. 1425; Regnault, *Praxis*, XXV,16: Vol. II, p. 411; Molina, *De contr.*, Disp. 348: cols. 566–7; Lugo, *De iustitia et iure*, Disp. 26,4: Part II, p. 312; Laymann, *Theol. moral.*, III,iv,17: p. 423.

out his master's business diligently and prudently, so that, if the servant loses, the master loses. In the case of the merchant, on the other hand, who is his own master, just as he enjoys the benefit when his business is successful, it is right that he should feel the loss when it is not.

The rule of Scotus, Bañez concludes, may be useful if the government wants to fix the price of some necessary, such as corn. "Then the labor and industry incurred by farmers ought to be taken into account, so that they can support themselves by their labor. This, however, the government should consider in general and on the whole, for it cannot provide for every farmer in every event."[34]

7.3   Labor and value: crafts and professions

John Duns Scotus and his late Spanish critics are obviously to some extent arguing at cross-purposes. The canonists and early theologians argued that merchants labor for the benefit of all and should be paid for this, just as craftsmen are. Scotus, in effect, made the additional point that this is not only right because the individual merchant deserves it, but it is in fact socially necessary because no one would be a merchant unless he was paid for it. He never suggests that the merchant should, or could, draw a fixed salary. Authors in the tradition represented by Bañez argue as though this is what he meant and object to it. A merchant will get only what the market allows, sometimes less, sometimes more, than a straight salary. This emphasis on the market is significant. It does not follow that merchants in strong bargaining positions are free to manipulate the market or even, to any considerable extent, deliberately to play on market variations for personal profit. The documentation in Chapter 5 of massive and explicit condemnation of such practices offers proof enough of this. They represent misuse of economic power. What does follow, however, is that merchants and other sellers in weak bargaining positions are subject to market forces. As documented in Chapter 6, the idea that taking advantage of such weak bargaining positions represents misuse of economic power as well was clearly on the wane. This is the aspect most relevant to late-scholastic wages doctrine.

The relation between labor and value in scholastic thought is more sharply outlined if focus is shifted back from the case of the merchant to that of the craftsman. In commerce, the merchant's labor and professional skill are rewarded through a profit margin on purchase price, transport and storage costs, insurance, etc. These factors normally

[34] *Decisiones*, to II–II,77,4: p. 366.

make up a relatively large part of the sales price. In the price paid a craftsman for his product, the percentage allocable to labor will vary with the nature of his skill and the value of his raw material but will normally be much higher. It may amount to nearly all that is paid some qualified professionals, such as a physician or a lawyer, for whom material costs are sometimes quite negligible. As a matter of fact, in the case of some crafts and professions, the very distinction between a *price* for services rendered and a *wage* paid for rendering such services may become blurred. The artisan prototype is therefore not unproblematical as regards how much he is paid for his labor and how this is determined. With the translation of Aristotle's *Ethics*, the scholastics were presented with a text that invited reflections on these questions. A brief account of medieval comments on this text, and of the tradition that developed from it, will bring us to wages theory proper.

Classical scholars do not agree about the meaning of Aristotle's formula stating the ratios of exchange between builder and shoemaker, farmer and doctor. Some admit that they cannot make sense of it. Most would maintain that Aristotle cannot have intended either of the two main interpretations proposed by the medieval Latin commentators, simply because the scholastics read into the formula the terms of a market economy nonexistent in ancient Greece. These interpretations are (1) that the exchange rate is determined by the relative need *(opus, indigentia)* for the products or services bartered (as felt by the parties themselves or by the community), and (2) that it is determined by the labor and expenses laid down in these products or services. The former interpretation and its development in scholastic literature were discussed in Chapter 5.[35] The latter interpretation may have been invited by the confusion between *opus* as "need" and *opus* as "work" in the original version of the Lincoln translation. Another possibility is suggested by a gloss mentioning labor in one of the extant manuscripts of the Lincoln corpus,[36] but whether this gloss is due to Grosseteste or added later is difficult to determine. Anyhow, Albert the Great launched this interpretation in his first commentary on the *Ethics* and confirmed it in his second commentary: The number of shoes in exchange for a house should be as the proportion of builder to shoemaker *in laboribus et expensis.* This was supported somewhat halfheartedly by Thomas Aquinas and most enthusiastically by Henry of Friemar.[37] Subsequent textual commentators often repeated it, as some

---

[35] See section 5.2.
[36] To 1133b2 in Oxford All Souls College 84, f.90rb.
[37] Albert, *Super Ethica*, V,7: 343–5; *Ethica*, V,2,9–10: 357–9; Thomas, *Sent. Eth.*,

modern interpreters still do.[38] It soon spread beyond the commentary tradition proper and no doubt influenced some of the authors already quoted on labor and value in this chapter.

It may well be that most of those lecturers on the *Ethics* advocated (or took Aristotle to advocate) the simple idea that craftsmen ought to be adequately recompensed for their efforts and outlays and thought that there was little more to it than that, but there is no firm textual evidence to support this. There is some evidence to show that the leading scholastic masters looked more deeply into the matter. Albert the Great reveals what lies at the root of his labor doctrine when he points out that a certain craft would no longer be exercised if it did not pay the craftsman what he lays down in labor and expenses. Henry of Friemar states that no one would apply himself to a piece of work on which he would not recover his labor and cost.[39] This recalls Scotus's remark about the need to engage salaried merchants if no one volunteered to perform their function. The price of a commodity cannot stay for long below total costs if it is to remain on the market. The anticipation of the so-called Law of Cost, which has in fact been attributed to Scotus, is at least as much in evidence in these Aristotle commentators. Thomas Aquinas did not pursue this line of argument on the part of his teacher Albert, and some later authors faulted him for what they took to be a primitive explanation of labor in his *Ethics* commentary. This criticism is unwarranted. There is nothing at all to indicate that Aquinas envisaged hours of labor or some other measure of the amount of labor being the determinants of exchange ratios between builder, shoemaker, and farmer. In other works, he repeatedly points out that different kinds of labor are paid differently. Thus, in the matter of crafts, an architect who plans a building earns more than a manual worker under his direction.[40]

Peter Olivi, who did not accept Thomistic doctrine uncritically, reproduces this example in his treatise on buying and selling. The men who actually quarry and cut the stones, albeit putting in more bodily effort, earn less than the architect who guides and instructs them with skill and industry. Why so? All things rare are precious, says Olivi, citing an ancient adage. When gold and corn are plentiful, they are not es-

V,8–9: XLVII,292–5; Henry, *Comm. Eth.*, V,5: Basel UB F.I.14, ff.133rb–134vb; Toulouse BMun 242, ff.277va–278rb.

[38] Cp. Langholm, 1979, Chapter 2.

[39] Albert, *Super Ethica*, V,7, to 1133a14–16: 343; Henry, loc. cit: f.133rb; f.277va.

[40] *De regno*, I,9: XLII,460; *Quodl.* I,14: IX,468.

timated as highly as when there is a shortage of them, and it is the same when there is plenty or scarcity of doctors or advocates, soldiers or ditchdiggers. As regards skilled crafts and professions, practitioners are scarce because few are suited for such occupations and because their training is long and expensive.[41] Gerald Odonis, who was critical of Aquinas and drew on Olivi, in his commentary on the *Ethics* takes the former to task for one of his remarks about labor and proceeds to explain Aristotle's formula in terms of the relative scarcity of different skills. If the shoemaker is a costlier craftsman than the farmer, his work will be more expensive and fetch a higher price than the farmer's work. It is not labor as such that is a measure of value in exchange. A farmer works more for a small quantity of wheat than an advocate drawing up a deed, and yet the farmer pays the advocate a hundred times as much for that brief document, and such is the case of all rare crafts.[42] In his treatise on contracts, Odonis copies Olivi's example, with an addition: When there is a scarcity of doctors, advocates, or persons of other particular professions, it follows that they can hire out their work more dearly.[43]

This statement contains a number of clues. First: As I see it, and as already pointed out, the scholastic cost and market estimates of the just price are not in conflict but are mutually supporting and complementary. In the context of the *Ethics*, Albert the Great's alternative explanations of Aristotle's exchange model in terms of need and in terms of labor and expenses are not in conflict, either. On the contrary, they fasten on two aspects of the underlying reciprocal relationship between product value and factor value that is the very crux of modern value theory. I have argued elsewhere that their persistence side by side through centuries of Aristotle commentaries furthered this insight.[44] Second: The larger the percentage of total cost allocable to labor, the more obvious is this relationship. If all is due to labor, as in some higher professions, it is reduced to a truism, because the service of the professional is product or factor, depending on the point from which it is viewed. The distinction between price and wage is blurred. Aquinas refers to the architect's income as wages *(merces)*. Olivi and Odonis discuss the value of services *(obsequia)*. In the last line quoted, Odonis says that professionals can hire out *(locare)* their work. If, in Albert's labor and expenses formula, the latter term is eliminated or materially re-

---

[41] *De emptione et venditione*, Q.2: 459–60.
[42] *Sent. Eth.*, V,9: f.207ra–b.
[43] *De contr.*, Q.5: f.82v.
[44] Langholm, 1979, Chapter 6.

duced, what developed from his explanations of Aristotle's exchange model may be interpreted as a theory of wages.

The third clue in Odonis's statement is the word "can" *(possunt)*. It recalls the Roman law value maxim. Wage, like price, may be a matter of power. Statements of the analogy between price and wage determination are not unusual in medieval scholastic sources. Wage is the price of labor and is subject to the rules of commutative justice.[45] In the fifteenth century, Olivi's analysis was restated and transmitted by prominent authorities like Bernardino of Siena and Gabriel Biel.[46] Odonis's choice of terminology indicates a further analogy, namely, a focus on the wage earner in a strong bargaining position, just as the merchant was usually seen as a seller in a strong bargaining position. It is sometimes difficult to know whether commentators on the chapter on exchange in *Ethics*, V, explain how wage/price is in fact determined or how it ought to be determined. Odonis's "can" suggests the former. The skill and scarcity of a much-sought-after craftsman enable him to drive a hard bargain and earn a high wage. This may be justified unless he oversteps certain limits in his use of power. Odonis does not add this, but it was done by scholastic authors both before and after him. Thus, Thomas Aquinas, in the *Summa theologiae*, states that a professional receives his fee as a *stipendium laboris* (using the exact phrase that was to be applied a little further on to merchants); however, if he wickedly extorts *(extorqueat)* an immoderate amount, he sins against justice.[47] In his work with the same title, Antonino of Florence, a century and a half later, says much the same: The professional sins if he extorts an excessive salary.[48]

7.4   Wages and the will of the laborer

When a salaried craftsman or professional is in a strong bargaining position where he is able to dictate or materially influence the terms of his employment, it is to the position of his employer that concepts like economic compulsion and conditional will might apply. This would seem to be relevant enough. The pressure on the sick to overpay for medical attention against his absolute will can be as strong as the pres-

---

[45] Aquinas, *Comm. Sent.*, III,33,3,4: VII,376; *Summa contra gentiles*, III,149: XIV,439; *Sum. theol.*, I–II,114,1: VII,344; Giles of Lessines, *De usuris*, III: 415; IV: 417; Godfrey of Fontaines, *Quodl.* XIII,10: LPB 5 (1935) 265.

[46] Bernardino, *Quadr.*, Serm. 35,2,2–3: IV,197–8; Biel: p. 202.

[47] *Sum. theol.*, II–II,71,4: IX,126.

[48] *Sum. theol.*, III,6,3,6: col. 276.

sure on the starving to overpay for food. Neither Thomas Aquinas nor
Antonino of Florence states the cases referred to in those terms, and I
can point to no other use of them in this type of context in scholastic
literature. When they finally appeared in connection with wages, they
applied to the laborer in a weak bargaining position being underpaid
by the employer. If a single scholastic author is to be credited with
having called attention to that form of exploitation, it must be Antonino. His knowledge of labor conditions in the Florentine textile industry, with its abuse of economic power on the part of employers, caused
him to revert to this subject repeatedly in his *Summa theologica*, as well
as in his *Confessionale*. The following is a highly condensed account.

The laborer seeks employment in order to provide for himself and
his dependants. For a labor contract to be lawful, its terms must be
just, and there must be no fraud on either part. The wage should be
based on a common estimate. To pay less is contrary to the equality of
justice; it is like buying a commodity for less than the just price owing
to the need of the seller. Laborers are poor people and easily exploited.
Employers sin not only by paying them too little but also by paying
them too late or in bad money. Much of Antonino's attack is directed
at the truck system, whereby wages were paid in food, or cloth, or other
things, instead of money. This system is above reproach if the laborer
voluntarily *(sponte)* agreed to a contract like this, but not if the contract
stipulated payment in money and the substitutes received had to be
sold at a loss. This loss should be made good by the employer, for the
laborer received other things against his will *(involuntarius alias res re-
cepit)*. As a matter of fact, it is not always possible to go by an expression
of will. The employer is not excused "if the laborer agrees in order
not to be out of a job, but to earn something, even if not enough" *(si
assentit ne sit otiosus, sed aliquid lucretur, etsi parum)*.[49]

Antonino's criticism of the truck system was repeated by later authors in the penitential tradition.[50] Others suggested that workers
should be paid what was usual if such a standard was available, and
otherwise according to a good man's estimate.[51] As in the case of
buying and selling, these criteria served to limit compulsion. This as-

---

[49] *Sum. theol.*, II,1,17,7–8: cols. 267–9; II,2,1,18: col. 352; III,8,1,1: col. 293;
    III,8,2: col. 297; III,8,4,4–5: cols. 313–17; *Confessionale*, art. *De avaritia*: f.42v;
    art. *De artificibus*: f.94r.
[50] Ariosto, *Enchir.*: f.119ra–b; Pacifico, *Summa*, Ch. 17: f.114v; Trovamala,
    Summa: f.255rb; Azpilcueta, *Enchir.*, XVII,108: p. 340.
[51] Cagnazzo: f.220va; Mazzolini: I,384; Fumo: p. 387; as well as Azpilcueta, loc.
    cit.

pect of Antonino's teaching was forcefully confirmed by some prominent authors. Gabriel Biel quotes him verbatim on the just wage, adding that the laborer should be paid what his labor is worth, unless he should voluntarily donate what is outstanding *(sponte residuum donaret)*, referring to Scotus's gift principle. This, however, cannot be presumed in the case of poor people lacking bread, "who, compelled by their need, accept less, although they long for a just value" *(qui sua necessitate compulsi minus recipiunt, quamvis iustum pretium desiderent).*[52] Francisco de Vitoria discusses this question as well. He solves it by explicitly introducing the Aristotelian principle of a mixed will overruling the legal principle that no injury is done to the willing. A doctor or an advocate who exacts an unjust salary is bound to make restitution, says Vitoria by way of introduction. What about a master with respect to his servant?

> Suppose the master says to the servant, "If you wish to stay in my house, do so; if not, go where you will," and with this wants it to be agreed between them as though the master had said to the servant, "I pay you nothing by way of recompense." What is then to be said about the master? I say that he should make restitution, even if he agreed in this way with the servant. Contra, because no injury was done to the willing servant. I say that it would not have been simply voluntary but would have had something of the involuntary mixed with it, because he was powerless to do more, seeing that he was about to die of hunger and had nowhere else to go.[53]

With authorities like Antonino of Florence, Biel, and Vitoria, the traditional scholastic view that need is a form of compulsion not to be exploited, long since established as regards price, thus gained belated recognition as regards wages, but its time was about to run out. Increased concession to the forces of supply and demand, first clearly expressed by Cajetan and supported by Spanish authors in the case of buying and selling, was soon to be embraced in discussions of wages as well.[54] Domingo de Soto, an almost exact contemporary of Vitoria, interprets Cajetan analogously from price to wage and heralds a new doctrine that was to be supported and developed in the Salamanca

[52] Op. cit.: p. 210.
[53] *Comentarios*, to II–II,77,1: 128–9. In the report on which the critical edition of Vitoria's work is based, the author tends to switch to the vernacular at key points. The important last full period reads: "Dico quod non fuit voluntarium simpliciter, sed habuit aliquid admistum de involuntario, porque no pudo más, por ver que se moría de hambre y non hallaba do ir." To "involuntario," there is a marginal note: "Scilicet necessitatem qua coactus fuit ad serviendum illi."
[54] See section 6.4.

tradition, virtually without opposition. When there are many sellers or few buyers, the rate of exchange will be lower. Likewise, a thing offered for sale will tend to be estimated lower than a thing asked for by a potential buyer. What holds for goods will hold for labor. A poor servant asking for employment need not be paid the same wage as one approached by the employer.[55] Soto and later authors in the Salamanca tradition seem mainly to have had domestic service in mind. From the thirteenth-century theologian Richard of Middleton, Mazzolini transmitted the question whether a servant whose master will not pay him a due wage can help himself to the difference in secret. This question of the secret wage, a tempting and presumably often readily accessible source of supplementary income in a large household, became a standard one in the Salamanca texts. Richard had taught that the servant sinned but need not make restitution.[56] Soto's treatment is harsher: It is never permitted to steal from one's master. If the wage agreed upon cannot be obtained by other means, the servant is excused, but not if he seeks to augment his wage, believing himself to be underpaid by the contract, unless this was obtained by force or fraud. Force by need is not mentioned. "For no injury is done to the willing. And therefore, if you will not serve for that reward, leave!" *(Volenti namque non fit iniuria. Et ideo si non vis illo pretio servire, abi).*[57]

Molina confirms this doctrine on most points but takes some account of economic compulsion. Secretly supplementing a wage agreed on is strictly condemned. A servant should be paid a just wage, but this is something that varies with circumstances, including how many or how few there are who seek the employment in question at any given time. There is no obligation on the part of an employer to pay more, even if the servant lives miserably on such a wage and is unable to support his family on it; however, if someone, compelled by need because there is no other employment available for him, accepts an inferior wage, and there is no reason why his labor should be valued below that of others, his wage should be raised to a level of justice. The just wage in fact has three levels, like the just price; a lower, medium, and higher level. If the servant in question was urged to take the job, his wage should be raised at least to the medium just level.[58] If not, the lower level would suffice. How to determine it? According to Lessius, it is sufficient to look to the market. If there are others who would willingly

---

[55] *De iustitia et iure,* VI,3,1: ff.196v–197r.
[56] Richard, *Comm. Sent.,* IV,15,5,7: p. 225; Mazzolini, loc. cit.
[57] Op. cit., V,3,3: f.150v.
[58] *De contr.,* Disp. 506: col. 1635–8.

(*libenter*) take the job at the wage offered, it is proof that it is just.[59] Expositions along these lines are to be found in the works of Azor, Regnault, and Laymann.[60]

Price and wage are governed by the same principle, according to Lugo. The labor contract is freely entered into, but once concluded, it carries the obligation to pay a just wage, just as a sales contract carries the obligation to pay a just price. It is the same with a loan contract. No one is forced by another's need to lend him money, but if he does lend, he must comply with the rules of justice and charge no usury. Unlike a loan contract, however, the just terms of sales and labor contracts vary with supply and demand. A price may be low because there are few buyers, and a seller may be forced by his need to sell at this low price, though a buyer should never pay less than what is just, given the circumstances, for this is intrinsically evil. Similarly, if someone will hire a servant, he cannot pay less than the just wage because of the servant's need, but ought either to abstain from the contract or to fulfill the intrinsic obligation. Both can look to the market. If someone is forced by need to accept employment at a wage he considers to be below his worth, it does not follow that the master is obliged to raise it. It depends on whether there are other masters willing to pay more. Then his present master should pay more, or the servant can easily find another job. It may be, however, that the just wage is low because there are few masters seeking this kind of service. In short, let the servant seek employment elsewhere. If he can find no one willing to pay him more, it means that his wage is just.[61]

---

[59] *De iustitia et iure*, II,24,4: pp. 325–6.
[60] Azor, *Inst. mor.*, III,8,(2),13: cols. 738–9: Regnault, *Praxis*, XXV,44: Vol. II, pp. 465–6; Laymann, *Theol. moral.*, III,iii,1: p. 313.
[61] *De iustitia et iure*, Disp. 16,4: Part I, p. 434.

PART III

Rejection and revival
in postscholastic thought

Non aspettar mio dir più né mio cenno:
libero, dritto e sano è tuo arbitrio,
e fallo fora non fare a suo senno:
per ch'io te sovra te corono e mitrio.

Dante, *Purgatorio*, XXVII, 139–42

CHAPTER 8

Hobbes: the antithesis

8.1 Hobbes against "School-divinity"

The concluding pages of each of the chapters of Part II of this book demonstrate a common tendency of decline of a certain set of doctrines concerning need, the will, and justice, which lie at the core of what may be called scholastic economic ethics. After having been applied for different lengths of time to questions regarding capital, commodities, and labor, these doctrines started to lose ground in each of the three areas in the first half of the sixteenth century and continued to do so until we closed the record some hundred years later. This was a period of increasing secularization of intellectual life and of nascent capitalism. New ideas about economics, based on altered material and institutional and religious premises, found expression in other literary media than those examined in Part II; however, the late scholastics' growing doubts about the validity of traditional doctrines also herald these new developments. It is the purpose of Part III to trace them further, with special reference to the question of choice and compulsion or (as it is now mostly called) coercion in economic relationships. As told in broad outline in Chapters 9 and 10, this is a story of virtually complete rejection of the medieval paradigm in academic and political circles, followed, after centuries, by its reappearance, in different shapes, partly without any acknowledgment of a scholastic heritage. Before embarking on that general historical survey, I propose, in the present chapter, to establish a point of observation and departure in the works of the seventeenth-century philosopher whose position on these issues is absolutely unique, namely, Thomas Hobbes.

For students of the origins of modern social science, Hobbes is an author of perennial fascination. Every year sees one or more new studies, and every decade a significant new approach to his thought. In principle, Hobbes wrote the same book about the nature of society and sovereignty three times (or more, if English and Latin versions are counted separately), refashioning his terms and arguments and spinning off (in these and other writings) comments and reflections that leave his readers guessing: Was he a (somewhat bizarre) Christian or a hypocrite? Was he a modern author or a medieval one in a new dress? Were his values those of the burgeoning bourgeoisie or those of the aristocracy, which he personally served throughout his long life? Was his natural law system merely a set of prudential rules of conduct or truly ethical? Was it a utilitarian system or a deontology? Did he recommend a minimal state securing peace and defense or a close regulation of social life? Reasonable answers, both ways, have been given to most of these questions. It is partly this ambiguity or, to put it differently, these many facets to his thought, which make his work such a useful point from which to observe future developments in the social sciences, including economics.

In the present context, Hobbes's importance is enhanced by his explicit and extensive preoccupation with the subjects discussed in Parts I and II and his opposition to Aristotle and to "School-divinity." His particular bugbears among the scholastics are Peter Lombard, Thomas Aquinas, and John Duns Scotus as well as Francisco Suárez, the political ideologist of the School of Salamanca. Aquinas is singled out because he "set up the kingdom of Aristotle."[1] In a recent study of Hobbes, it is claimed that he "transformed the Aristotelian paradigm."[2] This claim may be questionable as a general characterization. If applied to the subjects at issue here, it is exactly correct. The principal analytic concept of Hobbes's social philosophy is fear (*metus*). Two of his fundamental arguments, to which this concept is crucial, concern compulsion and the will, and justice. His frame of reference on these subjects is very largely Aristotle's *Ethics*. He uses the terms and alludes to some of the examples of *Ethics*, III, and *Ethics*, V, only to replace Aristotle's conclusions with his own, contrary, conclusions. In support of the latter, he draws on another literary source familiar to the scholastics, introducing, one after the other, the libertarian economic principles of the Roman law, which they had fought for so long and so persistently to keep at bay. No other author active in this crucial formative period of modern thought did anything even remotely similar. For the history of economics, in accounts of which Hobbes seldom appears as other than a background figure, if at all, it is an intervention of vital importance.

8.2   Necessitation, compulsion, and the will

Regardless of how the structural relation between the main parts of Hobbes's philosophical system is to be understood, that is, whether he

---

[1] V,64.
[2] Spragens, 1973, 43.

shaped his metaphysics so as to support his political philosophy, or shaped the latter as a necessary consequence of the former, or developed them independently of each other, the logic of the system requires that actions proceeding from fear are conceived of as entirely voluntary. Hobbes therefore insists on this in his three main philosophical works, *The Elements of Law, De cive*, and *Leviathan*, and it is one of the subjects explored in his discussion with Bishop Bramhall.[3] All human action is movement, and all movement is necessitated, that is, determined or caused by prior movement, though Hobbes recognizes the existence of a first cause, an unmoved mover, who is God.[4] Voluntary actions are actions that have their beginning in the will.[5] They are the result of deliberation, that is, the alternate appearance in the mind of appetites and aversions associated with a thing, a successive consideration of good and evil consequences of doing it and not doing it.[6] In such deliberation, the last appetite, or aversion, is the will.[7] A voluntary action is thus in a sense self-determined, by the will, as one of its causes, but the will itself is not free in the sense that it is not necessitated.[8] It is as much necessitated as anything else. All actions, even of free and voluntary agents, are necessitated. Liberty from necessity is meaningless.[9] Freedom, or liberty, should rather be defined with reference to external opposition; it is the absence of impediments

[3] In view of the many editions of Hobbes's works in circulation, I shall simply refer, by volume and page, to the Molesworth editions of the Latin *Opera* (with the prefix L) and the English *Works* (without a prefix). The following works are quoted (some titles abbreviated). Latin: *Vita* (L I,lxxxv–xcix); *De homine* (L II,1–132); *De cive* (L II,133–432); *Leviathan* (L III). English: *De cive* (II, translated as *Philosophical Rudiments*, but, following the convention, I shall refer to the English version as *De cive* as well); *Leviathan* (III); *The Elements of Law* (IV,1–228, as two works, under different titles); *An Answer to Bishop Bramhall* (IV,283–384); *The Questions Concerning Liberty, Necessity and Chance* (V, containing an earlier piece, *Of Liberty and Necessity*, with Bramhall's replies and Hobbes's animadversions); *A Dialogue between a Philosopher and a Student of the Common Laws of England* (VI,1–160); *Behemoth* (VI,161–418); *The Whole Art of Rhetoric* (VI,419–528); *Decameron Physiologicorum* (VII,69–177); *Six Lessons to the Professors of the Mathematics* (VII,181–356).

[4] III,198; V,450.

[5] IV,68–9.

[6] III,47–8; V,358.

[7] III,48–9; IV,68; V,317; 360.

[8] II, 68–9; IV,69.

[9] V,47; 56; 106; 229; 329; 373; 424.

of motion.[10] This applies to inanimate matter as well as to rational creatures. Water has no liberty to run when enclosed in a jar. In a river it is enclosed by the banks but is free (though necessitated) to run downward between the banks. Similarly, a prisoner's liberty may be impeded by walls or by chains, but there is greater liberty, in the sense of freedom of movement, in a large prison than in a narrow one.[11]

All deliberate actions are voluntary. Spontaneous actions are of two kinds, namely, certain involuntary actions done without prior deliberation or election and all deliberate actions "where the thing that induceth the action is not fear."[12] Fear, like lust, or hope, is an element in deliberation.[13] Men call that good for which they have an appetite and evil that for which they have an aversion.[14] Fear is "an aversion, with opinion of hurt from the object."[15] Hence, "not only actions that have their beginning from covetousness, ambition, lust, or other appetites to the thing propounded; but also those that have their beginning from aversion, or fear of those consequences that follow the omission *(a metu eventum qui consequuntur facti alicuius omissionem)* are voluntary actions."[16]

To do something voluntarily but not spontaneously is, for instance, "to give one's money willingly to a thief to avoid killing."[17] Aristotle's case of the jettison of cargo is used repeatedly. Thus, in *Leviathan*: "Fear and liberty are consistent; as when a man throweth his goods into the sea for fear the ship should sink *(quando aliquis metu neufragii bona sua in mare projicit)*, he doth it nevertheless very willingly, and may refuse to do it if he will: it is therefore the action of one that was free."[18] In *The Elements of Law*: "The example of him that throweth his goods out of a ship into the sea, to save his person, is of an action altogether voluntary: for there is nothing therein involuntary but the hardness of the choice, which is not his action, but the action of the winds."[19]

In his discussion with Bishop Bramhall, Hobbes says of someone

---

[10] II,120; III,116; 196; V,62; 367; 389–90.
[11] III,196; V,264–5; 367–8.
[12] V,79.
[13] III,47–8; IV, 68; V,358.
[14] III,41; IV,32.
[15] III,43 (L III,44: "*Aversio* cum opinione damni secuturi, *metus*"). Cp. L II,104: "Si incumbente bono concipimus modum aliquem quo amittatur, vel si malum aliquod illi connexum trahi imaginamur, *metus* dicitur."
[16] III,49 (L III,49); cp. II,63; IV,92; V,260.
[17] V,79.
[18] III,197 (L III,160).
[19] IV,69.

whose fear makes him willing to jettison cargo, that he is compelled.[20] The terms *vis absoluta* and *vis compulsiva* are not used by Hobbes, but the legal distinction is clearly drawn and maintained throughout his works. He accuses the bishop of obscuring it by calling compulsion force. "I call it fear of force, or of damage to be done by force, by which fear a man's will is framed to somewhat to which he had no will before."[21] This is an unconditional endorsement of *coactus volui*. Force eliminates the will; compulsion does not. Hobbes goes to great lengths insisting on this. As with the early Latin Aristotle commentators, the criterion is "election."[22]

When a man is compelled, for example, to subject himself to an enemy or to die, he hath still election left in him, and a deliberation to bethink which of these two he can better endure; and he that is led to prison by force, hath election, and may deliberate, whether he will be haled and trained on the ground, or make use of his feet.[23]

Bramhall introduces Aristotle's notion of mixed actions to describe behavior such as that of the captain who jettisons cargo. In the given situation, such actions are voluntary, but "hypothetically, supposing a man were not in that distress, they are involuntary."[24] Hobbes, who was not above that sort of thing, pounces upon this unfortunate formulation, pretending to misunderstand his opponent and, by implication, Aristotle: How can the throwing of cargo overboard be said to be involuntary supposing there was no storm, considering that no such action would then be performed at all?[25] One critic remarks that the doctrine criticized in Bramhall was held by Hobbes himself when he wrote *The Elements of Law*.[26] This is a little misleading. It is true that Hobbes, in the earlier work, describes some actions as mixed, but the mixture is quite different from that of *Ethics*, III:

Voluntary actions and omissions are such as have beginning in the will; all other are involuntary, or mixed voluntary; involuntary, such as he doth by necessity of nature, as when he is pushed, or falleth, and thereby doth good or hurt to

---

[20] V,248.

[21] V,290.

[22] See section 1.2.

[23] V,272; cp. V,287.

[24] V,275–6.

[25] V,288. A note in Hobbes's handwritten summary of the *Ethics* (Chatsworth A.8, p. 8) proves him to have been well familiar with what Aristotle meant by a "mixed" act.

[26] Hood, 1964, 47.

another: mixed, such as participate of both; as when a man is carried to prison, going is voluntary, to the prison, involuntary.[27]

We must assume that the prisoner has elected to make use of his feet rather than being "haled and trained on the ground." Thus subjected to *vis compulsiva*, he walks voluntarily, but to get him to prison, the guards subject him to *vis absoluta* as well, pushing him in the right direction, against his will. What is mixed here are two kinds of motion, one voluntary, the other involuntary, being caused by the two kinds of *vis* of the medieval legal traditions.

Hobbes's familiarity with one of these traditions is demonstrated by an observation made in continuation of the lines where he criticizes Bramhall for confusing compulsion and force. It takes us back to the canonistic doctrine of sin and the will: "Force taketh away the sin, because the action is not his that is forced, but his that forceth. It is not always so in compulsion; because, in this case, a man electeth the less evil under the notion of good."[28] Culpability, however, was a secondary issue. Hobbes was mainly concerned with compulsion and the will from the point of view of justice.

8.3   Justice

Because compelled actions are voluntary, it follows that compelled instantaneous exchange of goods and services is voluntary as well. To Hobbes, this was merely a trivial limiting case. His preoccupation with fear was due to the role that it plays in making and keeping covenants. In the state of nature, it is men's fear of one another, combined with the rational instinct of self-preservation, that causes men to covenant and to institute the mighty Leviathan to keep peace among them. Generally speaking, a covenant is a contract with a time internal. It may involve two parties or several. If one or more parties to a contract perform first, they must trust the remaining party or parties to perform later according to the terms agreed upon. In *De cive*, Hobbes states this in economic terms: A covenant involves credit (*credo*: I trust).[29] Many economic contracts are, of course, formally of this nature. Now granted that a covenant is voluntary at the time when it is made, even if made from fear, the crux of Hobbes's theory is that it is also binding in the future. Hobbes insists that this is true even in the state of nature. "To

[27] IV, 68–9.
[28] V,290–1.
[29] II,20 (L II,173: "Ubi vero vel alteri, vel utrique creditur"); cp. also III,121; IV,90.

perform contracts, or to keep trust" is one of the laws of nature, a requirement in order to establish peace and to end the senseless war of all against all.[30] To break a covenant is illogical, says Hobbes; to go back on one's word is somewhat like that which in scholastic disputes is called an absurdity – it is to contradict oneself, much as when someone by argument is driven to deny an assertion that was previously maintained.[31] These propositions have been variously received by critics of Hobbes's political philosophy. Once commonwealth is instituted, however, it is possible to some extent to bypass them, because the sovereign is then empowered and authorized to see that private contracts are kept. A man "ought to perform for his promise sake," says Hobbes in *De cive*, but the law "compels him to make good his promise for fear of the punishment appointed by the law."[32]

This picture may seem bleak, indeed. Fear reigns throughout. Men are compelled to make contracts from fear of what would come to pass if they decline (for instance, borrow at usury so as not to be short of money for food or clothing), and they are compelled to perform from fear of legal repercussions (settle with usury in order to stay out of prison), all done voluntarily. But this is a caricature of Hobbes. One of the benefits of commonwealth is that the sovereign may prohibit certain contracts or may release contractors from unreasonable obligations. In *Leviathan*, Hobbes considers a case in point: "Covenants entered into by fear, in the condition of mere nature, are obligatory. . . . And even in commonwealths, if I be forced to redeem myself from a thief by promising him money, I am bound to pay it, till the civil law discharge me."[33] In other words, while embracing *coactus volui*, Hobbes recognizes *actio quod metus causa* as well, at least in principle, the assumption in this quotation being that the sovereign will annul claims thus obtained by duress. In the particular case of extortion by a thief, it is reasonable to think that he would indeed do so, though it may be worth noting that the Latin version of *Leviathan* (which is the later one) does not offer a direct translation of the last line but reads, *nisi lex civilis prohibeat* ("unless the civil law should prohibit it").[34] Moreover, what the sovereign would permit or prohibit in cases of economic compulsion is a different matter altogether.

To keep valid covenant is justice. Breach of covenant is injury or

---

[30] II,29–30; cp. III,130; IV,95.
[31] II,31; cp. III,119; IV,96.
[32] II,185.
[33] III,126–7; cp. also II,23–4; IV,92.
[34] L III,109.

injustice. This famous definition, frequently stated,[35] may seem much too narrow, but it is broader than it sounds. The fundamental covenant is the social contract, whereby the sovereign is appointed and authorized. The sovereign will enact civil laws. These laws are, so to speak, part of the bargain. From the natural obligation to seek peace by making a social compact, there follows the artificial obligation to keep the civil laws. Hence, everything that is done in accordance with civil law is just, and everything that is done against civil law is unjust.[36] It is true that Hobbes offers another definition of justice as well. It is that of Ulpian in the *Digest*.[37] Hobbes most often states it as follows, with minor variants: "Justice is the constant will of giving to every man his own."[38] The word "own" suggests property and gives an economic emphasis to this definition. Hobbes considered property to be a creature of the civil law.[39] In the war of all against all, no one can claim property in a thing that others cannot claim as well. The sovereign assigns and protects property. At one point, Hobbes attributes Ulpian's definition to Aristotle.[40] At another point, he presents it with a wording that is also common in other English translations of Ulpian: "Justice . . . is a constant will of giving to every man his due."[41] Replacing "own" with "due" generalizes the definition and lessens its economic emphasis. It also provides an opportunity to pinpoint the essential differences between Aristotle's and Hobbes's conceptions of justice. Aristotle asks what is "due" in any given instance; in the case of an economic contract, justice pertains to its terms, and the respective "dues" of the parties should be equal. Hobbes, on the other hand, takes "due" as voluntarily agreed on by the parties involved and focuses on "giving," that is, on keeping the contract according to its terms.

The libertarian legal maxims quoted in Parts I and II are fully embraced by Hobbes. The proposition that no one suffers injustice voluntarily follows immediately from his definitions of justice and the voluntary and are to be found in all three main statements of his political philosophy.[42] Within the limits of the civil law, it follows as well

---

[35] II,30; 34; 101; III,130–1; 134; 137–8; 254; IV,95; 98; 140.

[36] II,151; III,251; VI,29; 219.

[37] D.1,1,10, pr.

[38] VI,29; cp. II,vi; 267; III,234; 254.

[39] II,265–6; III,131; IV,216.

[40] VI,8.

[41] II,301.

[42] Poignantly, in *The Elements of Law.* "Volenti non fit iniuria" (IV,140). Repeated, in the Latin *De cive*, copied, with a translation, in the English

that anyone is moderator and arbiter of his own thing. In Hobbes's words, in *The Elements of Law*, "Every man may dispose of his own and transfer the same at this pleasure."[43] As a corollary to these principles, the traditional scholastic concept of a just price must lose its meaning. In each of the three works, Hobbes examines the two branches into which Aristotle's particular justice was conventionally divided. In *The Elements of Law*, he has this to say about the branch considered to apply in economic exchange: "And for commutative justice placed in buying and selling, though the thing bought be unequal to the price given for it, yet forasmuch as both the buyer and the seller are made judges of the value, and are thereby both satisfied, there can be no injury done on either side, neither party having trusted, or covenanted with the other."[44]

The subject is discussed at some length in *De cive*:

The justice of actions is commonly distinguished into two kinds, commutative and distributive; the former whereof, they say, consists in arithmetical, the latter in geometrical proportion; and that is conversant in exchanging, in buying, selling, borrowing, lending, location and conduction, and other acts whatsoever belonging to contractors; where, if there be an equal return made, hence, they say, springs a commutative justice: but this is busied about the dignity and merits of men. . . . But what is all this to justice? For neither if I sell my goods for as much as I can get for them, do I injure the buyer, who sought and desired them of me; neither if I divide more of what is mine to him who deserves less, so long as I give the other what I have agreed for, do I wrong to either.[45]

And in *Leviathan*:

Commutative [justice] they place in the equality of value of the things con-tracted for; and distributive, in the distribution of equal benefit, to men of equal merit. As if it were injustice to sell dearer than we buy; or to give more to a man than he merits. The value of all things contracted for, is measured by the appetite of the contractors: and therefore the just value, is that which they be contented to give. And merit. . . . To speak properly, commutative justice is the justice of a contractor; that is, a performance of covenant in buying and selling,

version: "Volenti non fit iniuria, the willing man receives no injury" (II,35; cp. L II,186). More elaborately in *Leviathan*, perhaps suggesting knowledge as well as will: "Whatsoever is done to a man, conformable to his own will signified to the doer, is no injury to him" (III,137; cp. L III,115: "Quod volenti fit, iniuria non est").

[43] IV,151.

[44] IV,98.

[45] II,33–4. The Latin version recalls the literal value maxim: "Nam neque si res nostras vendamus quanti possumus . . ." (L II,185).

hiring and letting for hire, lending and borrowing, exchanging, bartering, and other acts of contract.[46]

The reference, in *The Elements of Law* (the earliest of these works), to a thing bought being unequal to the price given for it might be read as an acknowledgment of a different principle of valuation than the relative bargaining powers of buyer and seller. Because it is not mentioned in the later versions, there might be a suggestion of a development in Hobbes's thought on the subject of commutative justice, an increasing emancipation from scholastic influence, but it is more likely that he is simply becoming surer of his own ground, less in need of referring to the paradigm being reversed. One of the most lucid contemporary Hobbes scholars has made the contrary suggestion that, by referring in *Leviathan* to the just value as that which the parties "be contented to give," Hobbes has "implicitly admitted an idea of 'the just' as meaning 'the fair' and not simply the performance of covenant."[47] In comment on that, reference may once more be had to the Latin version, which, literally translated, defines the just value as that to which the parties *consent*, not that with which they are *contented*.[48] To Hobbes, there is consent even in the case of *metus*, and justice is to pay the price consented to.

8.4   A blueprint of *laissez-faire?*

Justice, that is, the keeping of covenant, is not the only law of nature postulated by Hobbes. In each statement of his political philosophy, he presents a list of such laws. They vary in number, but their gist is the same. Laws of nature are precepts of reason, and what reason first and foremost tells us is that we should, for our own safety and preservation, seek peace.[49] Repeatedly, these various laws are summed up in the Golden Rule of Reciprocity, sometimes stated in the positive form, sometimes in the negative form, sometimes in both forms together: Do (not) to another, what you would (not) have done to yourself.[50] The problem of interpreting Hobbes's political philosophy really starts with the question of how the laws of nature apply in commonwealth, once the sovereign is instituted and authorized to make and enforce civil

---

[46] III,137–8.
[47] Raphael, 1990, 166.
[48] L III,116: "Pretium omium rerum contrahentium appetitu aestimatur; pretiumque iustum est in quod ambo emptor et venditor consentiunt."
[49] II,16–17; III,116–17; IV,85–7.
[50] II,45; 62; III,118; 144; IV,107.

laws. Most interpretations can be placed somewhere between two extremes, which I propose to examine in this and the following section. My purpose in doing this is to draw attention to a point generally overlooked in Hobbes studies, namely, that in one respect, of great importance to economics, the choice between these extremes makes little difference. It should be noted, before we start, that neither of them (nor any of those in between) can account for all that Hobbes says, but each of them is reasonable in that it finds support in some of what he says.

In both cases, it is useful to distinguish between two different kinds of obligation in Hobbes. The fear of death places upon men a prudential and natural obligation to seek peace and, particularly, to keep covenants. Once commonwealth is instituted, there is added a nonprudential and artificial obligation to obey the laws of the authorized sovereign. According to one extreme interpretation, this is all there is to social virtue. The sovereign makes laws and declares them publicly, "by which every man may know what may be called his, what another's, what just, what unjust, what honest, what dishonest, what good, what evil."[51] "The King tells us what is sin, in that he tells us what is law."[52] "The law of nature and the civil law contain each other, and are of equal extent."[53] "The laws of commonwealth . . . are the ground and measure of all true morality."[54] Effectively blotting out what could be found to the contrary, quotations like these formed the basis of what used to be the common reading of Hobbes; it shaped his reputation during his lifetime and for posterity until well into the present century. Among those who shared it was Adam Smith:

Mr. Hobbes . . . endeavored to establish a system of morals by which the consciences of men might be subjected to the civil power and which represented the will of the magistrate as the only proper rule of conduct. . . . Obedience to his will, according to him, constituted civil government, without which there could be no virtue, and consequently it too was the foundation and essence of virtue.[55]

It may be interesting to note that Kant said something rather similar about Mandeville.[56] It is an irony of economic doctrinal history that this conception of social virtue came to be associated with the strain of the

---

[51] II,77.
[52] IV,379.
[53] III,253.
[54] VII,75–6.
[55] *Lectures*: ed. Cannan, p. 2.
[56] *Kritik der praktischen Vernunft: Werke*, VII,153.

classical tradition that Smith transmitted from Mandeville. This is mainly due to a corollary, which is, at least in its most radical form, a non sequitur, but which has proved to be remarkably persistent both among adherents and among opponents of classical and neoclassical ideology. It runs somewhat as follows: Natural law commands that we seek peace in all things that we do, but in commonwealth, the civil law takes care of this for us. If any action of mine had threatened peace, it would have been prohibited by the civil law. Hence, when not thus restricted, I can do whatever I please to further my own interests. "Law is a fetter; right is freedom."[57] "In all kinds of actions by the laws praetermitted, men have the liberty of doing what their own reasons shall suggest, for the most profitable to themselves."[58]

How far this liberty actually extends depends on what the sovereign sees fit to allow or prohibit. Hobbes's statement that the government should concern itself only with measures that secure "peace and common defense"[59] suggested to Taylor, in an early work, an anticipation of a "negative *laisser aller* doctrine,"[60] but on Hobbes's premises, this does not necessarily follow. Peace and defense can be seen from the sovereign's point of view to call for quite a bit of government activity or very little. In his seminal study, Strauss emphasized the wide range of adaptability of Hobbes's doctrine, which could be said to expound "the ideal both of the bourgeois-capitalist development and of the socialist movement."[61]

Recent decades have witnessed a commendable new direction in Hobbes studies. Led by British scholars, the search is on for the genuine, historical Hobbes, in his very special and highly turbulent seventeenth-century background. The ideological potential of his system, however, continues to engage those who take the longer view, and the majority position among scholars about Hobbes's significance in this respect (and certainly the popular position) is still as a herald of *laissez-faire*. There is a certain paradox involved in this. Whereas, in the history of political science, Hobbes is seen as an advocate of absolutism, the emphasis being on the potentially limitless power of the sovereign, in the history of economic science, the emphasis is on the potentially almost limitless freedom granted the individual by that power and on the legitimacy of self-seeking protected by it. A major theme in social

[57] II,186; cp. III,117; IV,222–3.
[58] III,199; cp. III,206; 275.
[59] III,158; cp. III,235.
[60] Taylor, 1908, 101.
[61] Strauss, 1936, 1.

philosophy in the centuries prior to the triumph of capitalism and the establishment of classical economics was how to guide human pride and greed from negative and destructive activity into positive and productive channels. Hobbes did not envisage an inherent benevolent mechanism that might turn a free economy, protected only against fraud and physical force, into such a channel. In his pithy account of this gestation period of modern capitalism, Hirschman nevertheless fits Hobbes into his scheme as a special case. What in actual fact must be an evolutionary process is achieved by Hobbes by "founding a state so constituted that the problems created by passionate men are solved once and for all."[62]

Indications of a "channeling of passions into interests" in Hobbes's thought may then be sought in his description of social conflict. There is in all mankind "a perpetual and restless desire for power after power,"[63] but this desire is partly of an economic character, and power has an economic dimension. The value of a thing is what will be given for its use; the value of a man what will be given for the use of his power.[64] This power is a man's present means to obtain some future good.[65] Riches are power; need ("a desire, joined with grief, for the absence of the thing desired")[66] is dishonorable as a sign of powerlessness.[67] Society is for glory, but also for gain.[68] The most frequent reason why men desire to hurt one another is scarcity; it "ariseth hence, that many men at the same time have an appetite to the same thing."[69] Men's quarrels are caused by competition for gain, besides diffidence (for safety) and glory (for reputation).[70] Glory is the passion of the warrior class; gain is the passion of the merchant class. The desire for peace is universal and rational as Hobbes presents it, but it is obvious that the merchant will desire it more than the warrior. Peace will inactivate the latter, whereas it will activate the former; it is a requirement if the merchant is to ply his trade. Peace, therefore, is capable of transforming society, channeling war into commerce and changing men's aims from glory to gain or, perhaps, rather from glory in conquest to glory in wealth.

---

[62] Hirschman, 1978, 31.
[63] III,85–6.
[64] IV,39; cp. III,76.
[65] III,74.
[66] VI,461.
[67] IV,39; cp. III,79.
[68] II,5.
[69] II,8.
[70] III,112; cp. III,116.

The line of interpretation recorded in this section was brought to its ultimate conclusion by Macpherson's representation of Hobbes as the political theorist of "possessive individualism." Hobbes's man in the state of nature, according to him, is not some rude barbarian but "civilized man with only the restraint of law removed." Moreover, the "socially acquired behavior and desires" assumed by Hobbes are not those of any society but specifically those of seventeenth-century England, which "approximated closely to a possessive market society," that is, one made up of individual proprietors who "engage in continual, nonviolent competition for the power of others, which compels the others to enter the competition." What Hobbes only has to add in order to complete this picture of society is civil law, which defines justice, and the kind of justice required to protect these possessive individuals is, of course, contractual justice, the keeping of covenants. "Justice itself is reduced to a market concept."[71]

This is a Marxist interpretation of Hobbes and implicitly a criticism of the bourgeois morality that allegedly informed his analysis of man and society. As historical reconstruction, it has reaped a certain amount of negative criticism, for bias and for selective reading of Hobbes. As a powerful statement of one possible line of ideological development suggested by his works, it is not to be ignored. A single observation made against it by an early critic deserves to be mentioned here because it directly concerns the main topic of this book. One of the Marxist grievances against bourgeois economics is its failure to recognize the analogy between economic and physical compulsion, but by insisting that all acts performed under compulsion are voluntary, Hobbes, in fact, recognizes it:

Hobbes has the advantage of a consistent position, which serves to remind us that, if we shift our attention from the voluntariness of the act to the appetites or aversions which prompted it, we will find no qualitative distinction between actions impelled by physical fear and those prompted by economic coercion. In sum, Hobbes, far from subscribing to one of the most fundamental jurisprudential assumptions of laisser-faire capitalist society, has gone a long way toward removing its philosophical basis altogether.[72]

The obvious retort to this is that the analogy is stated in the reverse. Hobbes's position is consistent in that he extends *coactus volui* to include physical compulsion, rather than rejecting *coactus volui* in the case of economic compulsion, which would be the way to eradicate the basis of *laissez-faire*. Moreover, it all still depends on what the sovereign will

[71] Macpherson, 1970, 29; 22; 60–1; 64.
[72] Thomas, 1965, 235.

choose to permit or prohibit. Some remarks made elsewhere in his works may indicate an inclination to limit the exercise of private economic power, but the libertarian color of his specific comments on Aristotelian commutative justice and of his appeal to Roman law against the scholastic tradition is unquestionable. No Marxist, as far as I know, ever laid claim to Hobbes. Marx certainly did not do so.[73] Anyhow, if sympathy with those in economic need is to be searched for in Hobbes, the best place to look is not his doctrine of justice, but some of what he says about charity.

8.5   The role of charity

In an article published many years after the book previously quoted on the *laisser-aller* implications of Hobbes, Taylor initiated another line of interpretation, soon to be further pursued by Warrender and now generally known as the Taylor–Warrender thesis. According to these authors, the moral law, to Hobbes, is prior and superior to all human institutions and, in a certain sense, cannot be overruled or invalidated. Hobbes, therefore, cannot be understood to mean that moral obligation is limited to justice, that is, to keeping covenants and generally obeying the civil law. When the sovereign has laid down no specific command, the individual citizen is still obliged by the natural law summed up in the Golden Rule.[74] The sovereign provides an official and authentic interpretation of the natural law and thereby places his authority behind it. This interpretation, however, cannot cover everything; for the rest, each man must interpret it for himself, being accountable to his own conscience and to God.[75] "Laws of nature . . . are delivered by God in holy Scriptures."[76] "Because the law of nature is eternal, . . . all facts contrary to any moral virtue, can never cease to be sin."[77] "Whatsoever is done contrary to private conscience, is then a sin, when the laws have left him to his own liberty."[78] "In such cases where no special law is made, the law of nature keepeth its place."[79] Hobbes sometimes gives the impression that we are only in the forum of conscience obliged in the narrow sense of intention; however, ac-

---

[73] Cp., for instance, *Capital*, I,170; 390.
[74] Taylor, 1965, 42.
[75] Warrender, 1957, 146.
[76] II,49–50; cp. III,147; IV,109.
[77] III,278–9.
[78] IV,187.
[79] IV,227.

cording to this interpretation in its most extreme form, representing the opposite to the one discussed in the preceding section, Hobbes must be understood to mean that we are also obliged to carry out the precepts of nature in action, provided that we do not thereby break the civil law. I want to proceed from this assumption to a conclusion of great importance for the development of economic ethics and ideology in the classical tradition, because it brings us quite close to what is normally deduced from the opposite, traditional interpretation of Hobbes.

Discussing natural law, Hobbes would compile lists of virtues, "modesty, equity, trust, humanity, mercy,"[80] "justice, gratitude, modesty, equity, mercy."[81] Sometimes he would short-list them, naming one or two virtues in addition to justice. Thus, in *The Elements of Law*, he states that "equity, justice, and honor, contain all virtues whatsoever."[82] In the dedicatory epistle of *De cive*, he extols "justice and charity, the twin sisters of peace."[83] These phrases are not to be taken too seriously in themselves (Hobbes was fond of the bon mot); however, they indicate two dichotomies that are central to his political thought. In *Behemoth*, Hobbes calls an action vicious if it is "unconformable to the laws in such men as are subject to the law, or . . . unconformable to equity or charity in all men whatsoever."[84] Hobbes had quite a bit to say about equity. Justice versus equity is a legal dichotomy; the terms denote different aspects of jurisprudence. In a broader context, they are two different aspects of the same virtue. This is how they are to be understood when placed opposite charity. Justice versus charity has a twofold signification. Charity is "the greatest of God's commandments,"[85] and it is the sum and essence of purely moral virtue, founded on an obligation independent of civil law and unenforceable by civil law. In the Latin *De homine*, the last work by Hobbes that treats systematically of moral philosophy, there is a remarkable statement to this effect: "The moral virtue measurable by civil laws, which are different in different states, is only justice and equity; and that which we measure merely by natural law, is only charity. . . . But all virtues are contained in justice and charity."[86]

---

[80] II,48.
[81] III,146.
[82] IV,111.
[83] II,ii; cp. also VI,236.
[84] VI,218.
[85] VII,352.
[86] L II,117–18: "Virtus autem moralis, quam quidem mensurare possumus

Charity as a virtue is associated with charity as a function or an activity. Almsgiving, says Hobbes, that is, to help someone in need, is not done according to the civil law but according to the divine law, the precept of which is charity.[87] Charity in the sense of almsgiving is sometimes "an action that is good in itself,"[88] an unusual line from Hobbes's pen, but Hobbes felt strongly about this. His own charitableness impressed his contemporaries. An important point is lost if the famous episode in Aubrey is cited merely on account of the psychology by which Hobbes sought to explain his own behavior.[89] As regards private charity in others, he did not think much of it and suggested that the destitute be provided for by the commonwealth.[90] When men bestow benefits on strangers, it is often not charity, but either contract (purchasing friendship) or fear (purchasing peace).[91]

On Hobbes's philosophical premises, it is not unreasonable to single out as the greatest of God's commandments a virtue oriented to the supply of material needs. This aspect may no longer be as prominent when we think of charity as it used to be, but it was not new with Hobbes, and it still persists. Justice versus charity is (if not exclusively, then to a large extent) an economic dichotomy. Justice is the virtue of the marketplace. Charity is the virtue by which we share our surpluses with those who are too poor to participate in the market. In prescholastic thought, this distinction was not at all clear. It was established in the thirteenth century by a confluence of ideas transmitted by Gratian, Peter Lombard, and the translators of Aristotle. The scholastics would continue to preach charity, as the Fathers of the Church had done before them, but in a market economy, to base a systematic doctrine of ethics in exchange on charity would run counter to the purpose of maintaining a workable Christian economic system among fallen men. In practical applications, the ethical ideal of the Gospels must compromise with the facts of human nature, and it is a sad fact that the charitable must count on uncharitable response from the majority of their fellow men. Preaching charity as a general norm of market conduct would reach only those who desired to be virtuous, and the end effect

legibus civilibus, quae diversis civitatibus diversae sunt, sola est iustitia et
aequitas; quam autem mensuramus per leges mere naturales, charitas sola
est. . . . Contineri autem virtutes omnes in iustitia et charitate."
[87] IV,223.
[88] VI,37.
[89] *Brief Lives*: 157.
[90] III,334.
[91] IV,49.

would be an accumulation of wealth in the hands of the vicious. The most that could be aimed at in the moral sphere were some reasonable standards of justice, which assured that each party to an exchange received his due. This, on the one hand, puts a less heavy moral obligation on each party; on the other hand, the onus of omission is all the more severe. The unjust are failing in the duty of giving up what rightly belongs to another. The uncharitable are merely failing in the duty of giving up what is rightly their own.

And so the Church would proceed against usury, which is unjust profit on loans, and by and by against unjust prices and eventually against unjust wages, establishing norms and criteria regarding just terms of exchange, the primary purpose of which was to combat and limit the exploitation of need. These norms could be to some extent enforced in the Church's own external courts, but beyond all human jurisdiction, a stricter code of justice in exchange would remain as a purely moral obligation, for which lenders and borrowers, sellers and buyers, employers and employees would be answerable only to God, in the internal court of their own conscience. This was the economic justice propounded by the scholastic masters, preached in popular sermons, and explained in the handbooks for confessors. Gradually, in the late Middle Ages, when the fear of God was on the wane, it came to be realized that moral admonishments were an ineffective bridle on avarice; a workable economic ethics must be established on a different basis. A century or more after Hobbes, the early proponents of classical liberalism imagined that they had solved this problem by postulating the existence of an inherent benevolent mechanism that turned private avarice into a social blessing.

Thomas Hobbes anticipated no such vision. Hobbes, who, as he tells us, had shared his mother's womb with *metus*,[92] realizing that the fear of God was not sufficient, called for a mortal god who could scare men into behaving morally. Civil law, however, cannot regulate everything; recourse must be had to natural law as well. Hobbes, like the scholastics, appealed to charity. But Hobbes's natural law could not reach the marketplace, for, unlike the scholastics, he could not appeal to justice. He had stripped justice of all relationship with terms of economic contracts. Justice was the keeping of the contract according to its terms, voluntarily agreed upon whatever need had compelled it, an obligation fully enforced, if permitted, by the civil law. When the market is closed, there is always charity. From Locke to the latterday libertarians, charity

---

[92] L I,lxxxvi: "Atque metum tantum concepit tunc mea mater, Ut pareret geminos, meque metumque simul."

will reappear as a means of distributing wealth justly gained, but justice as a moral virtue, transcending civil law, disappeared with Hobbes from economic doctrine, leaving a void that remains the same, regardless of how men's obligation under natural law is to be understood in civil society.

CHAPTER 9

The economics of natural law

9.1 Natural law

The transition from medieval to modern thought on the economic subjects analyzed in this book is considered, by most doctrinal historians, to be related to a development in the theory of natural law. Thomas Hobbes is not in the mainstream of this development. In some respects, his approach harks back to that of the scholastics. Repeatedly, the various natural laws enumerated by him are crystallized in the Golden Rule of Reciprocity. Almost exactly half a millennium before the publication of *De cive*, Gratian defined natural law on the opening page of the *Decretum*: "Natural law is that which is contained in the Scriptures and the Gospels, by which anyone is commanded to do to another what he would have done to himself and prohibited to do to another what he would not wish to have done to himself."[1] In the context in which we quoted Henry of Ghent on economics, he states that "the justice of contracts pertains to natural law."[2] Peter Olivi, drawing on Henry, in his treatise on buying and selling refers to natural law, which forbids us to do to others what we would not have done to ourselves "according to our just and natural instinct."[3] It was not least this formal similarity between the traditional natural law approach and that of Hobbes that caused the substance of some of his precepts and the conclusions that he drew from them to appear so outrageous in the eyes of seventeenth-century ecclesiastics and, indeed, in the eyes of most of Hobbes's contemporaries. By naming God the prime unmoved mover of his deterministic world system, Hobbes was felt by these critics to make a similar travesty of the traditional idea of the eternal law.

In the course of the century following the resumption of Roman law studies and the publication of the *Decretum*, one of the concerns of the scholastics was to explain the nature of law and to clarify the distinction

---

[1] *Decretum*, I,1, pr.
[2] *Quodl.* I,40: V, 219.
[3] Q.1: 254. Cp. also the quotation from Scotus in section 6.1.

158

between different kinds of law. These enquiries peaked with Thomas Aquinas, who drew on Aristotle to supplement and systematize the ideas of the Romanists and canonists as well as those of previous theologians.[4] We may therefore take Aquinas as our medieval point of reference on the two kinds of law mentioned previously.[5] The eternal law, according to him, is the master plan of the universe, preexisting in God, who directs and controls all that happens.[6] What we now think of as the physical and chemical laws of inanimate matter are part of the eternal law, and so are as well the laws that guide the behavior of animate but irrational creatures, who feed, propagate, and tend their young, etc. According to a broad definition, however, this falls within the domain of natural law as well. Ulpian, copied in the opening title of the *Digest* and quoted by Aquinas,[7] defines the natural law as "that which all animals have been taught by nature," such as the conjunction of male and female. This does not apply to human beings alone, but is common to all living creatures on the ground, in the sea, and in the air.[8]

In other words, men are subject to the eternal law like stones, in that they fall when dropped (the law of gravity), and to the eternal-cum-natural law like brute beast (the law of animal behavior), but because they are supplied by God with reason, men are subject to the eternal-cum-natural law in a narrower sense as well. Men are able to understand the eternal law and can control their actions and the actions of others accordingly, obeying the eternal law because it directs them toward what is good. "They have a share of the eternal reason, whereby they have a natural inclination to its proper act and end; and this participation of the eternal law in the rational creature is called the natural law."[9] "There is in every man a natural inclination to act according to reason: and this is to act according to virtue. Consequently, considered thus, all acts of virtue are of the natural law: since each one's reason naturally dictates to him to act virtuously."[10]

Apart from the problems associated with the Socratic moral paradox

---

[4] On natural law in the canonistic and theological traditions culminating with Aquinas, cp. the classical study by Lottin. On Aquinas's doctrine in particular, cp. also O'Connor, 1967, 57–79, and d'Entrèves, 1970, 37–92.

[5] Omitting his discussions of divine and human law, which are important enough for the history of legal philosophy but less directly relevant here.

[6] *Sum. theol.*, I–II,93,1–5: VII,162–6.

[7] 94,2: VII,170.

[8] D.1,1,1,3.

[9] *Sum. theol.*, I–II,91,2: VII,154.

[10] 94,3: VII,170.

suggested by the latter proposition,[11] a modern critic might perhaps be inclined to object that this doctrine involves a confusion between law in two fundamentally different senses of the word. Insofar as it applies to inanimate matter and, to all accounts and purposes, insofar as it applies to nonrational animal behavior as well, the eternal law is a descriptive (or explanatory or predictive) law. Such laws tell us what happens or will happen, or why, but the participation of the eternal law in the rational creature, that is, Aquinas's natural law in its narrow sense, is not (or at least not mainly) a law of this character. It is true that an understanding of the eternal law by the light of reason may condition the behavior of some men toward virtue so firmly that it can be predicted (and explained and described), but the natural law is primarily a law of the same character as human positive law. It is a prescriptive (or normative) law. Such laws aim at directing and controlling behavior. As Aquinas has it, the natural law is reason's *dictate* to man to act virtuously.[12] In its various fields of application, for instance in the field of economics, it served for the scholastic moral philosophers and theologians as a basis for the establishment of ideal behavioral *norms*, like those discussed in Part II.

The first point that has to be made here is that an accusation of not taking account of such an important distinction between essentially different kinds of law is not one that can reasonably be laid at the door of any medieval author. The distinction is a modern one. According to an earlier, finalistic conception of the world, Aquinas's concept of natural inclinations can be made the basis of a different, uniform theory of law. Not only rational man, but all of God's creation, is infused with its proper natural inclination. Thus, what we would see as the subject of our descriptive laws of animal behavior was to the medieval theologian the acting out of natural inclinations on the part of animals.[13] Having said that, I hasten to add that a confusion between description and prescription was unquestionably invited by the medieval doctrine of natural law. It is also clear that such a confusion came, at a later

[11] See the opening lines of section 1.1.
[12] In order not to attribute to Thomas Aquinas a word that he did not actually use, I have altered one phrase of the most common English translation of the last quotation from the *Summa theologiae* above. What Aquinas says in the penultimate line is that *omnes actus virtutum sunt de lege naturali.* I render this neutrally "of the natural law," whereas the English Dominican Fathers, whose translation is otherwise often used, have "prescribed by the natural law."
[13] *Sum. theol.*, I–II,91,6: VII,157–8.

stage, to plague those sciences that developed from a natural-law mode of reasoning, and that economics was (and indeed still is) particularly harmed by this confusion. To that point, which is generally recognized, we must return. What I want to take up first is a different point, generally ignored, but to my mind equally important for a proper understanding of the transition from medieval to modern economic thought.

9.2   Economic laws

In the late Middle Ages, which saw speculations about natural law such as those discussed in the previous section, progress was being made in the empirical investigation of natural phenomena as well, leading eventually to the formulation of descriptive and explanatory laws in the modern sense: laws of motion, of light and color, etc. Some of the authors quoted in Part II stood in the forefront of this development. In 1941, Pope Pius XII named Albert the Great, the teacher of Aquinas, "patron saint of those who study the natural sciences." It probably never occurred to the pope to accord him a similar honor for his study of economic phenomena, but, as a matter of fact, the late Middle Ages already possessed a not inconsiderable body of knowledge about fundamental relationships in the economic sphere, and Albert stands out as one of its major contributors. The fact that such knowledge should be at hand is not surprising. Anyone who aspires to the formulation of workable norms of moral conduct in a certain area must take some account of the particular social mechanisms with which the norms are likely to interfere. Thus, for instance, scholastic criteria of justice in exchange were obviously based on the observation that price, if left unchecked, was a function of supply and demand. In the thirteenth century, the understanding of economic (as well as of natural) phenomena was still fragmentary and limited in scope. In the course of the centuries that separate Thomas Aquinas and Thomas Hobbes, it developed gradually into a certain conception (still quite hazy, it is true) of the economy as a comprehensive system. In step with this, and partly in consequence of it, norms of economic justice changed.

Different factors could be put forward to explain the breakdown of the scholastic paradigm of justice recorded toward the end of the chapters on usury, price, and wage in Part II. Material and institutional development of the economy toward early capitalistic modes of production and exchange are obvious factors. In the Catholic world, says the Italian economic historian Fanfani, the so-called spirit of capitalism is largely a matter of a "waning of faith," which is undeniably a factor as well.[14] For the norm-setters, however, whose works we have been studying, such factors operate indirectly, via an increased understanding of the mechanisms that will be touched by the norms and, by consequence, via a change in the level of moral perfection to which they find it realistic to aspire. The fundamental difference between descriptive laws in the social and natural sciences is that the former kind of laws are the aggregate expressions of human behavior, of which the latter are independent. Economists may insist that it is logically possible to envisage economies whose laws express behavior otherwise motivated, but from the very start of economics as an empirical science, realistic descriptive laws have had to be based on self-interest as the dominant motive of economic behavior. If price is a function of supply and demand, it is because buyers and sellers, on the whole, will exercise, to their own advantage, all the bargaining power the supply-and-demand situation lends them.

The scholastic norms of economic justice were designed to combat the self-interested exercise of bargaining power. They might well change with time and circumstances. The first principles of natural law merely provided a general basis for them. The simpler the economy and, equally important, the more limited the theoretical grasp of a more complex economy, the more narrowly will the scope of ethical analysis be limited to the individual loan, or sales, or labor contract, and to its consequences for the two parties immediately involved in it. To some of the early scholastics, it was still conceivable that the light of natural reason might impress on both parties to a given exchange their duty to combat avarice and to act justly. In the course of the centuries from Aquinas to Hobbes, changes in the material economy, its institutions, its "spirit," and, not least, the gradual extension of the norm-setters' theoretical grasp, all contributed to undermining this aspiration. The individual exchanger would be seen less and less as involved in a personal relationship but as confronting a system, a set of economic laws known, as a matter of empirical fact, to be driven by self-interest.

I wish to emphasize that this does not necessarily involve the conception of self-interest as socially beneficial. This is a parallel, but somewhat later, idea. What it typically involves is a certain depersonalization of the idea of the economy. This analytic depersonalization would be enhanced by the actual depersonalization that followed as a result of the development of the economy and of economic institutions. Exchange would no longer, as a rule, be conducted as a one-to-one

[14] Fanfani, 1935, 178.

confrontation between owners, typical of more primitive economies. The parties whose mutual needs and interests determined the rate of exchange more often than not would not meet face to face at all. Under these circumstances, when a faceless majority of economic actors must be expected to ignore the traditional norms of economic justice, it is counterintentional, and in a sense unfair, to demand such a moral standard of virtue from those who are still prepared to comply with it. The matter of justice in exchange is then (as Hobbes suggests) better left to the civil law, which sets a lower standard but one which can be enforced.

The emergent idea of the economy as a system governed by law finds expression in an altered interpretation of the role of the market. The different uses of this central economic concept are demonstrated in Chapters 5 and 6. In early scholasticism, the market price was an ideal norm (what a thing can be sold for, commonly, and in a public place, to many people, over several days).[15] This benchmark was intended to be used, along with other criteria such as cost, to judge whether one party to a given exchange, under different circumstances, behaved justly and did not exploit the economic need of the other party. To some of the late scholastics, the market had assumed some of its future abstract and impersonal character. The just price to them was not an ideal standard but what the forces of the market would bring about under various, empirically well-known, standard conditions: sale at auction, sale through a broker, etc. Moreover, if, in direct exchange between the interested parties, someone who approached another with a request to buy must expect a lower price than someone who is approached by another with a request to sell, this is merely a fact of life, an economic law of supply and demand.[16] It is nothing personal! No one is to blame.

In the eighteenth century, at the dawn of the British classical tradition, two Continental Jesuit moralists, prolonging the tradition of the School of Salamanca, applied this doctrine to the two cases of wage contracts examined in Chapter 7, that of the powerful professional and that of the powerless unqualified laborer. A patient's fear of death does not render an excessive doctor's fee invalid, says Claude Lacroix, commenting on Busenbaum. This is a fear arising from the man's intrinsic dilemma (*metus . . . proveniens ab intrinseca complexione hominis*). He was not compelled by anyone but entered into the contract freely.[17] Ed-

---

[15] See quotation from Bartolus in section 5.2.

[16] See section 6.4.

[17] *Theologia moralis*, III,ii,5: Vol. II, p. 248.

mund Voit, the author of another famous work on moral theology, considers the opposite case. If someone in need agrees to work for an inferior wage, he can seek no further compensation, for he was "forced by something intrinsic, for instance, on account of his poverty *(coactus ab intrinseco, v. g. ob paupertatem suam).*"[18] Fear of death and poverty are no one else's concern. Faced with an impersonal economic system, each person is on his own. Ironically, the somewhat inappropriate application of Aristotle's simile now fits the case. A person in economic need is not like the tyrant's subject but like the captain threatened by the elements.[19]

9.3   Natural rights

In its application to economics, medieval natural law doctrine was predominantly duty oriented. Another significant feature of the development of natural law philosophy in the centuries immediately preceding the origin of classical economics was a shift of emphasis from duties to rights. The two are, of course, usually (though not always) mutually corresponding, one person's right entailing one or more persons' duty, and vice versa. The change of emphasis is, therefore, best explained as the result of a change of focus from one duty-right relationship to another. The focus of medieval natural law doctrine in the economic sphere was on the immediate relationship between the parties to a given exchange. Its emphasis was on the duty of the more powerful party not to oppress the less powerful party. In the early modern era, natural law doctrine is of interest to economics mainly via developments in political philosophy, which focused on the relationship between citizen and government, its emphasis being on liberty, on the right of citizens. Right, as Hobbes has it, is liberty. Keeping Hobbes in mind, an idea of the relevance of this tradition can be had by considering briefly the works of four other leading proponents of natural rights theory, namely, Suárez (representing late scholasticism), Grotius and Pufendorf (of the Continental Protestant school), and Locke (one of the main British links to Adam Smith).

The root idea and part of the terminology of the natural rights tradition can be traced much further back through some of the authors quoted in Part II, notably Mazzolini and Summenhart, who, as we saw,

---

[18] *Theologia moralis,* I,809: p. 517.
[19] Though his terminology is different, this depersonalization following the emergence of the idea of economic laws is in line with Gordon's analysis of late scholasticism; cp. particularly his chapter on Lessius.

exerted a particularly strong influence on the School of Salamanca. It was precisely in that intellectual milieu, in which the medieval economic paradigm was gradually abandoned, that the rights doctrine emerged in its early modern form as well. Versions of it are to be found in Molina and several other authors quoted in Part II, but the definite statement of the position of this school is that of Francisco Suárez, set down in his monumental work, *De Legibus et Legislatore Deo*, formally a commentary on part of the *Prima secundae* of Aquinas. According to Suárez, the word *ius* may refer either to that which is fair and in harmony with reason or to the equity that is due to each individual as a matter of justice. In the latter sense it denotes a "right to claim, or moral power" *(actio, seu moralis facultas)*. A person may have such a right to something (for instance, right to wages of labor) or in something, as when the owner *(dominus)* of a thing is said to have property right *(dominium)* in the thing.[20] From their medieval predecessors, the early modern political philosophers inherited a conception of *dominium*, which comprises both ownership of material objects as understood here and power or authority over men.[21] Suárez's main contribution to political thought takes it in the latter sense. Man has an intrinsic right to liberty *(ius libertatis)*.[22] Being lord of his liberty *(dominus suae libertatis)*, he may alienate it.[23] A whole people may do so as well, submitting to a sovereign.[24] Political society can be conceived of as instituted by contract;[25] however, man is constitutionally a social animal requiring civil life.[26] This account is so similar and yet so different from that of Hobbes that it is not surprising that Hobbes should single Suárez out as the leading latterday exponent of the hated School-divinity.

It is in the theory of property, however, that the natural rights tradition touches upon economics. Citizens' rights include, and in some authors are presented as mainly consisting of, property rights. In order to appreciate what Suárez and his successors had to say about property, it must be viewed, for context as well as for contrast, against the background of traditional scholastic doctrine. Following Aristotle, as well as several other ancient sources, the medieval masters explained the in-

---

[20] *De Legibus et Legislatore Deo*, I,ii,4–5: V,4–5.
[21] Thus, for instance, Giles of Rome refers to "dominium super res temporales sive super personas" *(De ecclesiastica potestate*, II,7: p. 70).
[22] *De Legibus*, II,xiv,16: V,141.
[23] II,xiv,18: V,141.
[24] III,iii, 7–8: V,183–4.
[25] I,vi,19: V,28.
[26] I,iii,20: V,12; cp. III,i,3: V,176.

stitution of private property as a means to avoid strife and inefficient use of common resources, as well as, according to a typical suggestion by Thomas Aquinas, social disorder. Aquinas saw this institution in terms of an addition to natural law, which originally decreed community of property. This basic premise was not abandoned. Private property rights extended no further than to "the power to procure and dispense"; material things should remain common as to use, in that every man should be "ready to communicate them to others in their need."[27] Such "communication" was not restricted to charity toward the destitute in the form of alms. In principle, the scholastic doctrine of justice in exchange, prohibiting exploitation of the needy, rests on this basis. Medieval scholastic property theory, while acknowledging limited private rights as the most feasible practical arrangement, was thus essentially duty oriented. Suárez does not break with Aquinas but shifts his emphasis from a duty to share to a right to claim and keep. Under the original condition of common ownership, natural law decreed that no one should be prevented from making the necessary use of common property. Under present condition, when property is divided, the natural law forbids the taking of what belongs to another.[28]

On the subject of property, the Protestant natural law philosophers built on and developed the ideas of the late scholastics, stating them in terms which brought them closer to economic categories.[29] For their accounts of the institution of private property, Hugo Grotius and Samuel Pufendorf both make some use of Aristotle, and both refer to labor. The relevant locus is to be found in *Politics*, II,2, where the quarreling, which is an unavoidable concomitant of communism, is said to arise

---

[27] *Sum. theol.*, II–II,66,2: IX,85.

[28] *De Legibus*, II,xiv,17: V,141.

[29] Unlike Suárez, whose discussion of economic subjects is limited to some passing remarks about usury and unjust pricing (*De Legibus*, II,xii,3–6: V,131–2, and see the quotation from *De Iuramento* in section 9.4), Grotius deals directly with some of the matters reviewed in Part II in a chapter on contracts (*De Iure Belli ac Pacis*, II,XII: 228–41; 343–61), whereas Pufendorf examines them in greater detail in a series of chapters, discussing price and value, monopoly, money and usury, labor and wages (*De Iure Naturae et Gentium*, V,i–vii: 457–518; 675–762 – page references in both works to Latin and English of Carnegie editions). Though sometimes associated with the origin of classical economics, neither Grotius nor Pufendorf does much more than restate the positions adopted by some of the late scholastics, the traditional medieval paradigm having been abandoned or appearing in a hazier form. They are relevant as forerunners of Locke on property, not of Smith directly on economics.

between those who work more and receive less and those who work
less and receive more.[30] It is important to note that this is formally a
factual observation on the part of Aristotle and that this is how it was
interpreted in the medieval commentary tradition. The industrious feel
that they should be permitted to keep the fruit of their toil and will
not let go of it peacefully to others. It does not follow that this attitude
is justified. According to the patristic tradition, to which the early scholastics sought to accommodate the ideas of Aristotle, there was no natural right to keep things for oneself; on the contrary, there was a
natural duty to share them.[31]

Grotius, at one point, comes close to suggesting that labor entitles
the laborer to his product and that this is the basis of property rights.[32]
He later withdraws from this position, arguing that all things are made
from existing material and that this cannot be appropriated merely by
someone spending labor on it. If no one owned it before, it comes
under the head of acquisition by occupation.[33] Grotius bases his property theory on the social contract, whereby it is agreed that whatever
each one has taken possession of should be his property.[34] Pufendorf
does not agree that the mere seizure of a thing can prejudice the rights
of others, unless their consent is given, that is, unless it is ratified by
covenant.[35] The result of Pufendorf's somewhat involved covenanting
procedure then seems to be the institution of what was originally ac-

[30] 1263a11–15.

[31] The first Latin commentator on the *Politics* and the one to develop the
labor element in Aristotle's argument from strife was Albert the Great.
Quoting Matt. 20.12, Albert puts the complaint of those who work more
and receive less in the mouths of the laborers in the parable of the
vineyard: "These last have wrought but one hour, and thou hast made
them equal unto us, who have borne the burden and heat of the day"
(*Politica*, II,2: 108). There is nothing to suggest that Albert or his
successors would support the laborers' claim on the basis of natural law.
(Note that they were turned down by the householder in the parable).
Thomas Aquinas, in his commentary on the Politics, merely elaborates on
the text without committing himself (*Sent. Pol.*, II,4: XLVIII,131). In the
Summa theologiae, he states the argument from strife without mentioning
labor at all, though he refers to it in connection with the argument from
inefficiency, noting men's tendency to shirk labor on common property
(loc. cit. in note 27).

[32] *De Iure Belli*, II,II,ii,4–5: 114; 189.

[33] II,III,iii: 127; 206.

[34] II,II,ii,5: 114; 189–90.

[35] *De Iure Naturae*, IV,iv,5: 367; 539.

quired by labor. Without quoting Aristotle at this point, he notes the "quarrels and wars" that must arise over scarce common resources, adding that most things require labor and cultivation to produce them or make them fit for use and that it is "improper" *(inconveniens)* that one who contributed no labor to this should have the same rights as the one who did.[36] Grotius thus toys with the idea, and Pufendorf comes close to stating explicitly, that the laborer has a natural right to the fruit of his labor. They thereby take us, each one step further, toward John Locke's famous labor theory of property in the *Two Treatises of Government.*

Locke bases his theory on a metaphysical principle, that of workmanship. Man is God's property because God has created man; all creation is his workmanship. God wants that which he has created to last as long as it pleases him. Each man, therefore, has a duty to preserve himself and, provided it does not interfere with his own preservation, to preserve the rest of mankind. In the state of nature, where men are free and equal, these duties entail certain rights. One of them is the right to use the things that are necessary for one's preservation. Property is based on this. But each man also has the right to punish anyone else who breaks this law of nature.[37] Things were originally common but were not intended always to remain so. Every man has a property in his own person and thus in his own labor. That which he removes out of the state in which nature has left it, he has "mixed his *labor* with, and joined to it something that is his own, and thereby makes it his property." By his labor it has something "annexed to it," which excludes the common right of others.[38] If someone else, who has "as good left for his improvement, as was already taken up," should complain, it is clear that he desires the benefit of another's pain, to which he has no right.[39] This is one of several echoes in Locke, of the Aristotelian argument from strife, which Albert the Great and his successors explained with reference to labor,[40] but whereas the medieval commen-

---

[36] IV,iv,6: 368; 539–40.
[37] I,86–7: 243; II,4–8: 309–13; cp. II,56: 347. Cp. also *An Essay Concerning Human Understanding,* IV,iii,18: II, 154.
[38] II,27: 328–9; cp. II, 28–30: 330–1.
[39] II,34: 333.
[40] If distinct titles to property through labor could be established so that there was no doubt about right, there could be no room for quarrel, says Locke elsewhere (II,39: 338), just as there was little room for quarrels and contentions in the distant past, when natural provisions were plentiful and men to spend them were few (II,31: 332; cp. II,51: 344).

tators merely argue in favor of private property because trouble will *in fact* arise when people are not permitted to reap where they sow, Locke elevates labor to a *just title* to appropriation. The laborer has a natural right to that on which he has spent his labor and is justified in protecting it. Political society was established in order to relieve each person of undertaking that impossible task on his own. The purpose of government is to preserve property. This is stated in the *First Treatise* and repeated ad nauseam in the *Second Treatise.*[41]

There is thus something bordering on the sacred in the basis of property provided for it by Locke. God is the owner of his workmanship, and so is man as well. Men own property as though by virtue of having created it with their labor; however, as all critics of Locke agree, the whole argument turns on the phrase "as good left." When all cultivable land is appropriated, when further accumulation is made possible through the invention of money, and the propertyless must "mix" their labor with land or material owned by others, the workmanship model provides no easy solution. Just as the worker cannot well claim as his the soil or raw material on which he worked, its owner has no ready claim on the improvement. In retrospect, it may seem that Locke merely clears the ground for a new quarrel, one between labor and capital, as classes, and as social forces. It may be objected that he was concerned with the origin of property and society and not with the details of constitutions. It is true that while sometimes suggesting that the preservation of property is the only purpose of government, he more than once refers to its purpose as being that of regulating property, without explaining the nature and principles of such regulation, apparently leaving the question open for societies to find the best solution.[42] These issues divide Locke scholars,[43] in the historical situation, however, they could conveniently be overlooked. For the entrepreneurial middle classes, on whose behalf the new doctrine of political liberty was proclaimed, and for the new economics, which was primarily modeled on their activities, Locke seemed to have justified an idea of property untroubled by the moral conditioning of scholastic doctrine, one making the owner of economic resources in all respects their "moderator and arbiter." In consequence, rather than protect the weak

---

[41] I,92: 247; II,87; 88; 94; 124; 127; 138; 222: 367; 368; 373; 395; 397; 406; 460; and elsewhere.

[42] II,3; 50; 120; 139: 308; 344; 393; 407.

[43] Cp. the studies by Tully and Tuck (covering the tradition preceding Locke as well) and Simmons, with numerous references. On the history of property theory, cp. also Schlatter.

against the strong, it came to protect the latter against government interference on behalf of the former, permitting the exercise of economic power in lending and borrowing, buying and selling, as well as in the hire of labor, hampered by no obligation except to stay clear of fraud and (physical) force, and to keep contracts.

9.4   Compulsion in the natural rights tradition

In his treatise *De Voluntario et Involuntario*, which ranges far beyond the question of external compulsion and the will, which only concerns us here, Suárez, having commented on Aristotle's case of the jettison of cargo,[44] summons such additional authorities as Thomas Aquinas, Augustine, Gregory of Nyssa (Nemesius), and John Damascene to conclude emphatically that "forced will is simply will" *(coacta voluntas, voluntas est simpliciter)*.[45] The matter is touched upon only briefly in the major work on Law quoted in section 9.3. Acts done through fear are said there to be absolutely voluntary though involuntary *secundum quid*.[46] In two other works, questions relating to compulsion and the will are discussed at greater length. In the treatise *De Voto*, again referring to Aristotle and Aquinas, Suárez explains:

He is said simply and absolutely to will something who, with an absolute and effective act chooses it here and now, so that he does it with his will even though at the same time experiencing a simple displeasure whereby he would not have done it if that were possible without inconvenience. Such is the case of one who will promise something from fear of some evil; for here and now he chooses this means as convenient for himself, or as necessary for the purpose of avoiding an evil; . . . therefore the man is simply and absolutely willing, for forced will is will.[47]

I concede that the voluntary may be mixed with something of the involuntary, but . . . when a man is affected by two acts or qualities which are in some way repugnant, that simply wins, which is the stronger, and for the validity of a vow the simply voluntary suffices, even if mixed with the involuntary *secundum quid*.[48]

Given the long tradition on this subject, such a position on vows on the part of Suárez was perhaps to be expected. It is more of a surprise to find in yet another work by this author, whose voluminous production contains almost nothing on economics proper, an outright rejec-

---

[44] *De Voluntario*, II,i,8: IV,183.
[45] Op. cit., III,i,3: IV,201.
[46] *De Legibus*, VII,xii,11: VI,184.
[47] *De Voto*, I,vii,3: XIV,776.
[48] Op. cit., I,vii,16: XIV,780.

tion of any remnant of the medieval idea of need as compulsion. In *De Iuramento*, he writes:

It is in particular common here to find discussed the question of oaths made to a usurer that usury will be paid because he will not otherwise lend; the same is true of oaths not to rescind a contract of buying and selling, even if sold beyond one-half of the just price, and similar cases. In which no problem arises from compulsion or from a defect of will, because no absolute force is employed in this, the lender or seller forcing the other to receive the loan or to buy, and consequently neither to swear, but merely forces him to swear on condition, if he will have the loan or buy the thing he desires, and thus no *metus* strictly speaking intervenes here, but rather concupiscence, and therefore, on this account, there is little difficulty, but all is reduced to a question of injustice.[49]

Formally, this may be said to place Suárez in the tradition of Cajetan, who suggested that economic circumstances be considered rather than economic motivation, but the reduction of the needy borrower's or buyer's motivation to Suárez's terms removes him much further from medieval sentiments than the Italian Aquinas commentator.

The Protestant natural rights philosophers quoted in section 9.3 also mention compulsion and the will, but their attitudes to need as compulsion can, at most, be inferred. They are, on the whole, unsympathetic to the idea. Grotius makes present circumstances overrule absent conditions so that consent given because of fear is absolute and binding:

On the whole I accept the opinion of those who think that the person that makes a promise under the influence of fear is bound by it, if the civil law, which can annul or diminish an obligation, is not taken into consideration. For in such a case there is a consent, not conditional . . . but absolute. As Aristotle, in fact, has rightly stated, the man who throws his property overboard because of the fear of shipwreck would wish to save it conditionally, if there was no danger of shipwreck (*vellet res servare sub conditione si naufragium non immineret*). But, considering the circumstances of the place and time, he is willing to lose his property absolutely.[50]

Grotius adds that the person who inspired the fear is sometimes bound to release the other from his promise not because consent is lacking but on account of "damage wrongfully caused." This, once more, is the position adopted by some of the late scholastics discussing economic contracts. Motive is irrelevant, provided the terms of contract are just. Hobbes merely took this one step further, ruling our fear as a relevant factor and ruling out justice as well, because justice does not

---

[49] *De Iuramento*, II,ix,1: XIV,535.
[50] *De Iure Belli*, II,XI,vii,2: 223; 334 (with a minor alteration to the Carnegie translation).

pertain to the terms of a contract but only to its fulfillment according to the terms consented to.

Pufendorf does not hold with any of this. His natural-law treatise reads at times like a lengthy critical commentary on Grotius, and he is frequently at odds with Hobbes as well.

Aristotle, *Nicomachean Ethics*, III,1, calls those actions mixed, which are undertaken to avoid an evil, an example of which is the old one of throwing goods overboard when shipwreck is threatened. . . . Now although actions undertaken from fear of a greater evil should be classed as voluntary *(inter spontaneas sint referendae)*, and the less evil which we choose under such circumstances may really, in our present condition, be the thing we wish, such actions still cannot be the source of any obligation on our part toward another. For since an obligation looks to some person for whom something must be done, and so it implies in him a corresponding right, by reason of which he may compel the fulfilment of the obligation, the creation of such an obligation requires that, in the one, there be such principles as would produce an obligation, and in the other such as warrant his securing a right. . . . Therefore, that fear which causes a defect in the other party prevents the rise of an obligation, since the defect makes him incapable of acquiring a right.[51]

What Grotius adds regarding damage invalidating some promises is therefore irrelevant according to Pufendorf. Rather than demand release from an obligation because of such damage, the promisor should deny the obligation because the use of force rendered it defective. As regards Hobbes's notorious position on fear and the voluntary, it is countered at several points both in *De cive* and in *Leviathan*. It is absurd, for instance, says Pufendorf, to suggest that I am bound by some inner compulsion to give my property to a thief just because I promised to do so under threat. A thief can obtain no right to my property by such means. Concerning the idea of a social contract, which Pufendorf is, of course, interested in preserving in principle, he suggests that there is an ambiguity in Hobbes's use of the word *metus*. The social contract is made in order to obtain mutual aid against a common enemy; the fear that inspires such a pact is different from the fear that makes a person promise something in order to escape an evil threatened by another person.[52]

This is perhaps not an entirely convincing refutation of Hobbes. As Hobbes saw it, the social contract is also inspired by the mutual fear that men in the state of nature have of one another singly; however, it takes us closer to a crucial aspect of Pufendorf's highly competent analysis, an aspect that greatly reduces its relevance in an economic context.

[51] *De Iure Naturae*, III,vi,10: 282; 416.
[52] III,vi,12–13: 285–7; 421–3.

Pufendorf devotes a long section of his chapter on consent to the question of who causes the fear, drawing on Roman law as well as several other classical sources.[53] Here as well, it would seem that the author's conclusions regarding fear invalidating contracts, even if applied to economic exchange, are limited to threats of a noneconomic character, though not necessarily issuing from the opposite party to the exchange. Economic compulsion, that is, compulsion caused by poverty and need, is not mentioned and therefore not in principle ruled out; however, there is nothing to indicate that Pufendorf would consider someone profiting from such fear in another not to have obtained a right to this profit, provided the terms of the exchange in question were just in the sense understood by the late scholastics. When even this proviso begins to dissolve, as it does with Hobbes, and as Hobbesian ideas on this point take hold among his British successors in the natural rights tradition, Pufendorf's position offers no protection at all against exploitation of economic need.

On the subject of physical compulsion and consent, Locke, in the *Second Treatise*, also takes issue with Hobbes. The context is submission to a conqueror, but the argument proceeds in general terms:

It remains only to be considered, whether *promises, extorted by force*, without right, can be thought consent, and *how far they bind*. To which I shall say, they *bind not at all*; because whatsoever another gets from me by force, I still retain the right of, and he is obliged presently to restore. He that forces my horse from me, ought presently to restore him, and I have still a right to retake him. By the same reason, he that *forced a promise* from me, ought presently to restore it, *i.e.* quit me of the obligation of it; or I may resume it myself, *i.e.*, choose whether I will perform it. For the law of nature laying an obligation on me, only by the rules she prescribes, cannot oblige me by the violation of her rules: Such is the extorting anything from me by force. Nor does it at all alter the case, to say I *gave my promise*, no more than it excuses the force, and passes the right, when I put my hand in my pocket, and deliver my purse myself to a thief, who demands it with a pistol at my breast.[54]

Economic compulsion is nowhere subjected to a similar explicit analysis, but there is a revealing implicit reference to it in the *First Treatise*. Locke wishes to point out that property in itself does not give anyone authority over other men. Only compact might do that: "The authority of the rich proprietor, and the subjection of the needy beggar began not from the possession of the lord, but the consent of the poor man, who preferred being his subject to starving. And the man he thus sub-

---

[53] III,vi,11: 283–5; 417–20.
[54] II,186: 440.

mits to, can pretend to no more power over him, than he has consented to, upon compact."[55]

This is clearly a case of *coactus volui*. Threatened with starvation, the poor man gives his consent. Locke was fully aware of the terms that sometimes had to be consented to in order to obtain employment in contemporary England. In one of his *Considerations* regarding money, he comments on the poor bargaining position of laborers, as though it was a fact of life. This is a work of a very different kind, a typical mercantilist treatise offering advice to government. Locke refers to the truck system, according to which the commodities given (in lieu of money) for work rendered "such as they are, good or bad, the work-man must take at his master's rate, or sit still and starve."[56] Locke deplores this, as Antonino of Florence had once done, but he locates the cause of the evil in the general scarcity of money, not in the morals of the employers.

9.5   Natural liberty

In his *Traité d'économie politique*, first published in 1803, Jean-Baptiste Say treats briefly of the right of property: It is not the province of political economy to trace the origin of this institution, to regulate the transfer of property, or to devise means of protecting it. Political economy merely recognizes the right to property as the most powerful of all encouragements to the multiplication of wealth. It does not occupy itself much with the bases and safeguards of property, as long as it is in fact secure. It is proper to add, however, that the poor man, who can call nothing his own, is just as interested as the rich in upholding the inviolability of property. But for the protection of what the latter has previously accumulated, the former would find no employment for his services.[57] Interest on loans used to be condemned as profiting by one's neighbor's distress, which is still repugnant to the common maxims of morality. The advance of industry, however, has taught us to see the loan of capital in a different light. It is no longer usually a resource in the hour of need but an instrument of great benefit to all concerned. To charge interest is no more avaricious or immoral than, for example, to receive wages for labor; it is simply "an equitable compensation based on mutual convenience."[58] As regards the exchange of commod-

---

[55] I,43: 206.
[56] *Works*, IV,24–5.
[57] *Traité*, I,14: 133; 137.
[58] II,8: 385.

ities, the only fair criterion of the value of an object is its current price, expressing the quantity of all other objects that one can obtain *(qu'on peut obtenir)* for it the moment one desires to exchange. It is the province of ethics to examine the passions and virtues that may influence the price given or received in exchange: hope, fear *(la crainte)*, malice, etc.; political economy is solely concerned with the general laws in which they find expressions. Government intervention in these matters can be too dearly paid for.[59] The healthy state of industry is the state of liberty, where each interest is left to take care of itself and government activity is limited to protection against force *(la violence)*.[60]

When modern professional economics rose from its cradle in natural law philosophy in the century prior to Say's contribution, it carried with it the germ of the peculiar "Problemverschlingung" aptly so named by Max Weber in one of his methodological studies, a twisting and intertwining of description and prescription that it has never managed properly to straighten out.[61] It is true that the great French economist tended to guard his words less carefully than most of his British colleagues, but convolutions similar to those cited (no less serious for being subtler) are to be found in such authors as Smith and Mill and even in Marshall. Commenting on the natural law strain in economics, Schumpeter, in his *History*, found comfort in a possible remedy. He refers to something that was already mentioned, namely, that precepts always require some sort of factual basis or, in his own words, that "the normative natural law presupposes an explanatory natural law," the former being "natural law considered as a source of morally and legally valid imperatives," based upon "the facts and the relations between facts unearthed by the latter." Schumpeter's point here is that it is often possible, as, for instance, in the case of Smith (and presumably in that of Say), to distinguish and separate these elements. For the historian intent on tracing the progress of "economic analysis," shorn of "ideological bias," "special pleading," and "value judgments,"[62] there is indeed no other way to proceed than by attempting this kind of intellectual surgery, even when those extraneous factors so intimately influence the terms of analysis that the bits saved are meager. The operation, however, is both futile and misguided if its purpose is to reduce economics to less than a moral science, for it is not at all unreasonable to view its role in intellectual history as having been primarily normative. One of the questions before the historian

[59] II,1: 314; 320–1.
[60] I,17: 183.
[61] Weber, 1968, 274.
[62] Schumpeter, 1954, 110–1; 37.

then is precisely how factual analysis and insight, among other factors, at different times and in different circles, relate to ideologies and value judgments.

An alternative historiographical model, certainly no less controversial than that of Schumpeter but focusing specifically on these relations, was suggested by Fanfani, another statesman-economist as well as historian. According to Fanfani in his *Storia*, all early economic doctrines are expressions of a form of *voluntarism*. The idea of a rational economic order being foreign to them, they were rather in the nature of deliberate programs for the rationalization of economic life by imposing on it a large and detailed set of norms. Empirical observations (such as they were) served merely as aids to uncover areas of irrationality in need of regulation. It was only from the eighteenth century onward (and except for a revival of *neovoluntarism* in certain modern systems) that economic doctrines can rightly be called *naturalistic*, based on belief in the existence of a rational economic order, with which it is useless and harmful to interfere, and whose laws it is the object of empirical observation to discover and explain. Economic naturalism is not concerned with norms, or, more correctly, all norms are reduced by it to a single norm, that of letting the natural laws of economics operate freely.[63]

The merit of this model, whatever else may be said about it, consists in its focus on a prolongation of the natural law mode of reasoning in economics onto a new basis. In the classical tradition, this found its clearest expression in Smith's "obvious and simple system of natural liberty."[64] If one should venture to suggest a modification to the model on the basis of the arguments and findings of the present study, it would have to do with dating. Granted that there can be no sharp division into historical periods, one might be inclined to place the origin of economic naturalism in Fanfani's sense somewhat earlier. He obviously places it where he does because he wants to separate the Mercantilists (who were notorious norm-setters) from the Physiocrats. It seems, however, that he probably also, to some extent, falls prey to the common error of regarding the scholastic tradition as too uniform, overlooking the breakdown of the medieval paradigm at the hands of the late scholastics and their gradual assumption of some of the premises of the new economics.

The origin of liberalism is usually explained by the acknowledgment of two phenomena. The first is the ability of human society, without rational planning or intention but by some sort of evolutionary process,

---

[63] Fanfani, 1971, 25–9.
[64] *Wealth of Nations*, IV,9: II,184.

to develop beneficial mechanisms and institutions to support them. The second is the identification, particularly in the economic sphere, of self-interest as the prime mover of these mechanisms. According to this view, it is in the ideas of such authors as Mandeville and Hume, coupled with Benthamite utilitarianism, rather than in those of Locke and the natural law tradition, that the philosophical inspiration of liberalism is to be sought.[65] It is far from my intention to dispute the importance of these factors; however, I believe that a comparison with medieval scholasticism and a focus on the points of its breakdown can serve to highlight two other factors, without which the strength and longevity of liberalism are difficult to explain. These are the factors discussed in sections 9.2 and 9.3. To take them in the reverse order: There is obviously a reinforcement effect in the liberal ideology between the social utilitarian justification and the individual rights justification of the exercise of economic power for selfish ends.[66] It is clearly further enhanced by the broadening of the scope of economic analysis, from the personal exchange encounter to the impersonal laws of supply and demand. This is a point of the greatest importance, for when liberalism came under moral fire, it was these two, its doctrine of rights and its abstraction from the personal element, which proved to be the weakest of the legs on which the ideological structure rested.

[65] Compare Smith's two famous propositions, that it is the self-interest rather than the benevolence of suppliers that brings food and drink to our table (*Wealth of Nations*, I,2: I,16) and that man seeking his own gain will promote that of society without intending to do so (IV,2: I,421), with that of Hume to the effect that the contrary self-loves of different individuals, adjusting to one another, will bring about something "advantageous to the public; though it be not intended for that purpose" (*A Treatise of Human Nature*, III,ii,6: *Works*, II,296). The influence of Mandeville's "private vice: public virtue" formula on the classical ideology need hardly be stressed. The suggestion that Mandeville's ideas may be traced back to late scholasticism via Lessius seems to me highly questionable. The School of Salamanca influenced modern thought on the points discussed in section 9.2 and 9.3, not on those added in this section and more often cited by historians.

[66] Cp. Hume, commenting on property legislation: "There is no question, but the regard to general good is much enforced by the respect to particular" (*An Enquiry Concerning the Principles of Morals*, Appendix III: *Works*, IV,278). Note also that the first generation of classical authors regularly acknowledged the "sacred and inviolable" character of property (Smith, *Wealth of Nations*, I,10: I,123), the "sacred regard to the rights of property" (Ricardo, *Works*, V,501–2), or the same idea differently phrased.

CHAPTER 10

The neoclassical system
and its critics

10.1   The case of labor

In a recent critical assessment of the classical system, one of its most prominent features is derived from the Hobbesian conception of justice. By the classical system, I mean both the original set of models developed from Smith to J. S. Mill and the neoclassical reconstruction of which Alfred Marshall is usually considered to be the main architect (by reconciling the elder system with the marginal approach), though, in a narrower sense, it is sometimes reserved for post-Keynesian developments. A society embracing a jurisprudential theory according to which injustice "is no other than the nonperformance of Covenant" provides a "facilitative form" of law.[1] Such is the assumption of classical economics. The law is limited to adjudicating disputes arising in the private sector. The state provides a neutral, impartial framework. It does not intervene by engaging in "social engineering," that is, in ordering society by legislative action. This is the *laissez-faire* interpretation of Hobbes encountered in Chapter 8. In the economic sphere, the law permits economic actors to make their own contracts and restricts itself to ensuring that they are kept according to their terms properly interpreted. In addition, the classical system assumes markets to be perfectly competitive so that neither party to a contract has power over the other. Facilitative law and perfect competition ensure "voluntariness" in economic life.[2] In such a system, Galbraith observes, there "could be no misuse of private power because no one had power to misuse."[3]

No contemporary economist has insisted more strongly than Galbraith on the need to study economic power, focusing primarily on the large modern corporation wielding "power over markets, power in the community, power over the state, power over belief,"[4] which is met by "countervailing power" being organized from within the private sector

[1] Seidman, 1973, 554, quoting *Leviathan*: III,131.
[2] Id., 555–6.
[3] Galbraith, 1956, 12.
[4] Id., 1973, 6.

itself as well as from the public sector.[5] In the movement toward an integration of economics and political science, with which we shall be partly concerned in this chapter, Galbraith thus occupies a prominent position. It is, however, a position on the borderline of its main ideological controversy, for in his many works on power, he has avoided its characteristic terminology, fighting shy of words like *voluntariness, freedom*, and *coercion/compulsion*. It is, therefore, all the more interesting to note that Galbraith, in one of his infrequent excursions into economic history, makes explicit use of the Roman law concept of *metus* and that he does so in connection with labor. The context is a discussion of who, at different stages of economic development, were the typical possessors of power. The analysis recalls Max Weber's distinction between the two main kinds of "Herrschaft"[6] and thereby the scholastics' distinction between compulsion in the physical and the economic sense. In early agricultural societies, power was associated with land, which, as the strategic factor of production, made the use of compulsion highly advantageous. The feudal lord had command over serfs and helots who cultivated his land. With industrialization, power typically passed from land to capital. Urbanization offered a chance of escape from feudal bondage. "Nor has slavery been easily adapted to the factory. In the early stages of the factory system, wage labor compelled by the fear of hunger was also, almost certainly, cheaper than slave labor compelled by the fear of physical violence."[7]

This reference to *metus* as the fear of hunger motivating the wage laborer also recalls Alfred Marshall. The exact phrase appears in a sequence in Marshall's *Principles*, where the labor market is singled out as an exception to the general classical assumption of free competition. Explaining the marginal approach to equilibrium, the author discusses "buyers' need," their "willingness" or "unwillingness" to pay a certain price. As a general rule, a buyer's marginal utility of money, measuring, as it were, his unwillingness to part with more of it, is not materially affected by a single purchase, because it will involve a sum that is negligible compared with his total resources.

The exceptions are rare and unimportant in markets for commodities; but in markets for labor they are frequent and important. When a workman is in fear of hunger, his need of money :(its marginal utility to him) is very great; and if at starting he gets the worst of the bargaining and is employed at low wages, it remains great, and he may go on selling his labor at a low rate. That is all the

---

[5] Id., 1956, passim.
[6] See Introduction.
[7] Galbraith, 1978, 148–9.

more probable because, while the advantage in bargaining is likely to be pretty well distributed between the two sides of a market for commodities, it is more often on the side of the buyers than on that of the sellers in a market for labor.

It is no wonder, Marshall adds, that the working classes object to those economists who regard the labor market as like every other market whereas the differences, "though not fundamental from the point of view of theory, are yet clearly marked, and in practice often very important."[8] These observations were not a neoclassical novelty. It is well known that the first breach in the bulwark of liberalism occurred in the area of wage relations. They were the last to appear on the scholastic agenda, and they started to worry leading representatives of classical economics quite early. Smith, for one, commented on the disadvantage of the laborer in industrial disputes.[9] Mill, who repeatedly calls for government intervention against fraud and force[10] and, in his famous essay *On Liberty*, recommends leaving "producers and sellers perfectly free, under the sole check of equal freedom to the buyers for supplying themselves elsewhere,"[11] without wasting a word on need as compulsion, in his *Principles of Political Economy* acknowledges that the labor contract is a special case.[12]

It is special because labor is a special commodity (or, as some would say, because it was wrongly reduced to a commodity). It was special in early industrial society because of its lasting and all-embracing consequences, virtually yielding permanent domination to the employer in a range of secondary economic relations as well. Finally, it is special because the parties to it can be conceived of as representatives of conflicting social classes. When the needy laborer reappeared in ideological disputes in the nineteenth century, it was not as a person but as a class. The foremost Marxist interpreter of the British natural law tradition claims that these authors, and in particular Hobbes, went wrong because, by projecting contemporary conditions and mentalities back to the state of nature (except for civil laws) and postulating natural equality, they ignored class structure; what would ensue would not be a war of all against all but a conflict between two main, internally adhesive social classes.[13] This additional recognition permitted Marx to

---

[8] Marshall, 334–6.

[9] *Wealth of Nations*, I,8: I,68.

[10] *Principles of Political Economy*, V,xi,16: *Works*, III,971; *On Liberty*, V: *Works*, XVIII,293.

[11] *On Liberty*, loc. cit.

[12] *Principles*, V,x,5: *Works*, III,932.

[13] Macpherson, 1970, 84–5 and passim.

retranslate the classical labor theory of value and to predict a different society. It does not seem that Marx thought of the exploitation of labor specifically in Aristotelian terms, but he did consider need a form of compulsion,[14] and the conditional nature of the needy laborer's consent to his wages is clear enough in his biting ridicule of liberalism as "the very Eden of the innate rights of man," where the mighty capitalist and the pitiful seeker of employment "contract as free agents," "constrained only by their own free will."[15]

It is a curious comment on the ideological confusion of the late nineteenth century that it was in a papal bull, in reaction to Marxism, that the scholastic paradigm was once more, explicitly, brought to bear on the labor question. In *Rerum Novarum*, issued in 1891, Leo XIII all but quotes Aristotle verbatim when calling for a just wage:

Let workers and employers, therefore, make any bargains they like, and in particular agree freely about wages; nevertheless, there underlies a requirement of natural justice higher and older than any bargain voluntarily struck: the wage ought not to be in any way insufficient for the bodily needs of a temperate and well-behaved worker. If, having no alternative and fearing a worse evil, a workman is forced (*si necessitate opifex coactus, aut mali peioris metu permotus*) to accept

---

[14] On freedom and compulsion in Marx, cp. Elster, 1985, 204–16.

[15] *Capital*, I,176; cp. I,396; 766–9. These sentiments were expressed just as forcefully by John Ruskin, whose anger matches Marx's bitter irony. In *Unto This Last* (the title is a quotation from the parable of the vineyard at Matt. 20.14; cp. note 31 to Chapter 9), Ruskin relates the reversal of the medieval scholastic analytic paradigm, as well as Hobbes's perversion of the traditional idea of commutative justice, to the "politico-economical view of the case, according to the doctors of that science" of his own time (the book was first published in 1862): "We will suppose that the master of a household desires only to get as much work out of his servants as he can, at the rate of wages he gives. He never allows them to be idle; feeds them as poorly and lodges them as ill as they will endure, and in all things pushes his requirements to the exact point beyond which he cannot go without forcing the servant to leave him. In doing this, there is no violation on his part of what is commonly called 'justice.' He agrees with the domestic for his whole time and service, and takes them; – the limits of hardship in treatment being fixed by the practice of other masters in his neighborhood; that is to say, by the current rate of wages for domestic labor. If the servant can get a better place, he is free to take one, and the master can only tell what is the real market value of his labor by requiring as much as he will give" (op. cit.: p. 9). Ruskin's criticism, with Schumpeter's irritated comments (*History*: 411), nicely sum up this aspect of postscholastic ideological developments.

harder conditions imposed by an employer or contractor, he is the victim of violence against which justice cries out *(est subire vim cui iustitia reclamat)*.[16]

After the centenary of *Rerum Novarum*, and as communism has once more proved a political failure, it may be easier to lend ear to Marx's moral outrage and to recognize that the spokesmen of Church and Proletariat express, however differently, a common heritage. It is not to our purpose to assess their effect on the course of economic thought in the present century. I would hesitate to suggest that any major school has traceable links to medieval scholasticism. What can be demonstrated, however, is the gradual reappearance of analytical concepts that recall the scholastic paradigm regarding need, the will, and justice and of ideological controversies on issues resembling those that divided the medieval theologians and civilians. If this phenomenon is to be explained historically, the case of labor is essential. Shortly after the turn of the last century, Thomas Nixon Carver inadvertently reproduced Ricardo's definition of value in exchange,[17] with an addition (his emphasis): "Value is the *power* which an article or a service possesses of commanding other desirable things in peaceful and voluntary exchange."[18] It is easier to claim voluntariness when power is thus seen as an objective market phenomenon, as a matter of articles or services commanding things rather than a personal encounter. Numerous quotations could be added to those just given to show that at no stage in the history of classical economics was it possible to overlook entirely the human element when discussing labor. In the case of labor, the depersonalization of economics recorded in section 9.2 was never fully achieved. Modern critics of the classical system sometimes, but not always, draw on labor relations for their examples. The breakthrough made in the area of labor logically spread to other areas, bringing back the human element throughout the study of economic phenomena. It set in motion a reorientation of economic study, based on a relocation of its elemental unit in the personal exchange relation, in what the scholastics called a contract and institutional economists now call a transaction.

10.2   Transactions and rights

According to Fanfani's classification of economic systems, what is known collectively as modern institutionalism represents a sort of eco-

---

[16] *Rerum Novarum*, 45: 662. The English translation is that published in M. Walsh and B. Davies (eds.), *Proclaiming Justice and Peace*, London 1991.

[17] See section 5.1.

[18] Carver, 1915, 35.

nomic neovoluntarism.[19] Institutional economics comprises a number of different trends and programs, most of which are of little direct relevance here. We shall be concerned with two particular schools that form parts, respectively, of the "old institutional economics" and the "new institutional economics" (also known as "evolutionary economics"). These are the school originating in the works of John R. Commons, significantly updated by a number of recent followers, and the Austrian school, primarily associated with Friedrich A. von Hayek and his disciples. These schools clash over the issue of economic coercion and freedom, which will be discussed in sections 10.3 and 10.4. What is needed here is a brief introduction, conveniently provided by paraphrasing Commons, and a sketch of the main points of controversy between institutional and neoclassical economics.[20]

Since the time of the Physiocrats, Commons declares, economic theory has endeavored to get rid of the human will, which had been the main reliance of the Mercantilists and of the economic theory of the Church Fathers. The will was arbitrary, capricious, and contrary to natural laws. Hence there appeared, first, a natural rights theory, which prevailed from the eighteenth century, and, later, a natural selection or evolution theory inspired by Darwin. These theories seek to explain economic phenomena as the working out of natural forces, but this is all wrong: Economic phenomena are the results of artificial selection and not of natural selection. Such rights as we have are not natural but proceed from national and other collective action. The subject matter of economics is properly the habits, customs, and ways of thinking of producers, consumers, buyers, sellers, borrowers, lenders, and all who engage in economic transactions. These customs largely depend on state action, which aims at the establishment of reasonable values in economic life.[21] This ideal can be applied to value specifically in the sense of price. Reasonable price is a creature of the courts. It requires equal opportunity, fair competition, and equality of bargaining power.[22] Real value, says Commons, is that which a price ought to be, namely, "fair and reasonable as between all parties because there is no coercion or misrepresentation."[23]

---

[19] See section 9.5.
[20] On the development of the various branches of institutional economics, cp. the recent studies by Gruchy, Mulberg, Rutherford, and Vromen.
[21] Commons, 1924, 376–7; 1934, 680–4.
[22] Commons, 1934, 63.
[23] Ibid., 260.

The latter statement is made by way of a direct comparison with the price doctrine of "the theological school whose leader was Thomas Aquinas." Read in conjunction with several other references to Aquinas[24] and with the allusion to the economics of the Church Fathers, this deliberate coupling of "reasonable price" with medieval "just price" invites an interpretation of Commons's ideas as some sort of economic neo-Thomism. This interpretation would be of doubtful analytic merit.[25] There are, however, some notable similarities, not the least of which is the focus on the transaction as the unit of economic analysis. Generalizing what was said in the preceding section in connection with labor and quoting a recent authority, "Commons focuses his analysis upon the economy as a universe of human relations, . . . whereas conventional economics centers on the universe of commodity relations."[26] To Commons, economic science is the study of "the behavior of individuals while participating in transactions."[27] He defines a transaction as "two or more wills giving, taking, persuading, coercing, defrauding, commanding, obeying, competing, governing, in a world of scarcity, mechanism and rules of conduct."[28] There are three different kinds of transactions: Managerial and rationing transactions involve legally superior and inferior persons; bargaining transactions take place in the marketplace and transfer ownership of wealth between legal equals.[29] Commons does not like to call this exchange (as we did in Part II), because exchange is merely the physical act.[30] Only the state can transfer ownership "by reading intentions into the minds of par-

---

[24] Ibid., 39n; 110; 261, mostly on his alleged labor theory of value.

[25] Thomism has already been claimed as a blueprint for so many different schools of modern economics (from Marxism to Fascism via Welfarism and Capitalism) that I would warn against adding to the confusion by including Institutionalism as well. Commons personally conceived of the relationship in question as a *return* to something not unlike the value doctrine of Aquinas, after centuries of conflict and many other schools of thought (ibid., 116). In an as yet not published essay on the subject, one prominent contemporary Commons scholar interprets this to mean neither more nor less than that "Commons's theory of Reasonable Value should be categorized as a secularized, twentieth-century renewal of the quest for an economics of the Just Price" (Ramstad, 1996, 32–3). With that, I am fully in agreement.

[26] Parsons, 1985, 756.

[27] Commons, 1931, 654.

[28] Id., 1924, 7; cp. 1934, 323.

[29] Id., 1934, 68; cp. 1931, 652–3.

[30] Id., 1931, 651–2.

ticipants."[31] This difference was something that traditional economists had overlooked, confusing object and ownership of object.[32]

This brings us yet another step closer to our main theme. As just pointed out, the four centuries between, say, Cajetan and Commons witnessed a process whereby the personal element in economic study gradually receded and was replaced by aggregate relations between suprapersonal phenomena: volumes of supply and demand, and prices established by market forces. This process had recently been brought near its culmination with the idea of equilibrium and the marginal analysis. The focus on objects and market mechanisms does not only obscure the participating persons as such, it leads to a waning of interest in *the nature of the human motivational factors* that fuel these mechanisms. In the list of Contents of Marshall's *Principles*, there is a paragraph that states that motives are incapable of measurement.[33] In the corresponding text, the author observes that the study of an economic actor's mental states is bound to interest the philosopher. "But the economist studies mental states rather through their manifestations than in themselves; and if he finds they afford evenly balanced incentives to action, he treats them *prima facie* as for his purpose equal."[34]

This scientific manifesto by the founder of neoclassicism precisely pinpoints the position now adopted by mainstream economists. It is characterized by a curious disinclination to consider the existence of that which is not measurable. Need and greed count equally in statistical demand schedules. Necessaries and luxuries are all the same. It applies to power as well. In his presidential address to the American Economic Association, Galbraith told his colleagues, in effect, that their failure to take account of economic power was a defense strategy on the part of the powerful.[35] I have no quarrel with that but should like to add an analytic explanation by Allan Gruchy, an institutionalist and contemporary of Galbraith: "there is no index that measures power."[36]

By taking the formal and informal social framework as their point of departure and by restating the analysis of market behavior in terms of transactions, a major concern of the institutionalists would be the role of power and, thereby, the role of coercion and conflict in economic life. By the same token, economics and politics could not be kept an-

---

[31] Id., 1934, 60.
[32] Id., 1934, 251; cp. 1924, 18–19.
[33] I, ii, § 1.
[34] Op. cit., 16.
[35] Galbraith, 1973, 11.
[36] Gruchy, 1987, 94.

alytically separate. They are parts of the same social complex. Among other things, this insight exploded the theory of a neutral and natural *laissez-faire*. As regards its alleged natural character, it was no longer possible to ignore the fact that the market depends on government for its protection. In the words of Gunnar Myrdal, "there are no legal institutions which are natural merely because they are actual."[37] As regards value neutrality, it is sufficient here to point out that not only the word *value*, but a number of related economic terms, such as *right, optimality, efficiency*, and, indeed, *natural*, are inherently valuational words and that this value potential is consistently utilized, consciously or unconsciously, by economists. One way to react to the institutionalist challenge was to meet it on its own ground, by conceding value but insisting, if not on nature, then on the inherent ability of society to develop workable institutions independent of the state. Where the old institutionalists speak of *coercion* (a word as valuational as most of those just listed), authors in the Austrian branch of the new institutionalism therefore call for *freedom* or *liberty* in order for the invisible hand thus to guide economic evolution.

The alternative, typical neoclassical, response to the challenge of institutionalism was withdrawal to what may have seemed a safer position in utter abstraction, unreachable both by empirical falsification and by ideological critique. In this position, economics is no longer a social science but a set of analytical techniques, operated within a system where the social framework merely appears as so many parameters kept either constant or extraneous to the analysis. Human behavior is said to be studied as "a relationship between ends and scarce means which have alternative uses,"[38] but the focus is not, in fact, on human behavior at all. The model is closed as regards the human element by the simple assumptions of rationality and transitivity of preferences. The actual focus is on the allocation of scarce resources. Characteristic examples of this approach are the Pareto criterion and the Coase theorem.[39] In the respective optima of these models, individual differences

---

[37] Myrdal, 1965, 111.

[38] Robbins, 1937, 16.

[39] It can be argued that Coase's celebrated study of the nature of the firm (Coase, 1937) is formally in the tradition of Commons in that its key concept is transaction costs. The so-called Coase theorem (Coase, 1960) is valid only in the absence of transaction costs, which, on the author's premises, is a wholly unrealistic assumption. It is therefore possible to maintain (cp. Mulberg, 1995, 154) that Coase does not subscribe to the theorem that bears his name. From points of view similar to those

between marginal utility (which is just a euphemism of need) may seem overwhelmingly obvious and unjust to the untrained eye, but, since interpersonal comparison of utilities is impossible, the trained econo- mist can ignore the distributional aspect and concentrate on efficient resource allocation. Property rights, pointed out in section 9.3 as one of the ideological mainstays of liberalism, is now reduced to an arbitrary initial premise. Institutionalists object that if this is not questioned, the whole exercise is tautological, founded on an implicit defense of the status quo. We need not go into this further here, but it should be noted because rights and power correlate. It is thus at the core of the problem of economic coercion and freedom, to which we now turn.

10.3   Economic coercion

One of the expressions used to describe the scholastic paradigm of need and the will does not occur in the primary sources examined in Part II. There is no exact Latin counterpart to "economic compul- sion." As far as I can see, it is not used in previous studies of scholastic economics, either. It is not, however, my own invention. It appeared in early modern institutionalist literature in the slightly different form of "economic coercion."[40] According to Commons, economic power is the power to withhold from others what they need.[41] It is a kind of waiting-power, namely, a power to hold back until the opposite party

> indicated here in the text, the Paretian and Coasian analyses in their
> unqualified forms have been criticized by prominent recent institutionalists;
> cp. Samuels, 1974 and 1981; Schmid, 1978, 202–18.

[40] My choice of the word "compulsion" rather than "coercion" is partly a reflection of Hobbes's terminology and partly of the legal *vis compulsiva*, but it was primarily determined by the fact that "compulsion" is the standard English translation of Aristotle in *Ethics*, III,1, where "coercion" will not do because the model comprises an impersonal compelling force as well as a personal one. A distinction along those lines is suggested by one of the authors to be quoted in the following section, but I am inclined to reject it whenever there is a question of economic relationships. Both terms are used in modern economic literature, but the clear preference is "coercion." It may be felt that this is a stronger term than "compulsion." This is not intentional on my part, and the reader is free to substitute "economic coercion" for "economic compulsion" whenever it is used in this book.

[41] Commons, 1924, 52.

consents to the bargain.[42] Such power rests in property, which must be understood in an intangible, not a corporeal, sense. The reference to bargaining indicates that intangible property is the right to fix prices by withholding from others what they need *but do not own*.[43] On this note, the concept of economic coercion is introduced, and it must be distinguished from "duress of goods." The latter is "withholding from a person what rightfully belongs to him and is needed by him, but economic coercion is withholding from a person what does not belong to him, yet is needed by him."[44] Commons records the historical process through which an ever-widening concept of duress was recognized in common law. It is reminiscent of the one described in Part I regarding Roman and canon law. Whether Commons was aware of this parallel is not clear, but he was well familiar with the *vir constans*. A plea of duress was originally limited to grave physical violence involving such imminent danger to life, limb, or property as might overcome the will of a courageous and steadfast man. This personal requirement was subsequently reduced to mere ordinary firmness but still applied only to threats of physical violence. Finally, further modifications were made so that the law now recognizes almost any kind of threat rendering a person incapable of exercising free will, but there was never a question of duress or coercion residing in the mere unequal power of withholding things that others need.[45] This was the step now proposed by Commons, just as the medieval theologians had once translated the concept of *vis compulsiva* from noneconomic to economic categories.[46]

Elsewhere Commons makes a reference to the state of the market, also recalling subjects discussed in Part II. There are certain limits to

---

[42] Ibid., 54.

[43] Commons, 1934, 3.

[44] Id., 1924, 59.

[45] Ibid., 57.

[46] Sometimes Commons makes a threefold distinction. Under very primitive circumstances, the issue is decided by physical strength, the stronger robbing the weaker. Assuming the parties to be equal in this respect (or, one might add, assuming physical violence to be contained by law), the parties resort to economic coercion. Suppose, however, that waiting-powers are also equal. What then comes into play is persuasion, which is a wide category. Salesmanship will figure prominently, but bordering on this there is also fraud, misrepresentation, ignorance, and stupidity, factors vividly recalling those listed by the scholastics (Commons, 1934, 336–8). It is often difficult to draw the line between coercion and persuasion (Ibid., 333); however, we shall dwell no further on the latter category, just as we left out discussions of fraud in Parts I and II.

economic coercion. Suppose, for instance, that S (for Seller) is the stronger bargainer, having control of a commodity limited in supply but possessing such abundance that he can hold out longer than B (for Buyer). He can then force the price up, but only to the limit offered to B by the next strongest competitor, S^1. If, inversely, B is stronger than S, S will have a bottom-line price at which he can sell to the next strongest buyer, B^1. If S and B agree on a price, it will be found somewhere between these limits of coercion.[47] This model accommodates much of the scholastic discussion of collusion, monopoly, and the competitive market. At one point, there is an allusion (surely unintentional) to the Aristotelian model of restricted choice: "The value of the service which each renders to the other, when the exchange is finally made, is the greater pain he would suffer than the pain he actually suffers by giving up to the other what he does give up."[48]

Another early influence on this branch of institutionalism is Robert Lee Hale. In 1923 (a year before the appearance of the first book by Commons cited in this section), Hale published an article criticizing the work of Carver. There followed an exchange of letters between these two authors. In one of these letters, Hale defines coercion: "I should apply the word 'coercion' to every case where one person induces another to comply with his wishes, [provided] the second person complies for the purposes of avoiding the disadvantages of adverse behavior or adverse inactivity which the first person will otherwise practice."[49]

Here, again, we have a "mixed" act, like that of the subject threatened by the tyrant of Aristotle's *Ethics*. The general form of the definition is chosen because of Carver's reluctance to describe economic activity in such terms.[50] In the preceding article, Hale had applied it to

---

[47] Commons, 1934, 331–2.

[48] Ibid., 337.

[49] Hale to Carver, 3 December 1923; quoted in Samuels, 1984, 1041–2.

[50] Needless to say, no terminological consensus was reached. It is interesting to note that the discussion soon veered away from economics to the question of forced matrimony, a subject often discussed in medieval canon law and confessional literature. Carver insinuates that, on Hale's terms, "to win a lady's affection by the offer of love, loyalty, and devotion until she wants to marry you does not differ in kind from hitting her over the head with a club and dragging her to your cave" (Carver to Hale, 24 November 1923; Samuels 1039). Hale replies that neither of these cases involves coercion because coercion presumes a threat, which is not present in either case. On the other hand, threatening to kill a lady unless she agrees

economics. A person may choose to buy something at a certain price or to accept work at a certain wage. In either case, his conduct is motivated by a desire to escape a more disagreeable alternative.[51] This means, Hale claims, that the person in question acts under coercion by the seller or the employer, and such is the case throughout the range of what we call economic activity. It follows that the distribution of income "depends on the relative power of coercion which the different members of the community can exert against one another."[52]

Hale was a professor at the Columbia University law school, and much of his work centered on court decisions relating to economic activity. Only toward the end of his career did he return occasionally to the question of coercion in private economic exchange. There is a lingering notion, he then observes, that coercion implies lack of volition on the part of the person to whom it is applied and, conversely, that where there is volition and choice, there is no coercion.[53] Such is not the case, however. Coercion is in the nature of a threat. One chooses to enter into a transaction in order to avoid the threat of something worse. Each party yields to the threat of the other. There is thus both choice and compulsion.[54] What decides the issue is relative bargaining power, that is, power to exert pressure on the opposite party, in other words, to coerce him. Each person exerts some degree of coercion over other people's liberty, while at the same time his own liberty is subject to some degree of control by others.[55] In the economic system, "market values reflect the relative force of the threats which buyers and sellers of goods or services can make."[56] This is a matter of scarcity. "One who is capable of rendering service of a kind that is scarce in relation to the demand for it can, by threatening to withhold that service, obtain better terms for not carrying out his threat than can one with no such ability."[57]

In recent years, the ideas of Commons and Hale were developed by a group of authors who address the question of coercion from the point of view of property rights. According to Samuels, in an early work, the

to marriage and promising to pay her impoverished father's debts if she does are both instances of coercion (Hale to Carver, ibid.; Samuels 1040).

[51] Hale, 1923, 472.
[52] Ibid., 478; cp. 477.
[53] Hale, 1943, 616.
[54] Ibid., 606.
[55] Hale, 1952, 4.
[56] Ibid., 9.
[57] Ibid., 10.

economy is a system of mutual coercion, which is to be understood (following Commons) as withholding power. Property rights, granted by law, are capacities to participate in the economic process as a coercive force. This does not rule out freedom. The economic decision-making process is in fact a "pattern of freedom *and of exposure to the freedom of others and therefore* (my emphasis) a pattern of mutual coercion."[58] In later works, Samuels formalizes these ideas in terms of a paradigm centered on the concept of interactional "opportunity sets." The opportunity set structure in the economy is a function of the power structure and mutual coercion.[59] This paradigm emphasizes the presence of choice, but each person's choice is restricted, partly by law, and partly by choice made within the opportunity set of the opposite party to a given transaction.

When prices are paid in the market to secure or escape from something, they are paid in order to incur one cost so as to avoid a felt larger one; but all this . . . takes place within and as a function of the opportunity set structure generated by power play through mutual coercion. . . . Consensual choice is but a part, though an integral part, of this larger coercive process, a process which is no less coercive because individuals exercise choice, for paradoxically it is through the exercise of choice that mutual coercion takes place.[60]

Views similar to those of Samuels, as well as a conclusion that sums up the tradition sketched in this section, are to be found in a book by Schmid. A common grievance against neoclassicism on the part of contemporary adherents of the old institutionalism is the failure to recognize the fundamental role of property rights as a premise of economic analysis. They do not deny that a bargaining transaction is mutually beneficial in the sense that both parties are better off than before; however, "antecedent to the observed mutually beneficial trade is the prior mutual coercion that is given shape by the inescapable public choice of property rights."[61] Rights are transferable upon mutual consent.

Each party has an opportunity set with some content (not necessarily equal), and each is free within that limit to join or abstain from further transactions. Each party may deny access to another party who may have need but does not own the resource in question – that is, there is mutual coercion. Through a process of negotiation, the parties agree to transfer something they own in

[58] Samuels, 1971, 440.
[59] Id., 1974, 16.
[60] Id., 1981, 30–1.
[61] Schmid, 1978, 240.

exchange for what the other owns. Thus, a bargained transaction implicitly involves both coercion and consent.[62]

10.4   Aspects of liberty

Introducing the exchange of letters between Hale and Carver, Samuels urges the reader to distinguish between the pejorative and analytical uses of the term "coercion."[63] In the article that triggered the correspondence, Hale makes a plea for using the word in a sense that involves no moral judgment,[64] pointing out that it "frequently seems to carry with it the stigma of impropriety."[65] If this is true of "coercion," it is, by reversal, no less true of "freedom" (or "liberty" – I shall use them here to mean the same), for "to practically everyone 'freedom' is a laudatory term."[66] "Almost every moralist in human history has praised freedom."[67] For these reasons, it is difficult to make analytical uses of these words at all. If we agreed on a neutral terminology, much of what is said about economic coercion could be expressed in terms of economic liberty or freedom, but by the very fact that an author employs one terminology rather than the other, the reader can be led to suspect an imperfectly hidden ideological motive. Because I have just quoted a particular modern school on coercion and am about to close a book in which the terminology throughout has been that of "compulsion" (if not "coercion"), it is imperative, at least, that I state (among the scores of senses of that hallowed word) what I mean by freedom with respect to the legacy of scholasticism in economic thought.

For the Christian philosophers of the Middle Ages, says Gilson, the word "freedom" signified, above all, "the fundamental impermeability of the will from all constraint."[68] This includes freedom from necessitation in the metaphysical sense and freedom from compulsion in the sense of the power of the will to assert itself in adversity, by rising above material obstacles and accepting responsibility for one's actions. This idea, which finds expression in the Augustinian doctrine of culpability,

---

[62] Ibid., 11.
[63] Samuels, 1984, 1033.
[64] Hale, 1923, 476.
[65] Ibid., 471.
[66] Viner, 1961, 232.
[67] Berlin, 1958, 6.
[68] "La *libertas a necessitate, ou libertas a coactione*, signifie avant tout pour eux l'imperméabilité foncière du vouloir à toute contrainte" (Gilson, 1969, 289).

has most obviously influenced modern existentialist philosophy, but there is more than a pale impression of it in social philosophy as well. It is recognizable in the "rugged individualism" of the frontier farmer or in the decision of the struggling corner shopowner to decline the offer of a well-paid managerial position in a department store. In Aristotle's idiom, the captain may sometimes prefer to jettison cargo and master the stormy sea rather than being salvaged and towed into harbor. These are sentiments with which one can readily sympathize, but when libertarian authors invoke this ethos in connection with the subjects discussed in this book, they are confusing the issue.

More specifically, it is necessary to disregard, if only partly, two factors relating to Gilson's concept. They both appear among the versions of what Isaiah Berlin calls "positive freedom." One is freedom by retreat to the "inner citadel" of asceticism.[69] The other is enforced liberation of a worthier self in the "Temple of Sarastro."[70] The ideal of poverty, chastity, and obedience, professed by a majority of the authors quoted in Part II, is not reducible to the single motivation of breaking free from desires that cannot be realized in the face of natural and social obstacles, but that was undoubtedly part of the motivation for many of those who made that vow. Anyway, it influenced their economic teaching, even when addressed to the laity. It lies at the root of their warning against avarice as a false lure to happiness and their praise of charity and almsgiving. Beyond that, it is not germane to our inquiry. Although it is pre-Christian and has reached us through many channels, it is not on the agenda of any major contemporary school of economic thought (to say the least). As to freeing the inner potentiality for higher moral and rational insight in other people by forcibly educating them, that would seem to be what the medieval institution of the confessional was largely about. Moreover, the concern of the canonists and theologians teaching economic ethics was not only the spiritual needs of the stronger but equally the material needs of the weaker party. Freedom from economic need may sound like "negative" freedom, but according to modern libertarian authors, it is merely "positive" freedom in disguise. It would therefore seem to be highly relevant from the political point of view of the libertarians. It is less germane, however, if it is kept in mind that the aim of scholastic teaching, like the thrust of my arguments in this book, is ethical rather than political.

The commonsense concept of freedom is what Isaiah Berlin calls "negative freedom":

[69] Berlin, 1958, 19–25.
[70] Ibid., 29–39, referring to *The Magic Flute*.

I am normally said to be free to the degree to which no human being interferes with my activity. Political liberty in this sense is simply the area within which a man can do what he wants. If I am prevented by other persons from doing what I want, I am to that degree unfree; and if the area within which I can do what I want is contracted by other men beyond a certain minimum, I can be described as being coerced, or, it may be, enslaved.[71]

It has been pointed out that calling this "negative" is misleading. It defines freedom negatively as freedom *from* some restraint but also refers to what a person is free *to* do within these limits.[72] Granted that the scholastics taught restraint of behavior in order to free both the powerful from the shackles of their own avarice and the powerless from economic need, it is not problematical to apply the commonsense concept of freedom to the medieval paradigm as an analytical tool. To the extent that the moral norms permit it, each party is free to apply bargaining power but is compelled (or coerced) insofar as he is met by the bargaining power of the opposite party. As regards the Commons branch of institutionalism, opportunity sets are precisely areas of free exercise of bargaining power, that is, coercion, but this activity is restricted by interference from other opportunity sets, where opposing forces are at work. It should also be noted that the definition mentions political but not economic liberty (presumably because "economic freedom" usually carries the "positive" connotation of "freedom from need" previously mentioned). The institutionalists, however, view economics and politics as one interactive system, whereas the medieval scholastics had no (and the later scholastics only a hazy) idea of the economy as a separate set of social relationships at all.

Authors in the Austrian branch of the new institutional economics profess a negative concept of liberty. To Hayek, liberty is "that condition of men in which coercion of some by others is reduced as much as is possible in society."[73] To Machlup, "liberalism in the classical, individualistic sense" is "the mere absence of coercive interference."[74] These authors, prominent names in the field of analytic economics as well, do not tire of repeating this. They explicitly call their concept of freedom negative and point out that they are frequently criticized for this restrictive view.[75] The point where they run into conflict with the old institutional economics (and, mutatis mutandis, with scholastic eco-

---

[71] Ibid., 7.
[72] Raphael, 1994, 83.
[73] Hayek, 1960, 11.
[74] Machlup, 1969, 122.
[75] Hayek, 1960, 19; Machlup, 1969, 134–5.

nomics) is thus the proposition that regular economic activity can and should be free in the sense that it need not and should not involve coercion. According to the libertarians, their opponents ask for positive freedom, objecting that a person is not free if society denies him purchasing power.[76] This objection, it is claimed, involved a confusion of power and freedom,[77] and asking for power is dangerous. Positive freedom in the sense of power can be had only through political interference with the natural course of economic development, and political interference is the road not to freedom but to serfdom.[78] We need not go into this. The question before us is how it is possible to conceive of an economy that involves no coercion. The reply to this question by the two authors quoted, as well as by their teacher Mises, is essentially the same. It is stated most fully and explicitly by Hayek. Other leading economists have evaded it by a facile sleight of hand, deducing freedom from the fact that exchange is mutually beneficial to the parties.[79] Hayek faces the issue squarely.[80]

One might perhaps have expected Hayek to make his task easier by adopting the position of Hobbes and some of the late scholastics, namely, that "mixed acts" in the Aristotelian sense leave the actor free, but he does not even permit himself this. He does not refer to Aristotle but to Roman law. Having explained the difference between *vis absoluta*

---

[76] Machlup, 1969, 135.

[77] Ibid., 126; Hayek, 1960, 16–17. Hayek names Commons as one of those who spread this ideology.

[78] Hayek, 1944, passim.

[79] Friedman does this repeatedly (Friedman, 1962, 13; 1980, 1–2; 13). It is no more excusable because it is done in popular works. The "key insight" that exchange is mutually beneficial because the parties would not otherwise have exchanged, which Friedman attributes to Adam Smith, was common property among the medieval scholastics. Mises, 1949, 661, also refers to this principle, but his main argument is different.

[80] It should be noted that Machlup and Hayek were not chosen as spokesmen for the Austrians because they hold extreme positions within the school, but rather the contrary. They both make a point of disclaiming *laissez-faire* (Hayek, 1944, 13; Machlup, 1969, 127–8). They do not only welcome state protection against fraud and deception, theft, racketeering, blackmail, and physical violence (Hayek, 1944, 29; 1960, 137; 143; Machlup, 1969, 127), but also call for government measures to secure for everybody "some minimum of food, shelter, and clothing, sufficient to preserve health and the capacity to work" (Hayek, 1944, 90) and to "prevent misery which private charity cannot cope with" (Machlup, 1969, 128).

and *vis compulsiva* (without using these terms), he proceeds to declare that the former is not coercion because one who is subject to it does not act, whereas the latter *is* coercion: "Coercion implies . . . that I still choose but that my mind is made someone else's tool, because the alternatives before me have been so manipulated that the conduct that the coercer wants me to choose becomes for me the least painful one. Although coerced, it is still I who decide which is the least evil under the circumstances."[81]

The final period is an English rendering of *coactus volui*, which is quoted in Latin in a note.[82] What this tough position implies is that *vis compulsiva* is coercion but that there is no such thing in economic life if the categories involved are entirely economic, that is, if the threat is not physical, or noneconomic in a broader sense, such as in the case of blackmail, etc. Purely economic coercion does not exist. This is the only position that an author as stringently logical as Hayek can adopt. His political argument is that those who cry for power cry against their circumstances, which are *not* coercive, but what they get is interference by the state, that is, by men, and it is only the activity of men that can be coercive. Freedom is the absence of "coercion of some by others"; it is "independence of the arbitrary will of another"; "the only infringement on [freedom] is the coercion by men";[83] "liberty . . . describes the absence of a *particular* obstacle – coercion by other men" (my emphasis);[84] "coercion occurs when one man's actions are made to serve another man's will";[85] "government needs . . . power to prevent coercion (and fraud and violence) by individuals."[86]

Two corollaries follow from this conclusion, and Hayek goes through with them, almost without breaking his own logic. First, if there is no such thing as economic coercion, it follows that "the mere power of withholding [note Commons's term] a benefit will not produce coercion"[87] and that neither a competitive market nor a monopolistic market is coercive except (loosening the reins on logic a little) in extreme cases, such as when somebody deliberately monopolizes water supply in an oasis. "Unless a monopolist is in [such an extreme position] he

---

[81] Hayek, 1960, 133.
[82] Ibid., 449, note 2. It is not quoted verbatim from the *Digest* but from a commentary, in a slightly different form, "Etsi coactus tamen voluit."
[83] Ibid., 11–12.
[84] Ibid., 19.
[85] Ibid., 133.
[86] Hayek, 1967, 350.
[87] Hayek, 1960, 137.

cannot exercise coercion, however unpleasant his demands may be for those who rely on his services."[88] Next, it follows that the restriction placed on a person who faces a monopolist or someone who withholds a service from him is, in some sense, impersonal. Hayek suggests that his situation can be described as "compulsion" as distinct from "coercion." "While we can legitimately say that we have been compelled by circumstances to do this or that, we presuppose a human agent if we say that we have been coerced."[89]

Mises saw no problem in viewing economic circumstances as an impersonal and even a natural phenomenon. Two brief, separate quotations illustrate his position:

The member of a contractual society is free because he serves others only in serving himself. What restrains him is only the inevitable natural phenomenon of scarcity.

. . . What hurts the sick is the plague, not the physician who treats the disease. The doctor's gain is not an outcome of the epidemics, but of the aid he gives to those affected.[90]

Machlup insists "on separating the origins of any limitations on human choices and on regarding as limitations of freedom only those that are the result of restrictions and restraints which man imposes upon man." Moreover, even if "certain constraints on my actions are suspected by me not to have originated from impartial 'nature,' " there is a further criterion: "As long as I cannot blame anybody for the constraints, my freedom is not infringed."[91] Clearly, the patient's illness cannot be blamed on the doctor. What the doctor can perhaps be blamed for is refusing treatment except for an excessive fee, but this would be economic coercion, which, according to Hayek, does not exist. To Hayek, the criterion is intent:

So long as the act that has placed me in my predicament is not aimed at making me do or not do specific things, so long as the intent of the act that harms me is not to make me serve another person's ends, its effect on my freedom is not different from that of any natural calamity – a fire or a flood that destroys my house or an accident that harms my health.[92]

The problem with this criterion is that you are usually assumed to engage in economic activity with the intent of earning an income, which you get by rendering services to other people, all the while ar-

[88] Ibid., 136; cp. Hayek, 1967, 349–50.
[89] Hayek, 1960, 133.
[90] Mises, 1949, 280; 660.
[91] Machlup, 1969, 134.
[92] Hayek, 1960, 137.

ranging conditions for yourself in relation to other people so that your services are better paid. There need not be any particular person singled out by you for this purpose (though there often is), and there need not be any other person with a reason to blame you (though there sometimes is), but directly or indirectly your choices will be among the factors that determine the circumstances in which other people make economic choices. To paraphrase Samuelson, the economy is a universe of interacting wills, where complete freedom is impossible and coercion a necessary element,[93] or, in the words of Viner:

As a rule, what other men can or cannot do to us depends on their and our "physical circumstances," which may be acts of God or the product of laws of nature, like volcanic eruptions, but often are very much man-made creations, and often are the means whereby men find it possible to coerce other men or find it possible to resist the attempts of others to coerce them.[94]

It is a paradox that the individualists, by denying this, have been driven to a depersonalization of economics even more extreme than that which characterized the rejection of the scholastic paradigm in the seventeenth century, and it may be more than a coincidence that this has happened, at least partly, by way of reaction against a branch of institutionalism that occasionally recalls the scholastic system.

10.5   An ethical legacy

It will be obvious to those who read the preceding pages with a certain degree of detachment that the problem discussed is formally semantic but insoluble because the real issue is ideological. This is merely a confirmation of a point emphasized more than once in this book. It is true whether the problem is stated in terms of freedom versus compulsion or coercion, or in terms of the nature of the will behind "mixed acts." If I may make a suggestion by way of conclusion, it is that the ideological issue (taken in a broad sense) is no longer primarily political but moral. In the present century, all Western European democracies, that is, more or less, all countries at one time within the compass of medieval Christendom (as well as many countries in other parts of the world) have included in their civil codes paragraphs designed to limit exploitation of what the German *Bürgerliches Gesetzbuch*

[93] Cp. Samuelson, II, 1414–15.
[94] Viner, 1961, 232, in review article of Hayek, 1960.

calls "Zwangslage,"[95] along with other factors conditioning the value maxim of the medieval Romanists. These laws protect the needy party in all the types of economic contracts examined in Part II. To take only the examples just mentioned, civil law will set ceilings to the fees for medical services and to the price of water. Economists and politicians will argue for a little more or a little less regulation of economic life. Even in the Western world, this still makes some difference. I would nevertheless suggest that it is to the area within these legal limits, that is, to ethics, that we might more profitably direct our search for a possible (and possibly very important) legacy of scholasticism in our economic ideas.

In his *Philosophical Explanations*, discussing personal identification as a criterion in the structuring of social concepts, Robert Nozick takes the case of coercion as an illustration:

Writers on coercion have puzzled over why it is important whether another person intentionally directs your behavior in a certain direction. What is the difference, they wonder, between being kept inside a house by a lightning storm or by another person's playing with electricity outside your house, or by another person's threat to electrocute you if you leave the house. When the probabilities of electric shock are equal in the three situations, isn't one equally coerced in all three? Whether an act is yours, though, depends upon whose will is operating. In the lightning situation, your will keeps you indoors – no other's motives and intentions are as closely connected to your act. Whereas in the threat situation, it is another person's will that is operative. In the intermediate situation where another person acts but without intending to influence you to do act A, it is your intentions that are operating in your doing A.[96]

We need not pursue Nozick's conceptualization further. I quote him here because his "intermediate situation" indicates a most useful amplification of Aristotle's model in *Ethics*, III,1. Granted that the person who does not venture outside from fear of electrocution remains rather passive, as against those of Aristotle's examples who yield to compulsion by acting, the "lightning situation" corresponds precisely to that of the captain who jettisons cargo in a storm, whereas the "threat situation" is like that of the tyrant's subject. For Aristotle's analytic purpose, which was that of assessing the moral responsibility of the person compelled, there is no need for a third case. If the person in Nozick's cases had an important errand outside, he might be equally blamed for staying indoors or equally praised for facing the risk of electrocution, whether

[95] BGB § 138. Besides necessity, this paragraph refers to lack of experience or judgment as well as generally to weakness of will ("Willensschwäche").

[96] Nozick, 1981, 49. For an extensive analysis of the concept of coercion, cp. Nozick, 1969, and, partly in reply, Frankfurt, 1973.

its cause was impersonal, personal without intent, or personal with intent. When the perspective is reversed and the focus is placed on the compeller rather than the compelled, the relevance of the intermediate case becomes evident.

When the early scholastics turned Aristotle's model around and applied it to economics, they understandably avoided associating economic activity with tyranny and chose the impersonal case for their metaphor. I noted the sense of alienation that this brought to their use of it. There can be no doubt that this invited the depersonalization of economics, which began to make itself felt some three centuries after the Latin translation of the *Ethics*. It is futile to speculate about the course that economic doctrine might have taken had Aristotle supplied an intermediate case. What is clear is that of Nozick's three situations, this is the one that fits economic activity best. Exchange is by definition interpersonal, and though we do not normally engage in it in order to harm anyone in particular the moment he opens his door, we are always playing in someone else's garden. A realization of this fact calls for a certain sense of moral responsibility, a considerateness, or fairness, a certain justice if you will, in the Aristotelian not the Hobbesian sense, within the wider limits of the civil law. There is no reason to doubt the existence of such "moral sentiments" in the modern economy. There may even be cause to ask whether our Western societies have not, in fact, functioned as well as they have after all done *because of* such sentiments, in these last couple of centuries when mainstream economics has so consistently ignored them.

Bibliography

I. Manuscript sources

Averroës: *Liber Nicomachiae* (commentary on the *Nicomachean Ethics*, in the Latin translation of Herman the German). BVat Urbin. lat. 221.

Chiaro of Florence (fl. c. 1260): *Summa casuum conscientiae.* Florence BNaz Conv. Soppr. F.VI.855.

Compilatio tertia cum glossis. Paris BN lat. 3931A; 3932.

Decretum Gratiani cum Apparatu 'Ius naturale' (by Laurence of Spain). Paris BN lat. 15393.

Decretum Gratiani cum Glossa ordinaria (in the early version of Joh. Teutonicus, c. 1170–1245). Bamberg SB Can. 13.

Digestum vetus cum glossis. Bamberg SB Jur. 13; Paris BN lat. 4458.

Gerald Odonis (c. 1290–1349): *In quartum librum Sententiarum.* Paris BN lat. 3068.

    Tractatus de contractibus. Siena BCom U.V.8.

Guido Terreni (d. 1342): *Quaestiones in libros Ethicorum.* Bologna BU 1625.

Henry of Friemar (d. 1340): *Commentaria in decem libros Ethicorum Aristotelis.* Basel UB F.I.14; Toulouse BMun 242.

Hobbes, Thomas: *Aristotelis parva Moralia, sive De Ethicis Virtutibus.* Bakewell, Chatsworth Hobbes A.8.

Huguccio (d. 1210): *Summa decretorum.* Paris BN lat. 3892.

Infortiatum cum glossis. Bamberg SB Jur. 15.

John of Faenza (d. c. 1187): *Summa super Decretum.* Bamberg SB Can. 37.

John of La Rochelle (d. 1245): *Summa de vitiis.* Bruges BV 228.

Laurence of Spain (d. 1248, probable attribution): *Glossa Palatina* (to *Decretum Gratiani*). BVat Pal. lat. 658; Durham Dean and Chapter Library C.III.8.

Quaestiones super libros Ethicorum. BVat lat. 832; Paris BN lat. 15106.

Quaestiones super libros Politicorum. Bologna BU 1625; Paris BN lat. 16089.

Raymond of Peñafort (c. 1180–1275): *Summa de casibus cum apparatu sive glosulis* (by William of Rennes). Munich SB Clm 9663.

Richard of Middleton (c. 1249–c. 1308): *Quaestiones quodlibetales.* BVat Borgh. 361.

Robert Grosseteste (c. 1168–1253): *Notulae* to his translation of the *Nicomachean Ethics*, with the text. Stockholm KB V.a.3; Eton College 122; Cambridge Peterhouse 116; Paris Arsenal 698; Oxford All Souls College 84.

Sicard of Cremona (d. 1215): *Summa super Decretum.* Bamberg SB Can. 38.

201

Simon of Bisignano (d. 1215): *Summa super Decretum.* Ibid.
Stephen Langton (d. 1228): *Quaestiones.* Paris BN lat. 16385.
Summa Bambergensis super Decretum. Bamberg SB Can. 42.
Summa Monacensis super Decretum. Munich SB Clm 16084.
Tancred (c. 1185–c. 1236): *Apparatus in Compilationem primam.* Bamberg SB Can. 19.
Ulrich of Strasbourg (d. 1277): *De summo bono.* Erlangen UB Lat. 530/1–2.
Vincent of Spain (d. 1248): *Apparatus in Decretales Gregorii IX.* Paris BN lat. 3967; 3968.

II. Printed sources

I. Prescholastic sources

Ambrose of Milan: *De bono mortis,* in *Corpus Scriptorum Ecclesiasticorum Latinorum* 32/1.
Aristotle: *Metaphysica, Ethica Nicomachea, Magna Moralia, Ethica Eudemia, Politica,* in *Aristoteles graece ex recognitione Immanuelis Bekkeri,* Vol. 2. Berlin 1831.
  Ethica Nicomachea, Medieval Latin translations, critical editions by R.-A. Gauthier, *Aristoteles Latinus,* XXVI,1–3. Leiden-Bruxelles 1972–4.
  Ethica Nicomachea (by Ross), *Magna Moralia* (by Stock), *Ethica Eudemia* (by Solomon), in *The Works of Aristotle,* translated into English under the editorship of W. D. Ross, Vol. 9. Oxford 1915.
Augustine: *Retractiones, De libero arbitrio,* PL (Patrologia Latina, ed. Migne) 32.
  Epistolae, PL 33.
  De vera religione, Quaestiones in Heptateuchum, PL 34.
  Enarrationes in Psalmos, PL 36–7.
  De duabus animabus, PL 42.
  De spiritu et littera, PL 44.
Capitularia Regum Francorum, ed. A. Boretius, 2 vols., in *Monumenta Germaniae Historica,* Leges II. Hannover 1883–97.
Cassiodorus: *Expositio Psalmorum,* Corpus Christianorum, Series Latina 97–8.
Cicero: *De officiis,* LCL (Loeb Classical Library) 30.
  De inventione, LCL 386.
Corpus Iuris Civilis, ed. T. Mommsen, P. Krüger, and W. Kroll, 3 vols. Berlin 1888–95.
Corpus Iuris Civilis, cum commentariis Accursii, 6 vols. Lyon 1627.
The Digest of Justinian, translated by C. H. Monro, 2 vols. Cambridge 1904, 1909.
Epictetus: *Discourses,* as reported by Arrian, 2 vols. LCL 131, 218.
John Damascene: *De fide orthodoxa,* PG (Patrologia Graeca, ed. Migne) 94.
  The same, in the Latin translation of Burgundio of Pisa; critical edition by E. A. Buytaert. St. Bonaventure-Louvain-Paderborn 1955.
Moses Maimonides: *The Guide for the Perplexed,* translated from the Arabic by M. Friedländer. New York 1956.

Nemesius of Emesa: *De natura hominis*, PG 40.
The same, in the Latin translation of Burgundio of Pisa, critical edition by
    G. Verbeke and J. R. Moncho. *Corpus Latinum commentariorum in Aristo-*
    telem Graecorum, Suppl. 1. Leiden 1975.
Plato: *Laches, Protagoras*, LCL 165.
    Georgias, LCL 166.
    Republic, 2 vols., LCL 237, 276.
    Laws, 2 vols., LCL 187, 192.
Pseudo-John Chrysostom: *Opus imperfectum in Matthaeum*, PG 56.
Seneca: *De beneficiis*, LCL 310.
Scholia in Aristotelis Ethicam Nicomacheam, Lib. III, in *Commentaria in Aristotelem*
    Graeca, Vol. 20. Berlin 1892.
The same, in the Latin translation of Robert Grosseteste; critical edition by
    H. P. F. Mercken, in *Corpus latinum commentariorum in Aristotelem Graeco-*
    rum (CLCAG), Vol. VI,1. Leiden 1973.
Xenophon: *Memorabilia*, LCL 168.

II. Scholastic sources (including Roman and canon law)

Accursius (c. 1182–c. 1260). See *Corpus Iuris Civilis*.
Albert the Great (c. 1200–80): *Opera Omnia*, 38 vols. Paris 1890–9.
    Ethica, Vol. 7.
    Politica, Vol. 8.
    Super Lucam, Part I, Vol. 22.
    Super III Sententiarum, Vol. 28.
    Super IV Sententiarum, Part I, Vol. 29.
    Opera Omnia. Münster 1951–
        Super Ethica, Vol. 14.
        De bono, Vol. 28.
Alexander of Hales (c. 1175–1245): *Summa theologica*, 4 vols. Quaracchi 1924–
    48.
Andreae, Joh. (c. 1270–1348): *Super tertio Decretalium*. Trent 1512.
Antonino of Florence (1389–1459): *Summa theologica*, 4 vols. Verona 1740.
    Confessionale (Defecerunt). Milan 1472.
Antonio of Budrio (c. 1338–1408): *Super tertio Decretalium*. Venice 1578.
Ariosto, Alexander (d. c. 1485): *Enchiridion sive interrogatorium*, Lyon 1528.
    (Quoted in article, *De mercatoribus*, ff.116rb–119rb.)
    De usuris. Bologna 1486.
Astesanus of Asti (d. 1330): *Summa de casibus conscientiae (Astesana)*. Lyon 1519.
Azo of Bologna (d. c. 1220): *Summa Iuris Civilis*. Basel 1563.
Azor, Juan (1536–1603): *Institutiones morales*, 3 vols. Cologne 1602–12.
Azpilcueta, Martín de (1493–1586): *Enchiridion, sive Manuale confessariorum et*
    poenitentium. Antwerp 1608.
Baldus of Perugia (c. 1327–1400): *In Codicem praelectiones*, 3 vols. Lyon 1561.

Bañez, Domingo de (1527–1604): *Decisiones de iure et iustitia.* Venice 1595.

Bartolomeo of Brescia (d. 1258). See *Decretum Gratiani.*

Bartolomeo of San Concordio (Pisano, 1262–1347): *Summa de casibus conscientiae (Pisana).* Venice 1482. (Quoted in articles, *Emptio et venditio,* ff.127ra–129ra; *Negotiatio,* ff.278va–280rb; *Usura,* ff.465rb–489va.)

Bartolus of Sassoferrato (1313/4–57): *In primam (secundam) Digesti veteris partem.* Basel 1589 (1588).

In primam Codicis partem. Basel 1588.

Bernard Botone of Parma (d. 1266). See *Decretales Gregorii IX.*

Bernardino of Siena (1380–1444): *Quadragesimale de Evangelio aeterno,* in *Opera Omnia,* Vols. III–V. Quaracchi 1956.

Prediche volgari (Florence 1424), ed. C. Cannarozzi, 2 vols. Florence 1934.

Prediche volgari (Siena 1427), ed. C. Delcorno, 2 vols. Milan 1989.

Confessionale (Renovamini), in *Operette volgari,* ed. D. Pacetti. Florence 1938.

Biel, Gabriel (c. 1410–95): *Collectorium circa quattuor libros Sententiarum: Libri quarti pars secunda.* Tübingen 1977 (All references are to IV,15,10, pp. 189–215.)

Bonacina, Martin (c. 1585–1631): *De contractibus,* in *Opera Omnia,* Vol. II. Antwerp 1635.

Bonaventura of Bagnoregio (c. 1217–74): *Opera Omnia,* 11 vols. Quaracchi 1882–1902.

Commentaria in quatuor libros Sententiarum, Vols. I–IV.

Expositio super Regulam Fratrum Minorum, Vol. VIII.

Buridan, Jean (c. 1300–c. 1358): *Quaestiones super decem libros Ethicorum Aristotelis.* Paris 1513.

Busenbaum, Hermann (1600–68): *De contractibus,* in *Medulla theologiae moralis.* Paris 1657.

Cagnazzo, Giovanni (d. 1521): *Summa Summarum (Tabiena).* Bologna 1517. (Quoted in articles, *Emptio,* ff.164vb–168rb; *Familia,* ff.220ra–va; *Usura,* ff.477ra–490va.)

Caimi, Bartolomeo (d. 1496): *Confessionale.* Milan 1474.

Carletti, Angelo (c. 1414–95): *Summa de casibus conscientiae (Angelica).* Strasbourg 1513. (Quoted in articles, *Emptio et venditio,* ff.80va–82va; *Extimatio,* ff.107vb–108ra; *Negotium,* ff.212vb–213rb; *Usura,* ff.300vb–310rb.)

Tractatus contractuum (Anecdotum). Milan 1768.

Corpus Iuris Canonici, ed. E. Friedberg, 2 vols. Leipzig 1879.

Decretales Gregorii IX cum Glossa ordinaria (by Bernard Botone of Parma). Mainz 1473.

Decretum Gratiani cum Glossa ordinaria (by Bartolomeo of Brescia). Basel 1512.

De Vio, Thomas (Cajetan, 1468–1534): *Commentaria in Summam Theologiae Thomae Aquinatis,* in Aquinas, *Opera Omnia,* Vols. IV–XII. Rome 1888–1905.

Responsio ad dubia, in *Opuscula, quaestiones et quodlibeta,* Vol. 2. Lyon 1541.

De usura, ibid. Vol. 3. Lyon 1541.

Summa de peccatis. Rome 1525.

Duns Scotus, John (c. 1265–1308): *Quaestiones in quartum librum Sententiarum*

(Opus Oxoniense.) (All references to IV,15,2: *Opera Omnia,* Vol. 18, Paris 1894, pp. 255–357.)

Durand of Saint-Pourçain (c. 1275–1334): *Commentaria in quattuor libros Sententiarum.* Venice 1571.

Fumo, Bartolomeo (d. 1545): *Summa aurea armilla.* Venice 1558. (Quoted in articles, *Emptio,* pp. 281–8; *Familia,* pp. 385–7; *Monopolium,* p. 645).

Gerald Odonis (c. 1290–1349): *Sententia et expositio cum quaestionibus super libros Ethicorum Aristotelis.* Brescia 1482.

Gerardo of Siena (d. 1336): *Tractatus de usuris et de praescriptionibus.* Cesena 1630.

Gerson, Jean (1363–1429): *De contractibus,* in *Oeuvres complètes,* Vol. 9. Paris 1973.

Giles of Lessines (c. 1230–c. 1304): *De usuris,* in Aquinas, *Opera Omnia,* Vol. XVII. Parma 1864.

Giles of Rome (c. 1245–1316): *De regimine principum.* Rome 1556.

De ecclesiastica potestate, ed. R. Scholz. Weimar 1929.

Godfrey of Fontaines (c. 1250–c. 1306): *Quodlibeta,* in *Les Philosophes Belges* (LPB), 2–5; 14. Louvain 1904–37.

Godfrey of Trani (d. 1245): *Summa super titulis Decretalium.* Lyon 1519.

Guido of Baiso (c. 1250–1313): *Rosarium super Decreto.* Milan 1508.

Henry of Ghent (c. 1217–93): *Quodlibet I,* in *Opera Omnia,* Vol. V. Louvain-Leiden 1979.

Quodlibeta. Paris 1518.

Henry of Hesse (1325–97): *Tractatus de contractibus,* in Gerson, *Opera Omnia,* Vol. IV. Cologne 1484.

Henry of Oyta (d. 1397): *Tractatus de contractibus,* ibid.

Hostiensis (Henry of Susa, c. 1200–71): *Summa aurea.* Lyon 1537.

Lacroix, Claude (1652–1714): *Theologia moralis, seu eiusdem in H. Busenbaum Medullam commentaria,* 4 vols. Paris 1874.

Laymann, Paul (1574–1635): *Theologia moralis.* Munich 1630.

Lessius, Leonard (1554–1623): *De iustitia et iure.* Antwerp 1626.

López, Luís (d. c. 1595): *Instructorium negotiantium.* Salamanca 1589.

Lugo, Juan de (1583–1660): *De iustitia et iure.* Lyon 1646.

Luther, Martin (1483–1546): *Von Kaufshandlung und Wucher,* in *Werke,* Vol. 15. Weimar 1899.

Mazzolini, Silvester (1456–1523): *Summa Summarum (Silvestrina),* 2 vols. Antwerp 1581. (Quoted in articles, *Emptio,* I,292–7; *Familia,* I,383–4; *Monopolium,* II,200; *Negotium,* II,204–5; *Permutatio,* II,250–2; *Usura,* II,420–49.)

Medina, Juan de (1490–1546): *Codex de rebus restituendis,* in *De poenitentia, restitutione et contractibus.* Ingolstadt 1581.

Molina, Luís de (1535–1600): *De iustitia, Tomus secundus: De contractibus.* Cuenca 1597.

Monaldus of Capodistria (d. c. 1285): *Summa perutilis atque aurea (Monaldina).* Lyon 1516.

Navarra, Pedro de (fl. c. 1580): *De ablatorum restitutione,* 2 vols. Toledo 1585.

206   **Bibliography**

Nider, Johannes (c. 1380–1438): *Tractatus de contractibus mercatorum.* Antwerp 1486.

Odofredus (d. 1265): *Super Digesto veteri.* Paris 1504.

In primam Codicis partem praelectiones. Lyon 1550.

Pacifico of Novara (1424–82): *Summa confessionis (Pacifica).* Venice 1506.

Panormitanus (Nicola de' Tedeschi, 1386–1445): *Super tertio Decretalium.* Lyon 1550.

Peter of La Palu (c. 1280–1342): *Super tertium Sententiarum.* Paris 1517.

In quartum Sententiarum. Paris 1514.

Peter Lombard (c. 1095–1160): *Sententiae in IV libris distinctae,* 2 vols. Grotta-ferrata 1971–81.

Peter Olivi (c. 1248–98): *Tractatus de emptione et venditione,* ed. A. Spicciani. Rome 1977.

Tractatus de emptionibus et venditionibus, de usuris, de restitutionibus, ed. G. To-deschini. Rome 1980.

Peter of Tarentaise (Pope Innocent V, c. 1224–76): *In quattuor libros Sententiarum commentaria,* 2 vols. Toulouse 1649–52.

Quodlibet, ed. P. Glorieux, *Recherches de Théologie ancienne et médiévale* 9 (1937) 242–75.

Placentinus (d. 1192): *Summa Codicis.* Mainz 1536.

Quinque compilationes antiquae, ed. E. Friedberg. Leipzig 1882.

Raniero of Pisa (d. c. 1348): *Pantheologia.* Venice 1585. (Quoted in articles, *De venditione et emptione,* II,1151–8; *De usura,* II,1208–15.)

Raymond of Peñafort (c. 1180–1275): *Summa de poenitentia et matrimonio, cum glossis Joannis de Friburgo* (erroneous attribution; these glosses are by William of Rennes). Rome 1603.

Regnault, Valère (1543–1623): *Praxis fori poenitentialis,* 2 vols. Mainz 1617.

Remigio of Florence (d. 1319): *De peccato usurae,* ed. O. Capitani, *Studi medievali* 6/2 (1965) 611–60.

Richard of Middleton (c. 1249–c. 1308): *Super quatuor libros Sententiarum,* 4 vols. Brescia 1591.

Ridolfi, Lorenzo (c. 1360–1442): *De usuris,* in *Tractatus universi iuris,* Vol. 7. Venice 1584.

Rogerius (d. c. 1170): *Summa Codicis,* in A. Gaudenzi (ed.), *Biblioteca juridica medii aevi,* Vol. I. Bologna 1888.

Roland of Cremona (d. 1259): *Summae liber tertius.* Bergamo 1962.

Rufinus (d. 1192): *Summa decretorum,* ed. H. Singer. Paderborn 1902.

Salón, Miguel Bartolomé (1538–1620): *Controversiae de iustitia et iure,* 2. vols. Venice 1608.

Soto, Domingo de (1495–1560): *De iustitia et iure.* Lyon 1582.

Suárez, Francisco (1548–1617): *Opera Omnia,* 28 vols. Paris 1856–78.

De Voluntario et Involuntario, Vol. IV.

De Legibus et Legislatore Deo, Vols. V–VI (Lib. I–V; VI–VII).

De Iuramento, De Voto, Vol. XIV.

Summa Parisiensis, ed. T. P. McLaughlin. Toronto 1952.

Summa Trecensis, ed. H. Fitting *(Summa Codicis des Irnerius)*. Berlin 1894.

Summenhart, Conrad (c. 1455–1502): *De contractibus*. Venice 1580.

Tartagni, Alexander (c. 1424–77): *In priman et secundam Infortiati partem commentaria*. Venice 1595.

Thomas Aquinas (1224/5–74): *Opera Omnia*, 25 vols. Parma 1852–73.
    Scriptum super libros Sententiarum, Vols. VI–VII.
    Quaestiones quodlibetales, Vol. IX.
  Opera Omnia, Rome 1882–
    Summa theologiae, Vols. IV–XII.
    Summa contra gentiles, Vols. XIII–XV.
    De malo, Vol. XXIII.
    De regno, Vol. XLII.
    Sententia libri Ethicorum, Vol. XLVII.
    Sententia libri Politicorum, Vol. XLVIII.

Thomas of Chobham (c. 1160–c.1235): *Summa confessorum*, ed. F. Broomfield. Louvain 1968.

Trovamala, Battista (de Salis, d. c. 1495): *Summa de casibus conscientiae (Rosella)*. Strasbourg 1516. (Quoted in articles, *Emptio et venditio*, ff.74ra–76rb; *Negotiatio*, f.170va–b; *Usura*, ff.246vb–263rb).

Valencia, Gregorio de (1549–1603): *Commentaria theologica*, 3 vols. Ingolstadt 1603.

Vitoria, Francisco de (1492/3–1546): *Comentarios a la Secunda secundae de Santo Tomás*, Vol. IV: *De iustitia*. Salamanca 1934.

Voit, Edmund (1707–80): *Theologia moralis*. Würzburg 1769.

Walter Burley (c. 1275–c. 1344): *Expositio super decem libros Ethicorum Aristotelis*. Venice 1521.

William of Auxerre (d. 1231): *Summa aurea*, ed. J. Ribaillier, 7 vols. Rome 1980–7.

William of Rennes (fl. c. 1250). See Raymond of Peñafort.

III. Postscholastic sources

Aubrey, John: *Brief Lives*, ed. O. L. Dick. London 1958.

Baldwin, John W.: "The Medieval Theories of the Just Price: Romanists, Canonists, and Theologians in the Twelfth and Thirteenth Centuries," *Transactions of the American Philosophical Society* 49, 4 (1959).

Berlin, Isaiah: *Two Concepts of Liberty*. Oxford 1958.

Brundage, James A.: *Medieval Canon Law*. London 1995.

Burnet, John: *The Ethics of Aristotle*. London 1900.

Carver, Thomas Nixon: *Essays in Social Justice*. Cambridge, Mass., 1915.

Chafuen, Alejandro Antonio: *Christians for Freedom. Late-Scholastic Economics*. San Francisco 1986.

Coase, Ronald H.: "The Nature of the Firm," *Economica*, n.s. 4 (1937) 386–405.

"The Problem of Social Cost," *The Journal of Law and Economics* 3 (1960) 1–44.

Commons, John R.: *Legal Foundations of Capitalism*. New York 1924.

"Institutional Economics," *The American Economic Review* 21 (1931) 648–57.

Institutional Economics. New York 1934.

Dempsey, Bernard W.: *Interest and Usury*. London 1948.

d'Entrèves, A. P.: *Natural Law*. London 1970.

De Roover, Raymond: *San Bernardino of Siena and Sant'Antonino of Florence, The Two Great Economic Thinkers of the Middle Ages*. Boston 1967.

Dirlmeier, Franz: "Kommentare," to *Aristoteles, Nikomachische Ethik*. Darmstadt 1964 (= *Werke, in deutscher Übersetzung*, Vol. 6).

Elster, Jon: *Making Sense of Marx*. Cambridge 1985.

Epstein, Steven A.: *Wage Labor and Guilds in Medieval Europe*. Chapel Hill and London 1991.

Fanfani, Amintore: *Catholicism, Protestantism and Capitalism*. London 1935.

Storia delle Dottrine Economiche. Milan 1971.

Frankfurt, Harry G.: "Coercion and moral responsibility," in T. Honderich (ed.), *Essays on Freedom of Action*. London 1973, pp. 65–86.

Friedman, Milton and Rose: *Capitalism and Freedom*. Chicago 1962.

Free to Choose. New York and London 1980.

Galbraith, John Kenneth: *American Capitalism: The Concept of Countervailing Power*. Boston 1956.

"Power and the Useful Economist," *The American Economic Review* 63 (1973) 1–11.

The New Industrial State. Boston 1978.

Gauthier, R. A. and J. Y. Jolif: *L'Éthique à Nicomaque: Introduction, traduction et commentaire*, 4 vols. Louvain-Paris 1970.

Gilson, Étienne: *L'Esprit de la Philosophie Médiévale*. Paris 1969.

Gómez Camacho, Francisco: "La 'estimación común' en la teoría molinista del justo precio," *Revista española de teología* (1978) 85–111.

"Introducción," to *Luís de Molina, La téoria del justo precio*. Madrid 1981.

Gordon, Barry: *Economic Analysis before Adam Smith: Hesiod to Lessius*. London 1975.

Grice-Hutchinson, Marjorie: *The School of Salamanca: Readings in Spanish Monetary Theory 1544–1605*. Oxford 1952.

Early Economic Thought in Spain, 1177–1740. London 1978.

Grotius, Hugo: *De Iure Belli ac Pacis*, 2 vols. (Latin, reprint of ed. 1646, and English translation). Washington-London 1913–25. (Carnegie Classics of International Law, 3.)

Gruchy, Allan G.:*The Reconstruction of Economics: An Analysis of the Fundamentals of Institutional Economics*. New York 1987.

Hale, Robert Lee: "Coercion and Distribution in a Supposedly Non-Coercive State," *Political Science Quarterly* 38 (1923) 470–94.

"Bargaining, Duress, and Economic Liberty," *Columbia Law Review* 43 (1943) 603–28.

Freedom through Law. New York 1952.

Hardie, W.F.R.: *Aristotle's Ethical Theory.* Oxford 1968.

Hartkamp, Arthur Severijn: *Der Zwang im römischen Privatrecht.* Amsterdam 1971.

Hayek, F. A.: *The Road to Serfdom,* London 1944.

The Constitution of Liberty. London 1960.

Studies in Philosophy, Politics and Economics. London 1967.

Hirschman, Albert O.: *The Passions and the Interests: Political Arguments for Capitalism before Its Triumph.* Princeton 1978.

Hobbes, Thomas: *Opera philosophica quae Latine scripsit omnia,* ed. W. Molesworth, 5 vols. London 1839–45.

The English Works, ed. W. Molesworth, 11 vols. London 1839–45.

Hood, F. C.: *The Divine Politics of Thomas Hobbes.* Oxford 1964.

Hume, David: *Philosophical Works,* ed. T. H. Green and T. H. Grose, 4 vols. London 1882–86.

Irwin, T. H.: "Reason and Responsibility in Aristotle," in A. Oksenberg Rorty (ed.), *Essays on Aristotle's Ethics.* London 1980, pp. 117–55.

Joachim, H. H.: *Aristotle, The Nicomachean Ethics: A Commentary,* Oxford 1951.

Kant, Immanuel: *Werke,* 12 vols. Wiesbaden 1956–64.

Kenny, Anthony: *Aristotle's Theory of the Will.* London 1979.

Knuuttila, S., and T. Holopainen: "Conditional will and conditional norms in medieval thought," *Synthese* 96 (1993) 115–32.

Kuttner, Stephan: *Kanonistische Schuldlehre von Gratian bis auf die Dekretalen Gregors IX.* Vatican City 1935. (Studi e testi 64.)

Repertorium der Kanonistik (1140–1234). Vatican City 1937. (Studi e testi 71.)

Langholm, Odd: *Price and Value in the Aristotelian Tradition.* Oslo 1979.

"Economic freedom in Scholastic thought," *History of Political Economy* 14 (1982) 260–83.

Wealth and Money in the Aristotelian Tradition. Oslo 1983.

Economics in the Medieval Schools: Wealth, Exchange, Value, Money and Usury According to the Paris Theological Tradition, 1200–1350. Leiden 1992.

Lapidus, André: *Le Detour de Valeur.* Paris 1986.

Locke, John: *Two Treatises of Government,* ed. P. Laslett. Cambridge 1963.

An Essay Concerning Human Understanding, ed. J. W. Yolton, 2 vols. London 1964.

Some Considerations of the Consequences of the Lowering of Interest, and Raising the Value of Money, in *Works,* Vol. IV. London 1824.

Lottin, Odon: "Le droit naturel chez saint Thomas et ses prédécesseurs," *Ephemerides Theologicae Lovanienses* 1 (1924) 369–88; 2 (1925) 32–53; 345–66; 3 (1926) 155–76.

McLaughlin, T. P.: "The Teaching of the Canonists on Usury (XII, XIII and XIV Centuries)," *Mediaeval Studies* 1 (1939) 81–147; 2 (1940) 1–22.

Machlup, Fritz: "Liberalism and the Choice of Freedoms," in E. Streissler et al. (eds.), *Roads to Freedom: Essays in Honour of Friedrich A. von Hayek,* London 1969. pp. 117–46.

Macpherson, C. B.: *The Political Theory of Possessive Individualism. Hobbes to Locke.* Oxford 1970.

210   **Bibliography**

Marshall, Alfred: *Principles of Economics.* London 1907.

Marx, Karl: *Capital,* English ed. by S. Moore and E. Aveling, 3 vols. Moscow 1957–59.

Michaud-Quantin, Pierre: "Sommes de casuistique et manuels de confession au moyen âge (XII–XVI siècles)," *Analecta mediaevalia Namurcensia* 13 (1962).

Mill, John Stuart: *Collected Works,* 19 vols. Toronto 1963–79.

Mises, Ludwig von: *Human Action: A Treatise on Economics.* New Haven 1949.

Mulberg, Jon: *Social Limits to Economic Theory.* London 1995.

Myrdal, Gunnar: *The Political Element in the Development of Economic Theory.* London 1965.

Noonan, John T., Jr.: *The Scholastic Analysis of Usury.* Cambridge, Mass., 1957.

Nozick, Robert: "Coercion," in S. Morgenbesser, P. Suppes, and M. White (eds.), *Philosophy, Science, and Method. Essays in Honor of Ernest Nagel.* New York 1969. pp. 440–72.

Philosophical Explanations. Oxford 1981.

O'Connor, D. J.: *Aquinas and Natural Law.* London 1967.

Parsons, Kenneth H.: "John R. Commons: His Relevance to Contemporary Economics," *Journal of Economic Issues* 19 (1985) 755–78.

Pufendorf, Samuel: *De Iure Naturae et Gentium,* 2 vols. (Latin, reprint of ed. 1688, and English translation). Oxford 1934. (Carnegie Classics of International Law, 17.)

Ramstad, Yngve: "Toward an Economics of the Just Price: John R. Commons and Reasonable Value," Working Paper, University of Rhode Island, 1996.

Raphael, D. D.: "Hobbes on Justice," in G. A. J. Rogers and A. Ryan (eds.), *Perspectives on Thomas Hobbes.* Oxford 1990, pp. 153–70.

Moral Philosophy. Oxford and New York 1994.

Rerum Novarum: Litterae encyclicae Sanctissimi D. N Leonis Papae XIII de conditione opificum, in *Acta Sanctae Sedis* 23 (1890–91) 641–70.

Ricardo, David: *Works and Correspondence,* ed. P. Sraffa, 10 vols. Cambridge 1951–55.

Robbins, Lionel: *An Essay on the Nature and Significance of Economics Science.* London 1937.

Rocha, Manuel: *Travail et Salaire à Travers la Scholastique.* Paris 1933.

Rothbard, Murray N.: *An Austrian Perspective on the History of Economic Thought,* 2 vols. Brookfield 1995.

Ruskin, John: *Unto This Last.* London 1893.

Rutherford, Malcolm: *Institutions in Economics: The Old and the New Institutionalism.* New York 1994.

Saarinen, Risto: *Weakness of the Will in Medieval Thought.* Leiden 1994.

Samuels, Warren J.: "Interrelations between Legal and Economic Processes," *The Journal of Law and Economics* 14 (1971) 435–50.

"The Coase Theorem and the Study of Law and Economics," *Natural Resources Journal* 14 (1974) 1–33.

"Welfare Economics, Power, and Property," in W. J. Samuels and A. A. Schmid (eds.), *Law and Economics: An Institutional Perspective*, Boston–The Hague–London 1981. pp. 9–75.

"On the Nature and Existence of Economic Coercion: The Correspondence of Robert Lee Hale and Thomas Nixon Carver," *Journal of Economic Issues* 18 (1984) 1027–48.

Samuelson, Paul A.: *Collected Scientific Papers*, ed. J. E. Stiglitz et al., 2 vols. Cambridge, Mass., 1966–77.

Say, Jean-Baptiste: *Traité d'économie politique*. Paris 1841.

Schlatter, Richard: *Private Property: The History of an Idea*. London 1951.

Schliemann, Adolph: *Die Lehre vom Zwange*. Rostock 1861.

Schmid, A. Allan: *Property, Power, and Public Choice: An Inquiry into Law and Economics*. New York–London 1978.

Schulte, J. F. von: *Die Geschichte der Quellen und Literatur des canonischen Rechts von Gratian bis auf die Gegenwart*, 3 vols. Stuttgart 1875–80.

Schulz, Fritz: "Die Lehre vom erzwungenen Rechtsgeschäft im antiken römischen Recht," *Zeitschrift der Savigny-Stiftung für Rechtsgeschichte* 43 (1922) 171–261.

Schumpeter, Joseph A.: *History of Economic Analysis*. London 1954.

Seidman, Robert B.: "Contract Law, the Free Market, and State Intervention: A Jurisprudential Perspective," *Journal of Economic Issues* 7 (1973) 553–75.

Simmons, A. J.: *The Lockean Theory of Rights*. Princeton 1992.

Smith, Adam: *An Inquiry into the Nature and Causes of the Wealth of Nations*, ed. E. Cannan, 2 vols. London 1904.

Lectures on Justice, Police, Revenue and Arms, ed. E. Cannan (from a student report of 1763). Oxford 1896.

Sorabji, Richard: *Necessity, Cause, and Blame: Perspectives on Aristotle's Theory*. Ithaca 1980.

Spragens, Thomas A., Jr.: *The Politics of Motion: The World of Thomas Hobbes*. London 1973.

Strauss, Leo: *The Political Philosophy of Hobbes*. Oxford 1936.

Tawney, R. H.: *Religion and the Rise of Capitalism*. London 1936.

Taylor, A. E.: *Thomas Hobbes*. London 1908.

"The Ethical Doctrine of Hobbes" (1938), reprinted in K. C. Brown (ed.), *Hobbes Studies*. Oxford 1965, pp. 35–55.

Thomas, Keith: "The social origins of Hobbes's political thought," in Brown (ed.), *Hobbes Studies*, pp. 185–236.

Tuck, Richard: *Natural Rights Theories: Their Origin and Development*. Cambridge 1979.

Tully, James: *A Discourse on Property: John Locke and His Adversaries*. Cambridge 1980.

Viner, Jacob: "Hayek on Freedom and Coercion," *Southern Economic Journal* 27 (1961) 230–6.

212   **Bibliography**

Vromen, Jack J.: *Economic Evolution: An Enquiry into the Foundations of New Institutional Economics.* London–New York 1995.

Walzer, Richard: *Magna Moralia und Aristotelische Ethik.* Berlin 1929.

Warrender, Howard: *The Political Philosophy of Hobbes,* London 1957.

Weber, Max: *Der Sinn der "Wertfreiheit" der soziologischen und ökonomischen Wissenschaften,* in *Methodologische Schriften.* Frankfurt a.M. 1968. pp. 229–77.

The Protestant Ethic and the Spirit of Capitalism. English edition by T. Parsons. London 1930.

Wirtschaft und Gesellschaft. Tübingen 1925.

Economy and Society. English edition by G. Roth and C. Wittich. New York 1968.

Weber, Wilhelm: *Wirtschaftsethik am Vorabend des Liberalismus.* Münster 1959.

Geld und Zins in der spanischen Spätscholastik. Münster 1962.

Index

213